TOWARD A BLACKBOYCRIT PEDAGOGY

Critical and necessary, this book provides a window into the education and lives of Black boys in early childhood settings. Drawing on Black Critical Theory and Black Male Studies, and applying portraiture methodology, Bryan explores experiences of Black boys and their male teachers in ways that affirm their humanity and acknowledge the consequences of existing in a white supremacist system. Bryan's nuanced and comprehensive portraits honor the voices of Black boys and their male teachers, and counter the one-dimensional and essentialist perspectives that proliferate in our schools, which Bryan identifies as anti-Black misandry.

Introducing BlackBoyCrit Pedagogy, Bryan addresses the impact of socially constructed stereotypes and perceptions in the classroom and highlights the importance of educators who challenge such practices. In so doing, he provides a much-needed in-depth examination of pedagogies, literacies, and practices Black male teachers employ, as well as a perceptive view of the academic and social landscapes Black boys must navigate.

Nathaniel Bryan is Assistant Professor of Early Childhood Education at Miami University, USA.

NCTE-ROUTLEDGE RESEARCH SERIES

Series Editors: Valerie Kinloch and Susi Long

Rickford/Sweetland/Rickford/Grano
African American, Creole and other Vernacular Englishes in Education: A Bibliographic Resource

Guerra
Language, Culture, Identity, and Citizenship in College Classrooms and Communities

Haddix
Cultivating Racial and Linguistic Diversity in Literacy Teacher Education: Teachers Like Me

Brooks
Transforming Literacy Education for Long-Term English Learners: Recognizing Brilliance in the Undervalued

Baker-Bell
Linguistic Justice: Black Language, Literacy, Identity, and Pedagogy

Nash, Polson, Glover
Toward Culturally Sustaining Teaching: Early Childhood Educators Honor Children with Practices for Equity and Change

Bryan
Toward a BlackBoyCrit Pedagogy: Black Boys, Male Teachers, and Early Childhood Classroom Practices

Johnson
Critical Race English Education: New Visions, New Possibilities

The NCTE-Routledge Research Series, copublished by the National Council of Teachers of English and Routledge, focuses on literacy studies in P-12 classroom and related contexts. Volumes in this series are invited publications or publications submitted in response to a call for manuscripts. They are primarily authored or co-authored works which are theoretically significant and broadly relevant to the P-12 literacy community. The series may also include occasional landmark compendiums of research

The scope of the series includes qualitative and quantitative methodologies; a range of perspectives and approaches (e.g., sociocultural, cognitive, feminist, linguistic, pedagogical, critical, historical, anthropological); and research on diverse populations, contexts (e.g., classrooms, school systems, families, communities), and forms of literacy (e.g., print, electronic, popular media).

TOWARD A BLACKBOYCRIT PEDAGOGY

Black Boys, Male Teachers, and Early Childhood Classroom Practices

Nathaniel Bryan

NCTE
National Council of
Teachers of English

Routledge
Taylor & Francis Group
NEW YORK AND LONDON

First published 2022
by Routledge
605 Third Avenue, New York, NY 10158

and by Routledge
2 Park Square, Milton Park, Abingdon, Oxon OX14 4RN

Routledge is an imprint of the Taylor & Francis Group, an informa business

© 2022 Taylor & Francis

Library of Congress Cataloging-in-Publication Data
A catalog record for this title has been requested

ISBN: 978-0-367-25405-6 (hbk)
ISBN: 978-0-367-25403-2 (pbk)
ISBN: 978-0-429-28761-9 (ebk)

DOI: 10.4324/9780429287619

Typeset in Bembo
by Taylor & Francis Books

To my first early childhood teacher: my mother, Barbara Bryan, whose many sacrifices became the reason I am able to write this book.

To my sister, Melba, my brother, Shamir, and my one and only nephew, Jerrell: thanks for being there for me!

To my aunt and uncle, Mary E. and David Fickens—my *othermother* and *otherfather*—who constantly stand by my side in good and bad times.

To the host of family members, friends, and colleagues I have not listed here, I dedicate this book to you!

CONTENTS

ILLUSTRATIONS

Figures

Tables

FOREWORD

> The anti-Black mistreatment of Black boys is concretized in the fabric of the public schooling system (Warren, 2017) as Black boys continue to be positioned in negative ways. Much like COVID-19, the pandemic virus that, as I write this text, has disproportionately killed tens of thousands of Black people nationwide (Yancy, 2020), such mistreatment of Black boys is a virus that continues to spread throughout our schools and truncates Black boys' schooling and life opportunities. Currently, there is no cure in place or even widespread recognition of where the responsibility for change lies.
>
> – *Nathaniel Bryan*

Anchored in these realities, Nathaniel Bryan has crafted a text that provides the most comprehensive look at the education of young Black boys in educational literature today. In this compelling book, Bryan introduces his conceptualization of *BlackBoyCrit Pedagogy* by taking readers into issues, practices, and pedagogies that offer insights and antidotes. These antidotes, indeed, will help prepare educators to address and counter the viral attacks on Black boys that have been long recognized in the field of education. While this book focuses uniquely on the education of Black boys in early childhood education (typically seen as pre-kindergarten through third grade), strong implications can be extrapolated for the teaching of all Black students. However, the work is particularly critical for teachers in preK-to-grade three classrooms because the early years are precisely the time when Black boys will build identities that will either anchor their future successes or deny their brilliance, spirit, and desire to learn. The denial of their brilliance often derives from false claims that they are unteachable and unworthy, which leads to indelible labels that can negatively define how they will be seen and/or how they come to see themselves throughout the rest of their schooling and in society.

Bryan opens the book by inviting us into the classroom of his own kindergarten teacher, Mr. C, an educator determined to counter systemic structures, pedagogies, and biases that "conceal the academic brilliance and strengths of Black children." Through the stories he tells about his life as a Black boy in kindergarten, Bryan emphasizes how Mr. C instilled in students a belief in themselves and a passion for learning. Bryan shares Mr. C's joy in teaching, engagement with children in and out of the classroom, strategies for teaching within and beyond the curriculum to excite learners, and confidence in the students' brilliance—characteristics that inspired students to seek knowledge and wisdom.

From this introduction, the book provides a critically important look at the landscape of education in the lives of Black boys in the United States. This description of what Bryan aptly describes as anti-Black misandry and pedagogical malfeasance, in conjunction with Bryan's discussion of Black Critical Theory and Black Male Studies, are not merely academic exercises but essential understandings for all educators. It is by studying these concepts and realities that educators will be able to identify and understand why we need to dismantle and replace structures, practices, pedagogies, and attitudes that deny positive educational experiences for Black boys.

Deftly, Bryan draws us into the hearts and lives of five Black kindergartners—Maurice, Roland, Braden, Joshua, and Ameer—and their insightful, critically-minded Black male teachers, Mr. Javien, Mr. Tal, and Mr. Henry. Through their stories, we learn not only about the need for Black men as early childhood educators but about characteristics of their teaching that positively impact the academic, emotional, and psychological lives of Black boys. We gain insights into the teachers through the eyes of the boys and their family members in portraits created by Bryan based on his observations of and conversations with the boys, their families, and their teachers. While the entire book provides critical foundations and practical implications for educators, the portraits of three teachers through the eyes of children provide vivid images of educators who challenge the status quo. Zooming out from each portrait, Bryan extrapolates key characteristics of their teaching that can and should serve as a guide (and measure) for all educators.

Expanding on his earlier work through which he introduced the notion of Black PlayCrit Literacies (Bryan, 2020), Bryan uses the characteristics of successful Black men kindergarten teachers to introduce *BlackBoyCrit Pedagogy* as an antidote to the pedagogical, emotional, and psychological murder experienced by many Black boys in early childhood classrooms. Honoring scholars who change education with pedagogies designed to counter the Eurocratic and uncritical nature of schooling, he honors culturally relevant, responsive, critical race, culturally sustaining, and gender relevant pedagogies while explaining his yearning "for something more pedagogically empowering for Black children, and especially for Black boys." The result is *BlackBoyCrit Pedagogy* designed to "affirm and reaffirm the notion that Black boys and male teachers matter, and that they will always matter in and beyond early childhood education." Chapters follow that focus on the roles of play and literacy in *BlackBoyCrit Pedagogy* with specific instructional practices and foundational tenets to guide educators in teaching for transformation.

Like the other books in the NCTE-Routledge Research Series, this book takes a critical look at classroom practices as it speaks to both teachers and researchers and the ways in which research and practice must attend to the lives of People of Color within and beyond P-12 classrooms. *Toward a BlackBoyCrit Pedagogy* joins a series of books that includes foci on equity, justice, and antiracist education; critical qualitative, quantitative, and mixed methodologies; a range of cutting-edge perspectives and approaches (e.g., sociocultural, cognitive, feminist, linguistic, pedagogical, critical, historical, anthropological); and research on the literacies of minoritized peoples as well as on diverse contexts (e.g., classrooms, school systems, families, communities) and forms of literacy (e.g., print, electronic, popular media).

We hope you are moved to action in your own educational settings as you consider Nathaniel Bryan's description of the need to overhaul the education of young Black males and as you reflect on and learn from Black male teachers and the kindergarten boys who learned from and revered them. We are proud that Bryan's text joins other books in the series that have been carefully selected for their commitment to the role of educators in moving us toward a more equitable society. We welcome you into this necessary game-changer as a reframing of "the ways we think about Black boys and Black male teachers in early childhood education."

Valerie Kinloch
Renée and Richard Goldman Dean and Professor of Education
University of Pittsburgh, USA
and
Susi Long
Professor, Instruction and Teacher Education
University of South Carolina, Columbia, USA

ACKNOWLEDGMENTS

I would be remiss if I did not acknowledge all of the individuals who played a vital role in the conceptualization of this book. In a Westernized society that is steeped in whiteness and individualism, it is easy to forget the community that has provided so much of its expertise and resources to actualize this book. First, I thank God for allowing me to start and complete this project. Without Him, this book would not have been possible. Second, I am especially grateful to my family for providing insights and support along the way. Third, I am extremely grateful for Dr. Valerie Kinloch and Dr. Susi Long, who felt this book was worthy enough to be part of their series and provided the necessary guidance to ensure that my dream became a reality. I thank you for reading the many book drafts, providing an enormous amount of feedback, and pushing me to think even more critically about such important work. I appreciate your support.

Fourth, I am particularly thankful for those close friends who encouraged me and academics whose scholarship has inspired my own and from whose work I drew the necessary insights and strength to inform my work: Janice Baines, April Baker-Bell, Denise T. Baszile, Destiny Birdsong, Gloria Boutte, Eliza Braden, Anthony Broughton, Michelle Jay Bryan, Daniella Cook, Durell Callier, Tommy Curry, Michael Dantley, Donna Ford, Anthony James, Christopher Jett, Lamar Johnson, Joyce King, David Kirkland, Chance Lewis, Rachel McMillian, Rich Milner, A. J. Moore, Carlos Robinson, Toni Milton-Williams, Paul Okafor, Paula Saine, Dywanna Smith, Lanisha Tindal, Marlon Thomas, Rachelle Washington, Brian L. Wright, and Kamania Wynter-Hoyte, to name just a few. A special thanks to Miami University's College of Education, Health, and Society, and my graduate assistants Alejandro Baker and Adrian Parker, who assisted me in gathering sources and copyediting during stages of writing the book.

Finally, I give special thanks to the Black boys and male teachers who allowed me to enter their lives and classrooms. Without them, this book would not be possible. Thanks for answering my questions, asking questions, and thinking through solutions to clarify this work.

INTRODUCTION

(Re)membering Mr. C: Early Childhood Memories of the Classroom Practices of a Black Male Kindergarten Teacher

Franz Fanon (1963) once noted that imperialism has inflicted immense harm on colonized people and has caused germs to infiltrate their minds. He further added that colonized people cannot achieve full liberation until those germs are removed. Without such removal, the rot produces a mind that forgets all the *things* it should *(re)member* (Dillard, 2016; King, 2019; King & Swartz, 2014). *(Re)membering* requires one to "gather [his/her] stolen/forgotten/lost histories and knowledges" (Dillard, 2016, p. 222), including those of *people, places, and things*; it requires "turning the [enslavement] ships around" (p. 406), returning to one's place of heritage and humble beginnings to gather and reclaim the broken pieces of the *people, places, and things* long forgotten. For me, Charleston, South Carolina, is my place of (re)memberance, and all of the Black people there—both past and present—help remind me of all the things I should (re)member before they easily become the things I quickly forget.

My early years in school were filled with memories of my kindergarten teacher, Mr. Carter, someone who is worth (re)membering. "Mr. C.," as everyone referred to him, was one of the few male teachers who taught at the predominantly African American early learning development school, St. John Center[1] (Figure 0.1). St. John Center, a public early learning center for grades PreK-2 operated by a local, predominantly white, Episcopal church, was located on the east side in the heart of downtown Charleston. It was the neighborhood school, mostly attended by children who lived below the poverty line. St. John Center was located in the same community as Emanuel African Methodist Episcopal Church (Figure 0.2), affectionately known as "Mother Emanuel." In June 2015, tragedy struck Mother Emanuel, the oldest Black church in The South (Frazier et al., 2016), when 21-year-old Dylan Roof, an avowed White male

DOI: 10.4324/9780429287619-1

FIGURE 0.1 St. John Center

FIGURE 0.2 Emanuel African Methodist Episcopal Church

supremacist, entered the church doors during a regular Bible study and opened fire. This act of racial violence led to the physical death of the Emanuel Nine: Reverend Clementa Pinckney (Emanuel's pastor and a state senator), Cynthia Hurd, Susie Jackson, Ethel Lance, Depayne Middleton-Doctor, Tywanza Sanders, Daniel Lee Simmons, Sharonda Coleman-Singleton, and Myra Thompson (Frazier et al., 2016). Felicia Sanders, Polly Shephard, and Jennifer Pinckney were also in the church that evening and lived to tell the story of this heart-wrenching tragedy. I am including this information because it is important to remember the names of both the victims and the survivors, but also to highlight how this tragic event led to the *spirit murder* (Love, 2019; Williams, 1987)—the physical and psychological trauma associated with being Black in a white supremacist society—of many people (including me) who are forced to remember this heinous act that cannot and should not be easily forgotten.

My school, located a short distance from Mother Emanuel, like most urban schools, had its share of problems, including the school's negative statistics determined by school readiness tests designed to conceal the academic brilliance and strengths of Black children as a result of the Episcopal church's failure to provide adequate resources to meet the needs of its Black student population. The school's negative statistics often overshadowed and ignored its students' "community cultural wealth" (Yosso, 2005): the linguistic, academic, and cultural strengths, knowledge, wisdoms, skills, and talents that are inherently present, yet overlooked in Black communities.

Though the school is now defunct, during my years at St. John, teachers like Mr. C. made a lifelong difference in children's lives. The lack of funding that would soon shutter the school's doors explained the outdated, mold-infested school building, where ceiling tiles often fell after storms. As a young child, I vividly remember sitting in my kindergarten classroom, counting the number of water stains on low-hanging ceiling tiles, anxiously awaiting the opportunity to see them fall and the outpour of rainwater that would soon follow. At the tender age of five, watching Mr. C. conduct the dreadful clean-up—after which he was always annoyed—was very entertaining. Afterward, he would place the buckets and mops in a nearby closet; he knew his ritual would take place again soon.

Searching through boxes of old items at my mother's house evoked fond memories of my time at St. John Center. I found my *Lifetouch* yearbook, which included photographs of the students and teachers who attended and worked at the school. Perusing the photographs, I saw a host of Black children who had imaginable childhoods and foreseeable futures. I also counted a total of eight teachers, four Black women teachers, three White women teachers, and one Black male teacher. Looking as if he was in his early 20s, Mr. C. appeared to be the youngest of them all. From what I saw in the picture, he was a bald-headed, 6-foot-tall man, and I remember he was quite intimidating for a young boy like me, who had recently lost his father. At the age of 36 years old, my father, Nathaniel Bryan, Sr., died of a massive heart attack. Consequently, my mother, Barbara Bryan, became a single mother, raising three children by herself—my sister, Melba, my brother Shamir, and me—on Charleston's eastside.

Among the paucity of male teachers on faculty at our school, Mr. C. was the only Black male teacher I could remember seeing in the building. There were far more Black female than male teachers who worked at St. John Center. This demographic is consistent with current national data which suggest that Black female teachers represent 5 percent of the teaching profession, while Black male teachers represent a paltry 2 percent (Carver-Thomas & Darling-Hammond, 2017; Jackson & Kohli, 2016; Lewis & Toldson, 2013; Wynter-Hoyte et al., 2020; Farinde-Wu et al., 2017). Collectively, Black male and female teachers comprise 7 percent of America's teaching force, and this percentage is steadily declining (National Center for Education Statistics, 2017; Wynter-Hoyte et al., 2020). In the past 20 years, the percentage of Black male and female teachers has declined by 1 percent (National Center for Education Statistics, 2017).

The stubborn underrepresentation of Black male teachers has led to persistent and unrelenting national calls to recruit and retain Black male teachers in classrooms, especially at the early childhood level (Bristol & Goings, 2019; Jones & Jenkins, 2012). These calls come in response to a *majority-occupied* teaching force, which means that more than 80 percent of those who currently inhabit classrooms are White, middle-class and upper-class females (Landsman & Lewis, 2006; Love, 2019; Sleeter & Milner, 2011; U.S. Bureau of Labor, 2018). However, because the team (i. e., the teaching profession) is "all White" doesn't mean that it is "all right" (Ladson-Billings, 2005a); in other words, the academic and social needs of Black children remain unmet without the presence, pedagogies, and practices of Black (male) educators (Dingus, 2006; Foster, 1997).

I also remember that Mr. C's demanding presence, a result of his height was overwhelming enough to encourage the rest of the boys and me to take school seriously. We knew not to misbehave in the presence of Mr. C., and, if we did, we knew there would be corporal consequences. Mr. C. kept a ruler in his desk that he struck against the palms of our hands when we misbehaved. While some present-day scholars (Patton, 2017) may contest Mr. C's corporal punishment, I would argue that such was simply a product of his time. Corporal punishment in schools was quite prevalent before and during the early- and mid-1980s.

Despite this chastisement, we knew for sure that Mr. C. meant business and that he cared about our academic and social well-being as young Black students. His classroom was a colorful and decorative space filled with educational posters, pictorials, and other student-centered learning resources. Mr. C. spoke with such wisdom and confidence that my classmates and I believed he knew everything. We knew he was brilliant. He knew all the things we wanted to know and all of the things we wanted to *(re)member*.

It seemed that all the children in the school admired Mr. C., even children who were not assigned to his class. I remember that such admiration resonated throughout the school because he was visible and actively engaged with all children each day: he played basketball, football, and jumped rope with children in the mornings, before the school day began; during the day he taught tirelessly and after school he attended to children who awaited their parents to pick them up from school. For many of us, Mr. C. was the father we never knew, since most of us grew up in single-parent homes headed predominantly by young mothers who wanted the best for their children. Mr. C. took pride in being our teacher, and often emphasized the importance of acquiring a good education. His positive impact on children spread like wildfire throughout the school and its surrounding community.

Although I remember vividly Mr. Carter's mentorship, I also remembered he was an exceptional teacher who taught us requisite academic skills. He taught my classmates and me how to recite the alphabet, count from zero to 100, write our names, recall our birth dates, color within the lines, and so much more. Teaching us early literacy skills or how to read, however, seemed to be his top priority. He instilled in us the joy of reading by using books that highlighted Black experiences in America, and he paired our readings with music that was familiar to my classmates and me. This was his way of empowering us as readers. The way he read the books he shared encouraged my classmates and me to read. The intonation he used as he read aloud was captivating. He encouraged us to read aloud to each other in the same way, providing books that we could take home to promote our personal love of reading and pride as readers. He gave us the opportunity to write our own books that we could share with our classmates and take home to our families so we knew we were writers.

I believe that, when Mr. C. loaned us books and taught us that we were readers and writers, he was teaching us to transgress (hooks,1994) by providing tools to help my classmates and me free our minds from the clutches of racism, white supremacy, and anti-Blackness (Dillard, 2016): the social, phenotypical, contextual, and historical constructions of Blackness coupled with the unearned individual, institutional, and systemic privileges granted to White people at the expense of Black people (DiAngelo, 2018; Milner, 2020; Picower, 2021). I remember loving the books Mr. C. loaned me so much that I did not want to return them to school. Those books interested me because they were always connected to topics on Black historical facts that I loved learning about as a young Black child. They also interested me because they celebrated Black boyhood rather than upholding anti-Black misandry.[2] In other words, Mr. C's books did not express hate and disdain for Black boys (Curry, 2017; Curry & Curry, 2018) as do books typically found in classroom collections that draw on stereotypes (i.e., Black boys as bad and dangerous, and Black histories as exotic, uncivilized, or to be pitied). In this way, Mr. C. made the entire learning process both fun, engaging, and affirming.

I graduated from St. John Center (Figure 0.3) and then attended Wilmot J. Fraser Elementary School, which was also located on Charleston's eastside. Much like St. John Center, Fraser Elementary was a predominantly African American school that served most of the community's children. I use the past-tense verb because Fraser is also now defunct, closed by the Charleston County School

FIGURE 0.3 My Kindergarten Graduation

District due to supposed academic underperformance.[3] In the mid-2000s, community members and activists, who knew that most of Charleston County School District's financial allocations were invested in schools on "the other side of the track" (e.g., schools that were predominantly White and middle-class), fought to save Fraser to no avail. The old, vacant building still remains on the corner of Columbus Street, and has become one of the places I should (re)member before it easily becomes one of the places I forget.

In early grades at Fraser, I was cared for, taught, and nurtured by wonderful Black female teachers, including Mrs. Hazel, Mrs. Smalls, and Mrs. Ali, to name just a few. However, as I matriculated to upper elementary grade levels, I did not experience the same kind of care and concern from other teachers, who were mostly White. Similar to most present-day public K–12 schools, there was a lack of White teachers who believed in the academic and social potential of the Black children they taught (Boutte, 2016; Delpit, 1995; Gay, 2010; Ladson-Billings,

2005a, 2005b, 2009; Milner, 2020). They did not have high expectations for us, and were often unconnected to the Black communities in which they taught.

By the time I reached fourth grade at Fraser, I grew disinterested in reading. The books I was encouraged to read were very different from the ones I had read in Mr. C.'s kindergarten classroom. They often centered the lived realities and experiences of White children. Consequently, in fourth grade, I was labeled a "struggling reader" who did not perform well on national and state-level reading assessments. I hated taking multiple-choice tests and often bubbled in any response as an act of defiance and boredom. How did a young Black boy who started school being a brilliant reader and a lover of learning end up a struggling student? Rashid (2009) has noted that, due to the hegemonic or white-dominant schooling process and curricula, Black boys often transition from "brilliant [babies] to [children] placed at-risk" (p. 347). Given my "at-risk" status, I was often pulled out of classes to attend "the computer lab" to strengthen my reading skills. For Black boys, I believe the computer lab, like other pull-out (or rather *push-out*) programs, is the start of the school-to-prison pipeline (Losen, 2013; Losen & Gillespie, 2012). Whether it is the "computer lab," special education filled with mis-referred Black boys, or inequitable disciplining practices, Black boys are pulled out of mainstream classrooms and pushed out of equitable educational opportunities in ways that teach and then reinforce identities that become internalized. As a result, Black boys are left behind academically and pulled out over and over through their schooling experience, in effect forcing many into the criminal justice system. Much like Black girls (Morris, 2016), when Black boys are pushed out of classrooms, they are subjected to the disruption of "one of the most protective factors: [their] education" (p. 30) that can provide them life and educational opportunities. Fortunately, this was not the case for me, but it could have been.

The more I reflected on my "computer lab" experience, the more I began to realize that I was not a "struggling reader." In kindergarten, I was a reader guided by a Black male teacher who loved to read. Mr. C. was a mentor who modeled a love for reading and taught his students to do the same. Afterward, however, I was subjected to books and other texts that neither interested me nor reflected Black cultural ways of knowing and being and I was pushed into a computer lab existence that further dehumanized me. It wasn't until I grew older that I realized how deeply wounded I had been by school. The Eurocentric books they used to teach me (e.g., those I was required to read) were like bullets piercing my soul and thorns cutting my fingers every time I picked up a book. This was no different from the lashes many enslaved Africans received when they were caught trying to learn to read on enslavement plantations (Williams, 2005).

At home, however, I read books that interested me, but I was never assessed on these books in schools, another reason why I was considered a struggling instead of a fluent reader. I can only imagine what my reading comprehension and vocabulary scores would have been if I had been assessed using books I wanted to read. This example demonstrates the disconnect that often exists for Black children between their home and school cultures (Baines et al., 2018;

Ladson-Billings, 1994, 2009; Kinloch, 2010). In other words, the language and literacy practices found most often in schools do not mirror those practices in which many Black children engage at home. This is the experience of many Black boys in schools, who are misconstrued as struggling readers, but are able to read in a multiplicity of ways that are neither valued nor assessed in schools (Kinloch, 2010; Kirkland, 2011; Kirkland & Jackson 2009, 2019).

All of these memories, including those of Mr. C., were catalysts for my desire to become a teacher. Like him, I wanted to be a role model for the young children with whom I would come in contact. I felt that this would be my way of shaping and giving back to my community. Lynn (2006) has suggested that Black male teachers have always encouraged their students to give back to Black communities. When asked by pre-service teachers who most inspired me to become a teacher, I always tell my stories of Mr. Carter's mentorship. I strive to be just like him.

Honoring Mr. C. and consistent with his practices, this book—*Toward a Black-BoyCrit Pedagogy: Black Boys, Male Teachers, and Early Childhood Classroom Practices*—serves to highlight the pedagogies, literacy, and schooling practices of Black male teachers through the eyes of Black boys in early childhood education. More pointedly, the book addresses how Black boys highlight their male teachers as Role Models whose courage in challenging anti-Black misandry in the teaching and learning of early literacy skills, and the execution of those teachers' schooling practices.

Black Role Models

Like Mr. C., Black teachers have frequently been thought of as Role Models for Black children (Foster, 1997; Siddle-Walker, 1996). Similar to Gloria Ladson-Billings, however, who troubled the term *social justice* while introducing the term *Just Justice* in her 2015 American Education Research Association's (AERA) Social Justice award acceptance lecture, I also trouble the terms *role models* and *role modeling*. Ladson-Billings contends that applying the term *Just Justice* is not merely "a difference in semantics, but a fundamental rethinking of our work and tasks as human beings" (American Educational Research Association, 2015, n.p.). In that spirit and drawing from the scholarly works of DuBois (1903) in which he capitalizes the term "Negro" to honor, track, and remain connected to the exclusion, denigration, suffering, determination, resistance, and brilliance of Black people and their distinctive historical experiences in America, I purposefully capitalize the term *Role Model* to honor, track, and remain connected to a group of Black teachers, both men and women, who have historically remained committed to Black children in the face of anti-Black terrorism,[4] the enslavement of Black people, Jim Crow segregation and the "New Jim Crow" (Alexander, 2010), as well as their myriad reinventions existing under different names. *Role Models* teach Black children to (re)member so that they would not forget Black heritage knowledge (Dillard, 2016; King & Swartz, 2014), they teach Black children self-pride and love. I also consider *Role Modeling* a proper noun, demonstrating that the idea has always been grounded in dynamic and

TABLE 0.1 Differentiation between Role Modeling and role modeling

Role Models and Role Modeling	role models and role modeling
Teachers believe in the possibilities and highest potential of Black children and work(s) to empower them (Boutte, 2016; Foster, 1997; Siddle-Walker, 1996).	Teachers do not fully believe in the possibilities and highest potential of Black children and work to save them demonstrated through their expectations that the correct models reflect the white–dominant status quo.
Teachers see themselves as inherently connected to the Black community (Foster, 1997; Ladson-Billings, 2009; Lynn, 2006).	Teachers see themselves as separate from the Black community.
Teachers employ pedagogical and schooling practices that draw on Black students' diverse experiences and rely on strength-based practices that humanize Black children (Ladson-Billings, 1994, 2009; Lynn, 2006; Milner, 2020).	Teachers do not employ pedagogical and schooling practices that draw on Black students' diverse experiences, but rely on deficit-oriented practices that reify whiteness and dehumanize Black children.

idiosyncratic ways of thinking by Black teachers about Black children and families (Dingus, 2006; Foster, 1997; Perry et al., 2003; Siddle-Walker, 1996). I do the same with the words *Role Models* and *Role Modeling* to distinguish them from lower-case forms of the terms which I believe to be grounded in deficit-oriented views of Black teachers. Table 0.1 differentiates between the various concepts.

Black Role Models like Mr. C. have always believed in the possibilities and highest potential of Black children (Boutte, 2016; Boutte & Johnson, 2013; Foster, 1997; Siddle-Walker, 1996). Perhaps even to signify the importance of the Role, Black teachers have long been "othermothers"[5] and "otherfathers" who made students' dreams become realities in and beyond classrooms (Lynn, 2006; Williams, 2018). They also have histories of developing fictive kinships with Black children that are similar to those of biological family members (Cook, 2010).

During my childhood, Black Role Models typically lived in the same communities as their students (Foster, 1997; Ladson-Billings, 1994, 2009; Siddle-Walker, 1996), and often attended the same community functions and religious institutions (Foster, 1997; Perry et al., 2003; Siddle-Walker, 1996). They typically knew the names of every child and parent, and were what Murrell (2001) considers *community teachers,* or individuals who were actively involved in the educational affairs and politics of Black communities. They also developed positive relationships with their students as they taught them to work against the social, economic, and political boundaries imposed upon them (hooks, 1994; Ladson-Billings, 2009; Siddle-Walker, 1996). They enacted pedagogies in classrooms that drew from students' diverse lived experiences, and engaged in *culturally relevant teaching* (Brown, 2011; Ladson-Billings, 2009): teaching that centered and drew from the cultural experiences of their students. Concurrently, they produced high achievement outcomes, or what Ladson-Billings (2009) refers to as enabling Black students to develop "literacy, numeracy, technology, social, and political skills in order to be active participants in a democracy" (p. 160). This also entailed building student motivation and interest long-term and "student learning" or what students actually know and are able to do as a result of pedagogical interactions with skilled teachers (Ladson-Billings, 2006, p. 34). In summation, I believe that Siddle-Walker (1996) has best described Black teacher Role Models. According to her, they are "people who could bridge their current li[ves] with [the] possibilities [students'] lives might hold in the future" (p. 204).

All of the aforementioned characteristics describe Mr. C., who possessed strong compassion for and ability to nurture Black children, which came out of an Afrocentric history, African excellence, and the history of Black oppression in the forms of both the enslavement of Black people and decades of Jim Crow segregation (Foster, 1997; King, 2005). With such considerations in mind, I have long wondered what it would be like if all young Black boys in kindergarten classrooms could experience teachers like Mr. C., who was the quintessential Role Model for his Black students. Furthermore, I wondered about Black kindergarten boys' perceptions of their Black male teachers. During the study out of which this book is born, I sought to understand those perceptions and experiences as windows into what schooling can be for all Black boys. I did so by seeking answers to the following questions: (a) How do Black male kindergarten teachers perceive their abilities to support Black boys in early childhood education? (b) How do Black boys perceive the pedagogical and schooling practices of Black male kindergarten teachers?

The Impetus for This Book: Learning from Black Male Teachers and Black Boys

In 2016, I had the distinct pleasure of meeting three Black male kindergarten teachers—Mr. Javien, Mr. Henry, and Mr. Tal (pseudonyms)—who all reminded me of Mr. C. because of the ways they interacted with their Black boy students. These Black male early childhood teachers worked in elementary schools in South Carolina, and, over the course of nine months, I had the opportunity to learn about them and their practices. Because of the stellar reputations they had garnered among family members of students they had previously taught, these Black male teachers were selected to participate in my study. In fact, the purpose of my study was to explore the constructed identities and pedagogical styles of Black male kindergarten teachers and how those constructions positively impacted the academic and social outcomes of Black boys in early childhood classrooms. Little did I know that I would learn so much about these teachers' pedagogies, schooling, and literacy practices and how they supported the academic outcomes of their Black boy students that echoed my experiences with Mr. C.

As you will see throughout this book, based on the perceptions of their students, Mr. Javien, Mr. Henry, and Mr. Tal embodied and enacted teaching and literacy practices that countered anti-Black misandry in their own unique ways. At the same time, however, there were several themes consistent across their pedagogical, schooling, and literacy practices. They had the audacity to challenge pedagogical, curricular, and literacy norms (King & Swartz, 2014; Ladson-Billings, 2009) which often focus on White middle-class children, leaving Black children—and especially boys—behind. They had a deep level of concern for Black boys (and girls), and they deepened students' individual and collective critical consciousness by teaching to counteract anti-Black misandry and to help them understand at a young age what it means to exist in "Black [male] bodies under White gazes" (Yancy, 2017). Finally, they were courageous teachers who recognized and tapped into and promoted the individual and collective academic brilliance of Black boys, and provided them the essential academic and social tools to successfully navigate an educational system that was designed to fail Black boys. Instead of granting these boys what Ladson-Billings (2002) referred to as "permission to fail" (p. 107)—excuses for underperforming in schools—these Black male kindergarten teachers granted them permission/demands to succeed; e.g., reasons to believe in themselves and their own possibilities, and to perform well in and beyond schools, despite the odds against them (Ladson-Billings, 2002).

During my study, I also met five brilliant Black boys, ages 5–6 years old, who spoke about the pedagogical styles and literacy practices of these male teachers, and how these teachers impacted their lives in early childhood education. Ameer, Braden, Roland, Joshua, and Maurice (all pseudonyms) admired their Black male teachers. Based on my observations, these Black boys eagerly sought to learn with their teachers every day. For them, their teachers were not merely "mentors on paper," or positive images of Black men presented in books and other texts (Thompson, 1996), but they were what I call *living epistles* of *mentors in Black male flesh*. Drawing on Black body politics, which acknowledge the conditions of Black bodies in White spaces (Yancy, 2017), I assert that *living epistles of mentors in Black male flesh* means that these teachers were fully and physically present as "walking counternarratives" (Hicks-Tafari, 2018, p. 796) to dominant deficit views of Black boys: The boys' words let me know that their teachers' embodied criticality and critical perspectives of early childhood education that were essential to supporting Black boys in their early childhood classrooms.

The positive and diverse images of Black boys and boyhood in early childhood education, which are presented in this book, are often left out of the educational narrative. As early as preschool, Black boys are constructed as *problems* (Hopkins, 1997; Jackson & Moore, 2008; Proffitt, 2020; Nasir et al., 2019; Wright & Counsell, 2018). Consequently, Black male teachers are summoned to classrooms to *keep them in line* (Brown, 2012), the "silver bullets" (Brown, 2012) who are expected to change the conditions of Black boys in schools within systems that fail to critique the ways in which racism, classism, anti-Blackness, and anti-Black misandry have negatively impacted the experiences of the Black boys they are expected to, in White savior parlance, save.

However, as you will see, insights from these brilliant boys and their teachers will frame and reframe the ways we think about Black boys and Black male teachers in early childhood education. I invite you to learn with and from them and their Black male teachers. I hope their insights will not only influence educators' perceptions of Black boys and the critical role of Black male teachers, but also help you examine your own pedagogical practices and how you can positively influence, support, and engage Black boys in teaching and learning processes that counters anti-Black misandry (which I further define in Chapter 1). The aim of this book is to affirm and reaffirm the notion that Black boys and male teachers matter, and that they will always matter in and beyond early childhood education.

It is beyond tragic that we have so few books and other texts that accomplish what I am attempting to do here: to promote what Carey (2019) refers to as the comprehensive mattering of Black boys (and male teachers) beyond deficit and one-dimensional constructions. Comprehensive mattering deals with honoring the full humanity of and acknowledging all the positive attributes Black boys (and male teachers) have to offer (Carey, 2019). However, I fully understand that ignoring such mattering of Black boys and male teachers is among the consequences of living *in, under,* and *through* a white supremacist system where neither the lives of Black boys nor teachers matter. As such, it is my hope that this book helps us value the pedagogical practices of Black male teachers, and, more important, Black boys' perceptions of teaching and literacy practices in early childhood classrooms. In summary, I hope the memories of my kindergarten teacher and the insights and perceptions of the Black boys of their Black male teachers push us to see the importance of having Black male teachers who teach to transgress to better support the academic and social outcomes of Black boys in early childhood education. In school systems that have turned into prison pipelines for many of these boys, we owe it to them.

Organization of This Book

Because I see this book as an artful masterpiece, I position myself not only as a researcher and a teacher, but as a portraitist who is painting intimate portraits of each of the Black boys and male teachers who are introduced in this book. Therefore, I use Lawrence-Lightfoot and Hoffman Davis' (1997) notion of portraiture to provide detailed accounts about the experiences of five Black boys and male teachers in early childhood classrooms. Portraiture is the conjoining of both art and science to capture the essence of human life, experiences, and opportunities. It uses a variety of qualitative methodology, including autobiography, case study, and ethnography, to story the human condition—in this case, the experiences of Black boys and the pedagogies, literacy, and schooling practices of Black male teachers in early childhood classrooms (Lawrence-Lightfoot & Hoffman Davis, 1997). As such, I follow the tradition of Lynn (2006), who used portraiture to investigate the experiences of culturally relevant Black male teachers in an earlier study. Readers can find out more about how I co-constructed the portraits of each Black boy and male teacher in the Appendix of this book. In particular, I employ Warren's (2017) notions of "zoom in" and "zoom out" to share the findings and analysis of this work, which are also found in chapters that highlight the portraits of the Black boys and teachers (mainly Chapters 4, 6, and 8). "Zoom in" allows researchers to share the research data of a phenomenon; "zoom out" is the analysis of the data.

Before sharing the portraits of five Black boys and their teachers, however, some initial theoretical work is necessary so that teachers can be provided background to develop deeper understandings of the lived experiences and realities of Black boys. I believe that doing so is essentially important to teachers who, according to Emdin (2011), are often given a "boat without a paddle," (p. 284) or practical tools that are not grounded in the realities and experiences of Black children. Like most educational scholars, I believe that Black children's experiences must inform pedagogical, literacy, and schooling practices (Ladson-Billings, 2009). Thus, the first chapters of this book focus on guiding frameworks that ground those experiences with portraits of the Black boys and male teachers highlighted at the end of each chapter. In this way, I provide practical recommendations and examples for early childhood educators to consider in the teaching and learning process in order to better support Black boys in classrooms.

Finally, in order to show solidarity with the Black boys and male teachers, I position myself throughout this book by interweaving personal narratives about my early childhood schooling experiences as a Black boy who attended public schools, and my lived realities as a Black male teacher.

Overview of Chapters

Following this Introduction, Chapter 1 provides an overview of the academic and social outcomes of Black boys in early childhood education. Drawing on Black Critical Theory (BlackCrit) and Black Male Studies, I propose that, much like their Black male counterparts in middle and high schools, while little has been written about the schooling experiences of younger Black boys, they are not faring well. They face academic and social marginalization due to institutional anti-Black misandry. As such, I describe the academic and social landscapes of Black boys in early childhood education as an anti-Black misandric phenomena.

Chapter 2 serves to introduce what I term *BlackBoyCrit Pedagogy*. Guided by and grounded in Black Critical Theory (BlackCrit) and Black Male Studies, BlackBoyCrit Pedagogy is an inter-curricular framework that acknowledges and contests anti-Black misandry in the early childhood experiences of Black boys, and provides them educational experiences that are grounded in their lived realities and those of their Black male teachers.

Chapter 3 addresses how the recruitment and retention of Black male teachers is the solution and/or response to the so-called underperformance of Black boys in schools. Because Black male teachers are often socially constructed as solely "disciplinarians," father-figures, and role models rather than pedagogues who are able to support the academic and social outcomes of Black boys in classrooms, I suggest that, much like the academic and social landscape of Black boys in early childhood education, the reasons for recruiting and retaining Black males is also an anti-Black misandric phenomenon. I encourage a shift in stance so that Black male teachers can be perceived as pedagogues whose pedagogies and schooling practices benefit Black boys in and beyond early childhood education.

Chapter 4 highlights Black males as *BlackBoyCrit Pedagogues* in early childhood classrooms, and as teachers who Black boys perceive as Role Models in their young lives. In this chapter, I focus on the characteristics of three Black male kindergarten teachers—Mr. Javien, Mr. Henry, and Mr. Tal—through the eyes of Black boy kindergarteners. Drawing on Sims-Bishop's (1990) notion of *windows and mirrors*, I describe how five Black boys in kindergarten classrooms found that male teachers provided them mirrors in which they could see themselves, and windows through which they could see the world. In other words, these boys saw these teachers as BlackBoyCrit Pedagogues whose pedagogies, literacies, and schooling practices counteracted anti-Black misandry.

Chapter 5 highlights the importance of challenging literacy normativity (Pritchard, 2017) in the early childhood classroom. As such, teachers are encouraged to consider all the possibilities of working to dismantle an anti-Black misandric and White-centric literacy curriculum in early childhood classrooms, and to consider the dangers of not doing so. In particular, I offer Black Masculine Literacies (Kirkland & Jackson, 2009, 2019) as an alternative to literacy normativity.

Building on Chapter 5, in Chapter 6 I focus specifically on the literacy and schooling practices of Mr. Tal, Mr. Henry, and Mr. Javien as described by their Black boy kindergarteners. These boys' portraits help educators see how, through the integration of sports, both teachers used Black Masculine Literacies to engage their students in their teaching as well as in literacy learning. Here, I suggest that Black Masculine Literacies can counter the White-centric and anti-Black misandric literacy curricula Black boys face in early childhood classrooms.

Chapter 7 highlights Black boyhood play experiences. *Play* is both a language and literacy practice, and it is foundational to early childhood education and is an important aspect of the academic enterprise; however, Black boyhood play is under-discussed in early childhood education, despite the anti-Black misandric violence—hate and violence specific to Black boys—that these boys face from their schools and communities as their play is often treated as, in need of discipline, in contrast to similar behaviors regarded differently in the play of White boys.

Chapter 8 highlights the portrait of Mr. Henry, whose literacy practices are described by Black boy kindergartener, Roland. Understanding his students' interest in boyhood play, Mr. Henry used play to help his students better connect with reading—a subject matter that is often erroneously described by those who do not see or value Black boy knowledge or who cannot teach beyond White-centric practices as "difficult" for Black boys. He also helped them to see play as a part of the academic enterprise, helped them challenge deficit constructions of Black boyhood play, and see boyhood play as a weapon that can be used against social injustices. As such, I introduce what I term *BlackBoy (Play)Crit Literacies*: a pedagogical tool, language and literacy approach, and practice that challenges anti-Black misandry, and the deficit perceptions of Black boyhood play through Black-centric books and other texts.

Chapter 9 concludes with BlackBoyCrit Pedagogy in Action, which describes how the framework can provide a new way forward through the pedagogies, literacy, and schooling practices of Black male teachers in the lives and education of Black boys in early childhood education.

Suggestions for Using This Book

Before concluding this introduction, I provide a few suggestions for using this book. I believe it is important that early childhood teachers/educators[6] who read this book are provided a few suggestions for using its contents to advance their own practices and the research on Black boys and male teachers. As such, please consider the following suggestions explained in this section: (1) Do not use this book as a prescriptive text; (2) Understand that Black boys and Black male teachers are not monolithic groups—they are different and bring varying social locations and identities to classrooms; and (3) Be comfortable feeling uncomfortable. Below, I briefly address each of these suggestions, which are vitally necessary if teachers desire to grow in their own practices and engage in what Howard (2014) has referred to as paradigm shift, or a strength-based view of the ways we perceive Black boys and male teachers.

Do Not Use This Book as a Prescriptive Text!

There is a tendency for most teachers to seek out pedagogical and other resources that prescribe methods for engaging Black children—and boys in this case. However, this book is not such a text. Teaching which addresses anti-Black misandry is not about providing prescribed methods that teachers follow. The examples and portraits of Black male teachers in this book highlight teachers who engage in counter-hegemonic teaching, and who engage in those practices *in their own ways*. They examine their own dispositions toward Black boys, take time to acquaint themselves with the students they are teaching, and shape their pedagogy to fit those students' needs. In other words, while the examples in this book of Black male teachers' teaching are noteworthy, teachers are encouraged to find and develop their own pedagogical styles using their recognition of anti-Black misandry-based teaching to counter and replace it with teaching *with* and not *for* the population of students with whom they work and/or will work in early childhood classrooms.

Understand That Black boys and Black Male Teachers are Not Monolithic Groups

Most White people tend to essentialize Black boys and male teachers, or view them all as having similar characteristics and interests. This is taught and reinforced in media, popular press, curriculum, schools, and society writ large. There are many ways to be a Black boy and/or a Black male teacher. While some boys may enjoy sports, others may not (Bryan, 2019); while some boys may enjoy hand games, others may not; and so on. Dumas and Nelson (2016) proposed that we use the term "boyhoods" instead of "boyhood" to describe the varying ways one can be a boy. As such, I encourage readers of this book to consider Black boyhoods and acknowledge the varying ways one can be Black and boy. In my own work,[7] I have challenged teachers to respect the varying ways in which Black boys play, to contest normalized hegemonic/dominant masculine performances of Black boys' play styles, and to embrace the fluidity of Black boyhoods and the ways in which they play. Therefore, I encourage readers to see the mosaic of differences that exist among Black boys and contest their own stereotypes and biases about them. In this book, you will learn about Black boys' interests in sports; however, the emphasis on such interests should not discourage readers from valuing the multiple interests of Black boys beyond sports.

Furthermore, throughout this book, and similar to Wright and Counsell (2018), when referring to children, I use the term "Black boy" or "Black boys" and not Black males, and I encourage early childhood educators to do likewise. The use of the term "boy(s)" serves to acknowledge the humanity, innocence, and childhoods of the Black boys I highlight in this book. I fully understand that the use of the term "boy" is grounded in a racialized history of the dehumanization of Black men. White men and women have used the term to both dehumanize and disrespect Black men during Jim and Jane Crow segregation, and even presently (Curry, 2017; Siddle-Walker, 1996). However, I use the term "boy" here to honor the childhoods of these young learners, particularly since Black children are often criminalized (e.g., arrested, tried, and sentenced) as youth and adults. As such, my use of the term "Black boys" is an act of preserving Black children's rights to their childhoods.

Like Black boys, Black male teachers bring varying social identities to classrooms (Brockenbrough, 2012). Research studies (Brockenbrough, 2012; Woodson & Bristol, 2020; Woodson & Pabon, 2016) on Black male teachers have challenged the essentialization of this group. Challenging the traditional view of the Black male teacher, Brown (2012) has suggested that they have been socially constructed as what he has called *pedagogical kind*. According to Brown, the role of *pedagogical kind* is one in which the expectations of Black male teachers are essentially defined before they enter classrooms. As mentioned earlier in this chapter, Black male teachers across all levels, including early childhood education, are expected to serve as role models, father-figures, and disciplinarians. These expectations are often in response to the deficit construction of both Black men and boys (Brown, 2009, 2012). For example,

Black men are often constructed as absent fathers, despite research studies that suggest they are more involved in the everyday experiences of Black children than any other racial and ethnic group (Coles et al., 2010; Center for Disease Control, 2013). Anchored in the same anti-Black misandric biases, Black boys are socially constructed as disciplinary problems and troublemakers (Brooms, 2017; Harper, et al., 2014; Howard, 2008, 2013; Jenkins, 2006; Wright & Counsell, 2018; Wood & Harper, 2015). We know that these narratives—however dominant—are not true. Similarly, through the eyes of Black boys, this text hopes to encourage readers to let go of essentialist notions of what Black male teachers are and do. It is important to understand that the ways in which the teaching styles of Black male teachers and their engagement with Black boys may look similar in some ways, but are different in other ways.

Be Comfortable Feeling Uncomfortable!

At this point, given the emphasis on issues of race, racism, white supremacy, anti-Blackness, and anti-Black misandry, many readers may begin to feel uncomfortable. Scholars (DiAngelo, 2018; Love, 2019; Milner, 2020) have documented White and non-White teachers' discomfort with discussing such issues. However, I encourage you to relax, take a deep breath, and focus on learning something new. Boutte (2016) asserts that, when White and other teachers begin to feel uncomfortable discussing what many people consider *difficult* topics, they are on the verge of a learning edge. A learning edge is a liminal space where individuals can deepen knowledge about controversial topics (Boutte, 2016). When I teach courses at the university-level and conduct professional development training in schools and the typically white-dominant groups exhibit discomfort, I frequently ask them to consider the everyday discomfort of Black and Brown children, especially boys, who rarely find safe spaces in a world and in schools that are constructed to be "against the dark" (Dumas, 2016, p. 11): spaces that reflect everyday disdain and disgust for Black people and children. I admire the way Bettina Love (2019) reinforces this as she attempts to engage teachers who are participants in her professional development sessions. As she explains, "I remind them that it's okay to be uncomfortable but also to understand that while you may be uncomfortable for forty-five minutes, other people are uncomfortable their entire lives dealing with oppression" (Love, 2019, p. 148). If educators want to genuinely support Black boys and Black male teachers in schools, they must learn to feel comfortable having uncomfortable conversations about race, racism, white supremacy, anti-Blackness, anti-Black misandry, and other forms of oppression. Texts that can support educators in developing that comfort can be readily accessible and may be helpful reading alongside this book (Alexander, 2010; Coates, 2015; Cooper, 2018; DiAngelo, 2018; DuBois, 1903; Dyson, 2017; Love, 2019; Oluo, 2019; Perry, 2019; Picower, 2021; Saad, 2020; Woodson, 1933). Albeit far from exhaustive, I provide a list of sources, located throughout the book, so teachers can read and learn more about race, racism, and other forms of oppression.

Notes

1 St. John Center was a public early learning development center run and operated in the mid-1980s by a local Episcopal church in downtown Charleston, South Carolina. It consisted of grades PreK-2.
2 Scholars define misandry as a particular disdain for boys and men in general; however, given the history of enslavement and the historical and contemporary racialized and gendered victimization of Black men, Black Male Studies scholars (Curry, 2017; Curry & Utley, 2018) theorize anti-Black misandry which addresses ways in which American laws, policies, and institutions reflect disdain for Black men.
3 Dominant narratives and longtime excuses surrounding school closures suggest that schools are closed due to 'academic performance.' However, counternarratives assert that school closures are neoliberal projects used to justify takeover and gentrification, which remove Black people from their homes and communities (Kozol, 2005, 2012; Lipman, 2011; Saltman, 2007).
4 Butchart (2010) described anti-Black terrorism as "the overwhelming force and violence, ranging from simple intimidation through incendiarism, physical violence, shootings and murder against [Black] students and teachers" (p. 33), as enacted by White people.
5 Drawn from the Black womanist/feminist movement, *othermothers* and *otherfathers* refer to the active roles of caring and Role Modeling demonstrated by Black women and men educators toward children in Black communities (Collins, 2000; Lynn, 2006; Williams, 2018).
6 The term *early childhood teachers/educators* is used to describe stakeholders who are interested in the wellbeing of young children and particularly Black boys in grades PreK-3. They include, but are not limited to: teachers, teacher's assistants, administrators, and researchers who study and work with young children. Readers should also note that my use of the pronouns "we" and "you" throughout this book also refer to early childhood educators/teachers.
7 See N. Bryan (2019), "Playing with or like the girls": Advancing the performance of multiple masculinities in Black boys' childhood play in US early childhood classrooms, in *Gender and Education, 31*(3), 309–326.

References

Alexander, M. (2010). *The new jim crow: Mass incarceration in the age of colorblindness*. The New Press.
American Educational Research Association. (2015). *Social Justice Award lecture*. https://www.youtube.com/watch?v=ofB_t1oTYhI
Baines, J., Tisdale, C., & Long, S. (2018). *"We've been doing it your way long enough": Choosing the culturally relevant classroom*. Teachers College Press.
Boutte, G. (2016). *Educating African-American students: And how are the children?* Routledge.
Boutte, G., & Johnson, G. (2013). Funga Alafia: Toward welcoming, understanding, and respecting African American speakers' bilingualism and biliteracy. *Excellence & Equity in Education, 46*(3), 300–314.
Bristol, T., & Goings, R. (2019). Exploring the boundary-heightening experiences of black male teachers: Lessons for teacher education programs. *Journal of Teacher Education, 70*(1), 51–64.
Brockenbrough, E. (2012). "You ain't my daddy": Black male teachers and the politics of surrogate father. *Teacher College Record, 114*(5), 1–43.
Brooms, D. (2017). *Being black, being male on campus: Understanding and confronting black male collegiate experiences*. SUNY Press.

Brown, A. L. (2009). "Brothers gonna work it out": Understanding the pedagogic performance of African American male teachers working with African American male students. *Urban Review*, 41(5), 416–435.

Brown, A. L. (2011). Pedagogies of experience: A case study of the African American male teacher. *Teaching Education*, 22(4), 363–376.

Brown, A. L. (2012). On human kinds and role models: A critical discussion about the African American male teacher. *Educational Studies*, 48(3), 296–315.

Bryan, N. (2019). Playing with or like the girls: Advancing the performance of 'multiple masculinities in black boys' childhood play in US early childhood classrooms. *Gender and Education*, 31(3), 309–326.

Butchart, R. (2010). Black hope, white power: Emancipation, reconstruction and the legacy of unequal schooling in the US South, 1861–1880. *Paedagogica Historica*, 46(1/2), 33–50.

Carey, R. (2019). Imagining the comprehensive mattering of black boys and young men in society and schools: Toward a new approach. *Harvard Educational Review*, 89(3), 370–396.

Carver-Thomas, D., & Darling-Hammond, L. (2017). What black women teachers leave and what can be done about it. In A. Farinde-Wu, A. Allen-Hardy, & C. Lewis (Eds.), *Black female teachers: Diversifying the United States' teacher workforce* (pp. 159–184). Emerald Publishing.

Center for Disease Control and Prevention. (2013). Fathers' involvement with their children: United States, 2006–2010. *National Health Statistics Report*, 71, 1–21.

Coates, T. (2015). *Between the world and me*. Spiegel & Grau.

Coles, R. L., Coles, R., Green, C. (Eds.). (2010). *The myth of the missing black father*. Columbia University Press.

Collins, P. (2000). *Black feminist thought: Knowledge, consciousness, and the politics of empowerment*. Routledge.

Cook, D. A. (2010). Disrupted but not destroyed: Fictive kinship networks among black educators in post Katrina New Orleans. *Southern Anthropologist*, 35(2), 1–25.

Cooper, B. (2018). *Eloquent rage: A black feminist discover her superpower*. St. Martin's Press.

Curry, T. (2017). *Man-not: Race, class, genre and the dilemmas of black manhood*. Temple University Press.

Curry, T., & Curry, G. (2018). Taking it to the people: Translating empirical findings about black men and black families through a black public philosophy. *Dewey Studies*, 2 (1), 42–71.

Curry, T., & Utley, E. (2018). She touched me: Five snapshots of adult sexual violation of black boys. *Kennedy Institute of Ethics Journal*, 28(2), 205–241.

Delpit, L. (1995). *Other people's children: Cultural conflicts in the classroom*. The New Press.

DiAngelo, R. (2018). *White fragility: Why it's so hard for white people to talk about racism*. Beacon Press.

Dillard, C. (2016). Turning the ships around: A case study of (re)membering as transnational endarkened feminist inquiry and praxis for black teachers. *Educational Studies*, 52 (5), 406–423.

Dingus, J. (2006). Doing the best we could: African American teachers' counterstory on school desegregation. *The Urban Review*, 38(3), 211–233.

DuBois, W. E. B. (1903). *The souls of black folks*. Dovers Publication.

Dumas, M. (2016). Against the dark: Anti-blackness in education policy and discourse. *Theory into Practice*, 55(1), 11–19.

Dumas, M. and Nelson, J. (2016). Reimagining black boyhood: Toward a critical framework for educational research. *Harvard Educational Review*, 86(1), 27–47.

Dyson, M. E. (2017). *Tears we cannot stop: A sermon to white America*. St. Martin's Press.

Emdin, C. (2011). Moving beyond the boat without a paddle: Reality pedagogy, black youth, and urban science education. *Journal of Negro Education*, 80(3), 284–295.

Fanon, F. (1963). *The wretched of the earth*. Grove Press.

Farinde-Wu, A., Allen, A., & Lewis, C. (Eds.) (2017). *Black female teachers: Diversifying the United States' teacher workforce*. Emerald Publishing.

Foster, M. (1997). *Black teachers on teaching*. The New Press.

Frazier, H., Power, B. E., & Wentworth, M. (2016). *We are Charleston*. Emerald Publishing.

Gay, G. (2010). *Culturally responsive teaching: Theory, research, and practice*. Teacher College Press.

Harper, S. R.et al. (2014). *Succeeding in the city: A report from the New York City black and Latino male high school achievement study*. University of Pennsylvania, Center for the Study of Race and Equity in Education. www.gse.upenn.edu/equity/sites/gse.upenn.edu. equity/files/publications/Harper_and_Ass ociates_2014.pdf

Hicks-Tafari, D. (2018). "Whose world is this?" A composite counterstory of black male elementary school teachers as hip-hop other fathers. *Urban Review*, 50(5), 795–817.

hooks, b. (1994). *Teaching to transgress: Education as the practice of freedom*. Routledge.

Hopkins, R. (1997). *Educating black males: Critical lessons in schooling, community, and power*. SUNY Press.

Howard, T. C. (2008). Who really cares? The disenfranchisement of African American males in preK-12 schools: A critical race theory perspective. *Teachers College Record*, 110 (5), 954–985.

Howard, T. C. (2013). How does it feel to be a problem? Black male students, schools, and learning in enhancing the knowledge base to disrupt deficit frameworks. *Review of Research in Education*, 37(1), 54–86.

Howard, T. C. (2014). *Black maled: Perils and promises in the education of African American males*. Teacher College Press.

Jackson, T., & Kohli, R. (2016). Guest editors' introduction: The state of teachers of color. *Equity and Excellence in Education*, 49(1), 1–8.

Jackson, J., & Moore, J. (2008). Introduction: The African American male crisis in education: A popular media infatuation or needed public policy response? *American Behavioral Scientist*, 51(7), 847–853.

Jenkins, T. S. (2006). Mr. nigger: The challenges of educating black males within American society. *Journal of Black Studies*, 37(1), 127–155.

Jones, R., & Jenkins, A. (2012). *Call me mister: The reemergence of African American male teachers in South Carolina*. Advantage Media Group.

King, J. (2019). Staying human: Forty years of black studies practical critical activity in the spirit of Aunt Jemima. *International Journal of African Renaissance Studies*, 14(2), 9–31.

King, J., & Swartz, E. (2014). *"Re-membering" history in student and teacher learning: An Afrocentric culturally informed praxis*. Routledge.

King, J. (2005). *Black education: A transformative research and action agenda for the new century*. Routledge.

Kinloch, V. (2010). *Harlem on our minds: Place, race, and the literacies of urban youth*. Teachers College Press.

Kirkland, D. (2011). Books like clothes: Engaging young black men with reading. *Journal of Adolescent and Adult Literacy*, 55(3), 199–208.

Kirkland, D., & Jackson, A. (2009). Beyond the silence: Instructional approaches and students' attitudes. In J. C.Scott, D. Y.Straker, & L. Katz (Eds.), *Affirming students' right to their own language: Bridging language policies and pedagogical practices* (pp. 132–150). Routledge.

Kirkland, D., & Jackson, A. (2019). Toward a theory of black masculine literacies. In T. Ransaw, C. P. Gause, & R. Majors (Eds), *The handbook of research on black males: Quantitative, qualitative, and multidisciplinary* (pp. 367–396). Michigan State Press.

Kozol, J. (2005). *The shame of the nation: The restoration of apartheid schooling in America.* Crown Publishers.

Kozol, J. (2012). *Savage inequalities.* Broadway Paperbacks.

Ladson-Billings, G. (1994). *The dreamkeepers: successful teachers of African American children.* Jossey-Bass.

Ladson-Billings, G. (2002). I ain't writin nuttin: Permission to fail and demands to succeed in urban classrooms. In L. Delpit and J. K. Dowdy (Eds.), *The skin that we speak: Thoughts on language and culture in the classroom.* The New Press.

Ladson-Billings, G. (2005a). Is the team all right? Diversity and teacher education. *Journal of Teacher Education,* 56(3), 1–6.

Ladson-Billings, G. (2005b). *Beyond the big house: African American educators on teacher education.* Teacher College Press.

Ladson-Billings, G. (2006). From achievement gap to education debt: Understanding achievement in U.S. schools. *Educational Researcher,* 35(7), 3–12.

Ladson-Billings, G. (2009). *The dreamkeeper: Successful teachers of African American children* (2nd ed.). Jossey-Bass.

Landsman, J., & Lewis, C. (Eds.) (2006). *White teachers/diverse classrooms: Creating inclusive schools. Building on students' diversity and providing true educational equity* (2nd ed.). Stylus.

Lawrence-Lightfoot, S., & Hoffman-Davis, J. (1997). *The art and science of portraiture.* Jossey-Bass.

Lewis, C., & Toldson, I. (Eds.). (2013). *Black male teachers: Diversifying the United States' teacher workforce.* Emerald Group Publishing.

Lipman, P. (2011). *The new political economy of urban education.* Routledge.

Losen, D. J. (2013). Discipline policies, successful schools, racial justice, and the law. *Family Court Review,* 51, 388–400.

Losen, D. J., & Gillespie, J. (2012). *Opportunities suspended: The disparate impact of disciplinary exclusion from school.* UCLA Civil Rights Project.

Love, B. L. (2019). *We want to do more than survive: Abolitionist teaching and the pursuit ofeducational freedom.* Beacon Press.

Lynn, M. (2006). Education for the community: Exploring the culturally relevant practice of black male teachers. *Teachers College Record,* 108(12), 2497–2522.

Milner, H. R. (2020). Fifteenth annual AERA Brown lecture in education research: Disrupting punitive practices and policies: Rac(e)ing back to teaching, teacher preparation, and Brown. *Educational Researcher,* 49(3), 147–160.

Milner, H. R. (2020). *Start where you are, but don't stay there: Understanding diversity, opportunity gaps, and teaching in today's classrooms* (2nd ed.). Harvard Education Press.

Morris, M. (2016). *Pushout: The criminalization of black girls in schools.* The New Press.

Murrell, P. (2001). *The community teacher: A new framework for effective urban teaching.* Teachers College Press.

Nasir, N. S., Givens, J. R., & Chatmon, C. P. (Eds.) (2019). *We dare say love: Supporting achievement in the educational life of black boys.* Teachers College Press.

National Center for Education Statistics. (2017). Status and trends in the education of racial and ethnic groups 2017. https://nces.ed.gov/pubs2017/2017051.pdf

Oluo, I. (2019). *So you want to talk about race.* Seal Press.

Patton, S. (2017). *Spare the kids: Why whupping children won't save black America.* Beacon Press.

Perry, I. (2019). *Breathe: A letter to my sons.* Beacon Press.

Perry. T., Steele, C., & Hilliard, A.III. (2003). *Young, gifted, and black: Promoting high achievement outcome among African-American students.* Beacon Press.

Picower, B. (2021). *Reading, writing, and racism: Disrupting whiteness in teacher education and in the classroom.* Beacon Press.

Pritchard, D. E. (2017). *Fashioning lives: Black queers and the politics of literacy.* Illinois University Press.

Proffitt, W. (2020). From "problems" to "vulnerable resources": Reconceptualizing black boys with or without disability labels in U.S. urban schools. Urban Education.

Rashid, H. (2009). From brilliant baby to child placed at risk. The perilous path of African American boys in early childhood education. *Journal of Negro Education,* 78(3), 347–358.

Saad, L. (2020). *Me and white supremacy: Combat racism, change the world, become a good ancestor.* Sourcebooks.

Saltman, K. J. (2007). Schooling in disaster capitalism: How the political right is using disaster to privatize public schooling. *Teacher Education Quarterly,* 131–156.

Siddle-Walker, V. (1996). *Their highest potential: An African American school community in the segregated South.* University of North Carolina Press.

Sims-Bishop, R. (1990). Mirrors, windows, and sliding glass doors. *Perspectives: Choosing and using books for the classroom,* 6(3), ix–xi.

Sleeter, C., & Milner, R. (2011). Researching successful efforts in teacher education to diversify teachers. In A. F.Ball, & C. Tyson (Eds.), *Studying diversity in teacher education* (pp. 81–103). Rowman & Littlefield.

Thompson, M. C. (1996). Mentors on paper: How classics develop verbal ability. In J. VanTassel-Baska, D. T. Johnson, & L. N. Boyce (Eds.), *Developing verbal talent: Ideas and strategies for teachers of elementary and middle school students* (pp. 56–74). Allyn and Bacon.

United States Bureau of Labor Statistics. (2018). Employment situation summary. https://www.bls.gov/bls/news-release/empsit.htm#2018

Warren, C. (2017). *Urban preparation: Young black men moving Chicago's South Side to success in higher education.* Harvard Education Press.

Williams, H. (2005). *Self-taught: African American education in slavery and freedom.* University of North Carolina Press.

Williams, P. (1987). Spirit-murdering the messenger: The discourse of finger pointing as the law's response to racism. *U. Miami L. Rev,* 42, 127.

Williams, T. (2018). Do no harm: Strategies for culturally relevant caring in middle level classrooms from the community experiences and life histories of black middle level teachers. *Research in Middle Level Education,* 41(6), 1–13.

Wood, J. L., & Harper, S. (2015). *Advancing black male student success from preschool to through PhD.* Stylus Publishing.

Woodson, A., & Bristol, T. (2020). Male teachers of color: Charting a new landscape for educational research. *Race, Ethnicity, and Education,* 23(3), 281–287.

Woodson, A., & Pabon, A. (2016). "I'm none of the above": Exploring themes of heteropatriarchy in the life histories of black male educators. *Equity and Excellence,* 49(1), 57–71.

Woodson, C. G. (1933). *The miseducation of the negro.* Dove.

Wright, B., & Counsell, S. (2018). *The brilliance of black boys: Cultivating success in the early grades.* Teacher College Press.

Wynter-Hoyte, K., Long, S., McAdoo, T. M., Strickland, J. D. (2020). "Losing one African American Teacher is one too many": A critical race analysis of support for Praxis Core as African American students speak out. *Teachers College Record*, 122(11).

Yancy, G. (2017). *Black bodies, white gazes: The continuing significance of race* (2nd ed.). Rowman & Littlefield.

Yosso, T. J. (2005). Whose culture has capital? *Race, Ethnicity and Education*, 8(1), 69–91.

1

ARE BLACK BOYS WELL?

Anti-Black Misandry in the Academic and Social Landscape of Black Boys in Early Childhood Education

As I reflect on my own childhood schooling experiences briefly outlined in the Introduction to this book, I must admit: I was not well at all in school. Despite attending public schools on the heels of *Brown vs. Board of Education* (1954)—long-sought-after civil rights legislation that promised school desegregation and equality (Siddle-Walker, 1996)—my early childhood schooling experiences were still subpar due to institutional anti-Black misandry that ran rampant in the curriculum and pedagogical practices of my White teachers. I agree with scholars (Anderson, 1988; Perry et al., 2004; Williams, 2005) who have suggested that, for Black children and particularly Black boys, education is, has been, and will continue to be a constant struggle because their academic and social strengths are not recognized nor valued and, consequently, their needs misunderstood and barely met in and beyond early childhood education.

To understand why significant change is needed in the early education of Black boys, it is important for educators to recognize how the academic and social land-scapes of Black boys constitute anti-Black misandric phenomena. Defined in the Introduction, I use the term anti-Black misandry as a way to capture the disdain for Black boys that is reflected in American laws, policies, institutions, school curricula, pedagogies, literacies, resources, and practices (Curry, 2017). In this chapter, I explore those landscapes with a particular focus on early literacy, math, and school discipline. I hope that, by exploring such landscapes through anti-Black misandric lenses, teachers will understand the need to broach conversations in faculty meetings, classrooms, teachers' lounges, professional conferences, and other spaces that will allow them to ask about and center the well-being of Black boys. Similarly, I hope such examinations of academic and social outcomes will encourage teachers to identify their complicity in the ongoing anti-Black misandric violence and erasure of Black boys' academic and social potential, and to examine their own practices to

DOI: 10.4324/9780429287619-2

better support Black boys in early childhood classrooms. Finally, by understanding the landscape for Black boys, I set the scene for introducing BlackBoyCrit Pedagogy in Chapter 2.

In her book titled *Educating African-American Children: And How Are the Children?* Gloria Boutte (2016) drew on the story of the Maasai warriors to encourage teachers to consider the academic and social landscape of Black children, and the importance of culturally relevant teaching in K-12 schools. Maasai warriors are known to be the most intelligent, fiercest, and most community-oriented tribe in East Africa. In fact, the communicative exchanges between the Maasai reinforce the African notion of *ubuntu*—community. Boutte pointed out that, when a Maasai greets another Maasai warrior, they ask: *And how are the children?* An affirmative response—e.g., *the children are well*—not only signifies the well-being of the children, but that of the collective Maasai community. In an effort to provide a Black boy-centric examination and focus specifically on the academic and social outcomes of Black boys in early childhood education, Bryan and Wright (2019) have extended the question to ask, *And how are the Black boys?* Considering my own experiences and those of five Black kindergartners described in this book, I suggest that to create equitable learning environments for every child, we as early childhood educators must be willing to ask ourselves, *Are Black boys well?*

The aforementioned question is extremely crucial, particularly regarding the academic and social needs of Black boys in early childhood education that have been consistently left out of conversations about Black males in public K-12 schools. In 2003, James Earl Davis addressed the deafening silence in the research and a lack of focus on Black boys in early childhood education. In so doing, Davis reminded educational scholars about the tendency to neglect the needs and outcomes of young Black boys, and encouraged others to take up the charge of investigating their schooling experiences and outcomes. Recently, researchers responded to this recommendation by underscoring the brilliance of Black boys in early childhood education (Wright & Ford, 2016, 2019; Wright & Counsell (2018). Prior to this growing body of work, most scholars focused disproportionately on the academic and social outcomes of Black boys in middle and high schools. For example, in a special issue of *Teachers College Record* titled *In Their Own Words: Erasing the Deficits and Exploring What Works to Improve K-12 and Post-Secondary Black Male School Achievement* (Warren et al., 2016), the issue as a whole undertheorized and under-discussed the experiences of Black boys in early childhood education. Other scholars (Howard, 2014; Noguera, 2014; Kirkland & Jackson, 2009) have studied Black males at the middle and secondary levels. Indeed, for some scholars, the academic and social outcomes and experiences of young Black boys may not be considered to be as important or their experiences as seriously considered as those of Black males in secondary and post-secondary schools.

However, given the historical and contemporary anti-Black misandry Black boys face in and beyond early childhood education (Davis, 2003; Hopkins, 1997; Howard, 2014; Wright & Counsell, 2018), we cannot say with honesty and integrity that Black boys are well. As my own experiences attest, the academic and social outcomes of many Black boys stand on a shaky foundation; most teachers fail to recognize their strengths, buy into and perpetuate long-held anti-Black misandric stereotypes and biases as foundational to their perceptions of Black boys, and neglect the academic and social needs of Black boys in and beyond early childhood education (Rashid, 2009). As such, Black boys' schooling experiences are often negatively impacted by the types of anti-Black violence (e.g., physical, symbolic, curricular, linguistic, and systemic) that will be discussed in Chapter 2. Dumas and Nelson (2016) proposed that, as victims of anti-Black violence in schools, Black boys are also subjected to institutional Black suffering—the ongoing pain associated with being Black in an anti-Black world—which Duncan (2002) has attributed to teachers and administrators who treat Black boys as if they are "beyond love" (p. 131): they are denied the same kinds of empathy naturally afforded to White children.

In *And We Are Not Saved: The Elusive Quest for Racial Justice*, Bell (1988) asserted that, decades after the *Brown vs. Board of Education* ruling, Black children were still not saved from the clutches of white supremacy and racism in schools. Consequently, and in spite of the growing movement to bring attention to said conditions through books, research studies, and professional conferences, we cannot say today that Black boys have been saved from the clutches of anti-Black misandry (Toldson & Johns, 2016; Hotchkins, 2016; Warren et al., 2016). They are still victims of race, racism, white supremacy, and anti-Black misandry, which negatively impact their academic and social outcomes in and beyond early childhood education.

In efforts to help teachers understand why better support is necessary for Black boys, in this chapter, I make explicit the ways in which anti-Black misandry inform the academic and social outcomes of Black boys in early childhood education. However, before I address the academic and social landscape of Black boys in early childhood education, I first discuss a few characteristics of anti-Black misandric teaching and attitudes that help to shape that landscape: (a) deficit-thinking that often blames Black boys for their own schooling experiences and conditions; (b) academic achievement gap language; and (c) failure to listen to Black boys.

Deficit-Thinking

Civil rights leader Dr. Martin Luther King, Jr. asserted, "People with such a low view of the Black race cannot be given free rein and put in charge of the intellectual care and development of our boys and girls" (Minow at al., 2008, p. 268). Furthering this perspective, civil and human rights activist Malcolm X warned of the psychological erosion of Black children's minds when they are taught by those who hate Black people (X & Haley, 1965). It is customary to hear deficit-thinking about Black boys and their families in many educational settings, including early childhood classrooms, faculty meetings, teachers' lounges, higher education classrooms, and professional conferences. According to Patton-Davis and Museus (2019), deficit-thinking holds students from historically oppressed populations responsible for the challenges and inequalities that they face. Overall, these perspectives serve as tools that maintain hegemonic systems and in doing so, fail to place accountability with oppressive systems, policies, and practices within educational settings. (p. 119)

Although it may be unintentional, many early childhood teachers and researchers tend to engage in and uphold deficit-oriented language and beliefs about Black boys without fully understanding how such thinking negatively impacts teachers' mindsets, belief systems, pedagogies, literacy and schooling practices, and the educational experiences of Black boys (i.e., "lazy," "recalcitrant," and "unintelligent"; Howard, 2014; Warren, 2017). These practitioners and scholars tend to blame Black boys for the conditions under which they are schooled rather than self-reflect and interrogate the institutional inequities including anti-Black misandry that negatively inform young boys' schooling experiences.

School readiness deals with children's overall academic preparedness for school, which report and research studies have argued are strong predictors of later academic success in schools (Wright & Counsell, 2018). When discussing school readiness, early childhood educators typically rely on deficit views of Black boys (Wright & Counsell, 2018). This means subscribing to views about the kinds of tasks (e.g., sitting still, raising hands, playing quietly) they erroneously believe Black boys to be unable to perform rather than looking at school readiness in terms of abilities Black boys bring to the classroom as problem solvers, language users, consumers of a range of literacies, phonemically aware, and much more. This change in stance requires early childhood educators to rethink the idea of school readiness moving away from its Eurocentric origins to center the academic and social strengths and possibilities of Black boys (Wright & Counsell, 2018). In so doing, early childhood educators will see that it is the curriculum and attitudes about what constitutes knowledge that need to change, not the children which means that "many Black boys are ready for school, but school is not ready for them" (Wright & Counsell, 2018, p. 32).

In my professional capacities as teacher, teacher educator, and school administrator, I have heard the following statements directly from preservice and inservice teachers:

"Black boys are the worst behaved students in our school!"
"They just don't care about school!"
"They are lazy! If they put forth more effort, they can achieve [success]!"
"I wish his [referring to a Black boy's] father was more involved in his life."

These comments were made by teachers who claimed they loved *all* children; and yet, they upheld such deficit-thinking about Black boys. Johnson et al. (2019) have referred to such love as *fake love*. According to these scholars, fake love

> is inauthentic and it reproduces the disloyalty urban teachers have with Black children and youth. When teachers embody *fake love*, it produces this bogus relationship, which we describe as pretentious and masquerading the real hate White teachers have and give to Black youth (Thomas, 2017). Simply put, White teachers, like White people in general, 'love on' Black culture but do not 'love on' Black people. (p. 54).

These deficit comments reflecting a kind of fake love are neither new realities in schools nor in educational scholarship. Research studies (Anderson, 2019; Ferguson, 2000) have previously confirmed similar deficit and anti-Black misandric thinking about Black boys in schools. In a groundbreaking study on Black boys in an urban elementary school, Anne Arnette Ferguson (2000) found that teachers often labeled Black boys as bad, criminals, and problems. Similarly, Anderson (2019) found that teachers in a rural elementary school labeled Black boys as thugs and gangsters and as having disrespectful demeanors and attitudes. Other studies have suggested that many teachers stereotypically believe that Black boys are underachievers, lazy, and unintelligent (Bonner, 2003; Davis, 2003; Howard, 2014; Wright & Ford, 2016, 2019).

Recognizing the damaging impact of deficit views and fake love that dehumanize Black boys makes the need for *revolutionary love* very clear. This is a kind of love that centers Blackness and challenges the types of anti-Black violence Black boys face in schools (Johnson et al., 2019). Revolutionary love rejects deficit and anti-Black misandric thinking that creates negative models of Black boys. These models underlie the larger project of *schooling* or *being schooled* – teaching in ways that maintain the status quo which socializes Black boys into subordinate positions by disciplining and controlling rather than educating them (Shujaa, 1994). Schooling as a form of control originated in colonial projects used to subjugate Black boys, one strategy utilized in the creation of the U.S. empire (Howard, 2014). Under such systems which continue to guide education today, educators grant Black boys "permission to fail" (Ladson-Billings, 2002), thus blocking their academic and social pipelines towards success and future opportunities. In contrast, *educating* means that teachers provide Black children the tools to see the brilliance and ingenuity that lie in themselves and their own culture (Shujaa, 1994). Educating also means that educators must learn to recognize when actions, curriculum, and attitudes stymie Black boys' abilities to see their own brilliance and ingenuity (Wright & Counsell, 2018). This includes looking at broken systems of assessment and testing that continue to ignore/conceal the strengths of Black boys and rejecting the emphasis on standardized tests scores that narrowly define and proscribe Black boys' potential in early childhood classrooms (Davis, 2003; Howard, 2014).

It should be clear that the functions and mechanisms of schooling that reflect anti-Black misandric phenomena also impact any marginalized group in close proximity to Black boys. Black girls are also subjected to too much schooling and too little education; they face all of the consequences for living and schooling while Black (Morris, 2016). To put it simply, because of deficit practices, Black children experience "too much schooling, and too little education," with consequences that negatively impact them for a lifetime (Shujaa, 1994).

The negative impact of Black children's internalizations of deficit messages cannot be underestimated. When students do not perceive their teachers as believing in their full potentials, they will not embrace what Whiting (2009) terms their "scholarly identity"—the ability to see themselves as scholars in schools. Black boys themselves regularly acknowledge their teachers' deficit views about them, an internalization with potentially disastrous implications for their self-esteem, academic accomplishment, professional success, and emotional health. In one of many studies, Anderson (2019) shared how Black boys described how teachers labeled them as disciplinary problems and future prisoners. For example, referring to his White female teacher, David, a third-grade Black boy who participated in Anderson's study, remarked, "I always get in trouble and [am] told that I'm bad and she always thinks it's me doing something wrong but she never says anything to anybody else" (p. 30). David was one of two Black boys in his third-grade class. In contrast, when children, and especially Black boys, know that their teachers see them for their strengths, strong positive rather than contentious relationships are developed and students perform better academically and socially in schools (Howard, 2014; Milner, 2010; Warren, 2017).

In sum, rather than upholding deficit-thinking, overhauling pedagogy requires teachers to reframe the ways they think about Black boys and their intellectual abilities (Harper, 2010). This means an intentional shift from focusing on what Black boys supposedly *cannot* do in classrooms to a focus on what they *can* do (Harper, 2010), embracing assets-based thinking by focusing on the strengths, potentials, and possibilities Black boys bring to early childhood classrooms (Wright & Ford, 2019). In doing so, teachers can find joy in teaching Black boys by rejecting profiles of them as "broken" rather than asset-rich learners. This means rejecting models such as *The Guide for White Teachers Who Teach Black Boys* (Moore et al., 2018) which makes it appear that working with Black boys is a scripted phenomenon. Although many critical scholars have written chapters for this co-edited volume in an effort to encourage White teachers to rethink the ways they view Black boys, the title of the book constructs Black boys as children who are broken and need to be assembled and/or reassembled by White teachers. Black-BoyCrit Pedagogy (which will be introduced in Chapter 2), however, requires a reversal in stance to acknowledge what is broken in our teaching, attitudes, literacy practices, and systems that govern the teaching of Black boys.

Academic Achievement Gap Language in Early Childhood Education

Indeed, there is a great tendency in early childhood education research and practice to compare the academic and social outcomes of Black boys to White ones (Aratani et al., 2011). Early childhood educators are notorious for holding on to such comparisons. Many scholars, teachers, and administrators refer to such comparisons as the achievement gap. Comparing the academic outcomes of Black and White children, however, is an act of racism, white supremacy, and anti-Blackness (Hale & Bocknek, 2016; Hilliard, 2003; Love, 2019; & Toldson, 2019) particularly because measures of academic achievement are grounded in old colonized systems developed to uplift whiteness. These flawed comparisons between children of the dominant culture and those of minoritized cultures have created what Hale and Bocknek (2016) call "a biased risk perspective" (p. 79). This occurs when White children are centered as the norm (a racist construction and widely assumed "truth") to which Black children should aspire (Toldson, 2019). Clearly, this is an anti-Black misandric construction, as Black boys (and men) are neither mimetic of White men and boys (Curry, 2017), nor should they want to be. While Curry argues this outside of academic outcomes, I argue that this should also be the case academically and socially. Black boys demonstrate their brilliance in their own ways (Wright & Counsell, 2018); foundational knowledge for any teacher professing to support the learning of Black boys.

Allegedly, inequities in early childhood education are explained away by the so-called achievement gap in which most educators believe, instead of what Ladson-Billings (2006) has referred to as the *education debt*: the social, economic, moral, and educational wages owed to Black children for their historical and contemporary disenfranchisement in schools (Milner, 2010; Ladson-Billings, 2006). While most early childhood educators have a tendency to focus on the achievement gap, they should instead focus on opportunity gaps: the well-resourced early childhood programs and schools, neighborhoods, and highly-qualified teachers afforded to White children as early as early childhood education, and often at the expense of Black children (Milner, 2010/2020).

In my work, while I draw on comparative achievement data that may delineate differing levels of academic performance between Black and White boys, I do not aim to use it to center White children as the standard by which we should compare Black boys; rather, I use it to elucidate the negative effects of anti-Black misandry. I believe this is the only reason early childhood educators, educational researchers, and stakeholders should ever use such data. I would like to bring to the attention of early childhood educators that, due to Black people's resilience in demonstrating excellence despite institutional and structural marginalization in American society, they must compare Black children's present achievements to the past (and present) excellence and achievement of Africans/Black people in order to best determine academic achievement gaps (Hilliard, 2003). Because most early childhood teachers fail to respond to academic achievement in such a way, they have little information about "closing the achievement gap between Africans and excellence" (Hilliard, 2003, p. 131). However, early childhood educators should be aware that the personal and professional accomplishments of the Black male teachers in this book represent the kind of past achievement Black boys can presently strive to reach both in and beyond early childhood education. Indeed, Black male teachers have always been the examples by which Black boys are expected to—and can—measure their lives (Brown, 2012). As you will learn, this idea is also consistent with BlackBoyCrit Pedagogy.

Failure to Listen to (and Hear) Black Boys in Early Childhood Education

When space is provided for Black boys to share their perspectives regarding early childhood teachers and schooling practices, much can be learned (Dumas & Nelson, 2016). However, it goes without saying that Black boys' voices are "deafeningly silent in research [and in classrooms]" (Dumas & Nelson, 2016, p. 40). Teachers, and especially those who teach in early grades, rarely asks Black boys about their experiences in schools and the (adverse) schooling conditions that contribute to their demise or uplift in educational spaces (Davis, 2003; Howard, 2014; Wright & Counsell, 2018). In other words, while adolescent and pre-adolescent boys are often interviewed about their schooling experiences, we rarely see it in the early years. For example, in her groundbreaking and well-known work on Black boys, Ferguson (2000) interviewed pre-adolescent Black boys about their academic and social conditions. She was particularly interested in understanding how they survive in educational spaces that had already constructed them as problems and problematic. She found that these Black boys challenged the deficit labels placed on them when they were given the opportunity to critically examine the schooling process, teachers, and administrators. In his book titled *Black Maled: Peril and Promise in the Education of African American Males*, Tyrone Howard (2014) interviewed middle and high school boys, and found that they problematized White teachers for having the low expectations that contributed to the boys' underachievement in schools. Such narratives are extremely important in helping educators understand the academic and social landscape of Black boys in schools. However, it is rare that educators hear Black boys' concerns about their academic and social outcomes in early childhood education. As such, early childhood educators and researchers overly depend on quantitative research studies that inadequately explain the social and academic landscape of Black boys in schools. To that end, we need to understand the importance of listening to Black boys; their voices matter in classrooms. BlackBoyCrit Pedagogy is intentional about centering the voices and experiences of Black boys in the teaching and learning process.

The Social Landscape of Black Boys in Early Childhood Education

The socio-emotional needs of Black boys often go unmet in early childhood education (Wright & Counsell, 2018). Consequently, anti-Black misandry negatively impacts Black boys' socio-emotional outcomes. This includes zero-tolerance policies and teachers' biases and stereotypes about Black boys. Zero-tolerance policies criminalize Black boys for minor behavioral infractions in schools (Allen & Smith, 2014; Basile, 2020; Toldson, 2019; Wright & Ford, 2019). For example, when early childhood educators suspend and expel Black boys for normal child behaviors such as tantrums, they become complicit in educational systems that fail Black boys (Powell & Coles, 2020). Educational systems fail Black boys when they adopt systems of crime and punishment known to be racially biased in the larger society – racial profiling and unequal violence inflicted by police, inequitable sentences for Black males in contrast to sentences for White males convicted of similar crimes (marijuana possession and self-defense, for example). As Toldson (2019) wrote, the "controversial strategy [that] makes violating certain laws subject to immediate and harsh penalties, including mandatory minimum prison sentences [has been] inexplicably [adapted to] some schools … to make certain behaviors subject to immediate suspension or expulsion, regardless of the circumstance" (p. 86). Indeed, although school discipline was once handled by school administrators such as principals and assistant principals, it has now been placed in the hands of school resource officers (Toldson, 2019). Although zero-tolerance policies were implemented to decrease school violence—to wit, school shootings committed by White males—Black boys are negatively impacted by those policies including being suspended and expelled from schools in disproportionate numbers (Allen & Smith, 2014). As such, zero-tolerance policies are discriminating against Black boys and "priming the [preschool] and school-to-prison pipeline" (Wright & Ford, 2019, p. 21). The preschool/school-to-prison pipeline is an exclusionary discipline practice through which Black boys are funneled from early childhood classrooms into the criminal justice system at early ages (Wright & Counsell, 2018).

Explicit and implicit biases against Black boys also negatively impact their social outcomes at the classroom level. According to Wesley and Ellis (2017), "Explicit bias refers to the conscious beliefs, perceptions, and attitudes held about a person or group of people"; whereas implicit bias is "situated in unconscious thoughts that influence decisions and actions" (p. 23). A preponderance of research studies (Gilliam et al., 2016; Goff et al., 2014; Kirwan Institute, 2015; Skiba et al., 2002) continue to affirm the ways in which teachers' explicit and implicit biases – the deficit views described earlier in this chapter – contribute to the unmet social needs of Black boys in and beyond early childhood education.

It is important to note that teachers' stereotypes stem from the anti-Black misandric social constructions of Black boys (and men) as dangerous and less innocent than their White counterparts, ideas anchored in historical untruths and intentional misrepresentations and that are far too often reflected in society writ large and through media and popular press. To that end, teachers have been carefully taught to anticipate misbehavior from Black boys in early childhood classrooms, as a result, they read their behaviors negatively (Bryan, 2017; Wesley & Ellis, 2017; Wright & Counsell, 2018; Wright & Ford, 2019). Repeatedly, studies show that aspiring teachers typically enter preservice teacher education programs with stereotypical anti-Black (and anti-Latino) misandric views about Black and Latino boys. In a study by

Sealey-Ruiz & Greene (2015), teacher candidates identified films like *Boys in the Hood* (1991) and *Dangerous Minds* (1995)—films that negatively portray Black boys in urban schools and communities – as sources for those stereotypes. With these films as only two of many sources for erroneous anti-Black misandric messaging, if these negative images of Black boys are not interrupted prior to preservice teachers' entry into inservice teaching, these teachers have the potential to exacerbate the disproportionality in school discipline between Black (and Latino) boys and their White counterparts (Kunesh & Noltemeyer, 2019; Sealey-Ruiz & Greene, 2015). Although a few social justice and diversity-related courses and initiatives, including urban cohort initiatives designed to prepare preservice teachers to work in urban schools and communities have been instrumental in helping some White preservice teachers engage in self-examination to confront personal biases, teacher candidates may still struggle to discard their misguided beliefs about Black boys (Wynter-Hoyte et al., 2020). To that end, teacher education programs must ensure that courses that intentionally address anti-Black misandry are fully embedded in their entire curricula.

At the same time, inservice teachers, who serve as supervisors and mentors during field and practicum experiences, can also negatively influence how preservice teacher candidates will interact with Black boys in schools. Teacher education candidates are often assigned to schools during field and/or practicum experience, where they are supervised by inservice teachers who still uphold deficit beliefs about Black boys such as those discussed earlier in this chapter. For example, while supervising preservice teachers in an elementary school in the Southeastern U.S., I (Bryan, 2017) noted that a White female inservice teacher, Mrs. Kay (pseudonym), engaged in deficit-riddled conversations about Joshua, a Black boy in her third-grade classroom, with a White female preservice teacher, Chelsea (also a pseudonym). The inservice teacher used several deficit descriptors, including "bad" and "failing miserably" to describe him, and I noticed how such conversation influenced Chelsea's negative interactions with Joshua both in and beyond the classroom. Also mimicking Mrs. Kay, Chelsea often yelled at him in the classroom and the school hallway.

Collectively, all of these issues across the social landscape can lead to discipline crises for Black boys in schools (Howard, 2014); such mistreatment can also have anti-Black misandric impact on Black boys' racial identities, or the ways they perceive themselves as racialized beings (Wright & Counsell, 2018). While some teacher programs have infused social justice and diversity-related issues into courses (Wynter-Hoyte et al., 2020), most programs still depend on the same old pedagogies and schooling practices that do socio-emotional harm to Black boys. For example, courses such as *Classroom Management* are often required to meet education degree completion requirements; yet, they are still largely based on behaviorist models that focus solely on disciplining and controlling children in early childhood education (Milner et al., 2019). Based on my professional observation, in many early childhood classrooms, teachers still depend on classroom management systems, including *Positive Behavior Intervention and Support* (PBIS) and *Classroom Dojo*—both of which are systems of rewards and punishments—to manage students' behavior. These types of systems are not only dehumanizing to Black boys, but also mirror disciplinary practices found in prison systems (Wesley & Ellis, 2017). Milner et al. (2019) encourage teachers to instead use classroom practices that move away from punitive disciplinary tactics.

Teachers' emphasis—and in most cases, overemphasis—on disciplining Black boys is a growing concern in schools, and particularly in early childhood education (Basile, 2020; Hicks-Tafari, 2018; Howard & Reynolds, 2013). This crisis is part and parcel of what it means to be schooled instead of educated, which I described earlier in this chapter (Shujaa, 1994). Black boys represent 19 percent of preschool enrollment, but represent 45 percent of the population that is suspended and/or expelled at least once during their preschool year (U.S. Department of Education, 2014).

It should go without saying that these discipline data are troubling to Black families. Black families, and especially mothers who send brilliant, beautiful, loved Black boys to school hopeful that they will be as loved and supported by their teachers. While mothers of Black boys are certainly not oblivious to the realities of how Black males are positioned and persecuted in society, there is generally not the anticipation that their children will be criminalized (disciplined differently than White boys, viewed as less intelligent and capable than White boys, etc.) in preschool; such experiences often take them by surprise (Wesley and Ellis, 2017). For example, a Black mother, Tunette Powell (2014), expressed concern about early criminalization and the disproportional targeting as the result of firsthand experience, when her 3-year-old son was suspended five times from his preschool. According to Powell, while discussing her son's suspension and expulsion with White mothers whose sons attended the same preschool, she discovered that White boys who engaged in similar behavioral infractions were neither suspended nor expelled from school at the same rate as her son. Research shows that, in such cases, White boys are often perceived as "boys being boys": they are afforded the rights to childhood innocence, while Black boys are seen as having extreme behavioral problems (Essien, 2017; Powell & Coles, 2020; Wright & Counsell, 2018).

Similarly, Parker (2018) wrote about her personal trauma being a Black mother of a preschool son. Much of her trauma stemmed from incessant telephone calls from teachers who complained about her son's so-called inability to raise his hand and sit quietly on mats during lessons. Consequently, Parker began to see her son through the lens of the teachers, ultimately internalizing the belief that her son was "bad" rather than problematizing the anti-Black misandric system in which her son was being schooled. Early childhood educators should consider and work to dismantle the *adultification* of Black boys, which means that, rather than being viewed as children who make mistakes, they are perceived as men in need of manly consequences for their "behaviors" in both schools and society writ large (Dancy, 2014; Ladson-Billings, 2011). Such misperceptions of Black boys' behaviors capture the essence of the social landscape of life in an anti-Black misandric society and, by extension, to exist in its school systems and programs of early childhood education. These misperceptions of

Black boys perpetuate the historical and personal trauma mothers of Black boys must endure when they send their sons to school (Allen & Smith, 2018; Essien, 2019; Powell & Coles, 2020).

When Black boys like Powell's and Parker's sons and others are pushed out of school through suspensions and expulsions, they not only fall increasingly behind academically, but are forced into the preschool-to-prison pipeline. This pipeline exists as a result of the zero-tolerance policies earlier discussed. For Black boys, zero-tolerance policies contribute to hardships later in their school and life experiences (Allen & Smith, 2014; Lewis et al., 2010). For example, such policies contribute to poor academic outcomes which will be discussed later in this chapter.

Early Childhood Education as Prison

Given the anti-Black misandric social conditions in early childhood education that stymie Black boys' upward mobility, it is important to note that perhaps just as there are pipelines to prisons that originate in schooling, for Black boys, preschools and schools can also be prisons in themselves (Becker et al., 2017). Preschools and schools become prisons because Black boys are convicted in both the womb and the schoolhouse (meaning, they live under the assumption of guilt and criminality; Dancy, 2014; Ladson-Billings, 2011; Upchurch, 1997). In other words, when Black boys attend early childhood education, they become prisoners of such systems. Most educators refer to such phenomena as the preschool/school-to-prison nexus (Rodriquez, 2010; Stovall, 2018). As such, preschools and schools become what Wright and Counsell (2018) referred to as "school discipline hubs where the focus is extensively about maintaining [discipline] and order" (p. 26).

Academic Landscapes of Black Boys in Early Childhood Education

Characteristics of anti-Black misandric schooling and teaching such as those outlined in the previous sections underlie and perpetuate the academic landscape for young Black boys. It is widely acknowledged that early childhood education is foundational to school readiness and success, and often predicts the present and future life outcomes of Black boys (Bryan & Wright, 2019; Essien, 2017; Wright & Ford, 2016). In other words, the early learning years of Black boys are essential for capturing what they know and building further academic skills necessary to successfully navigate the rest of their lives. According to the National Association for the Education of Young Children (NAEYC, 2002), "The first years of life are critical for later outcomes. Young children have an innate desire to learn. That desire can be supported or undermined by early experiences" (p. 2). To that end, Black boys whose academic needs are not met in the early years of schooling become a part of the anti-Black misandric and institutionally-imposed "pipeline crisis … the disruption in what would otherwise be the normal progression of students from elementary, to middle, to high school, and eventually college" (Noguera, 2014, p. 117).

Due to anti-Black misandry, approximately 59 percent of Black boys graduate high school; even fewer attend and graduate from college (The Schott Foundation Report, 2015). In large cities including Detroit, Michigan, these graduate estimates are far more dismal. Roughly 23 percent of Black males graduate high school in Detroit, Michigan (The Schott Foundation Report, 2015). It is the responsibility of early childhood educators to name, understand, and do something about the ubiquitous nature of anti-Black misandry that underlies the failure of educational systems to educate Black boys. More than 20 years ago, esteemed professors Ronnie Hopkins (1997),Vernon Polite, and James Earle Davis (1999) documented the pipeline crisis and the negative impact of anti-Black misandry on the schooling experiences of Black boys from early childhood through high school. They found that Black boys were the most neglected population in PreK-12 schooling, resulting in dismal academic outcomes that were unlikely to provide them improved life outcomes and opportunities. More than 20 years later, it is clear in the academic literature that some of the same ubiquitous effects of institutional anti-Black misandry—threaded throughout the schooling experiences of Black boys—remain persistent, and Black boys are academically impacted in negative ways.

Academic Landscape in Early Literacy

The impact of anti-Black misandry in Black boys' early literacy learning is astounding. Early literacy entails young children's acquisition of basic skills as consumers and producers of written and spoken language, developing joy and purpose in using a range of literacies, positive literate identities, and the abilities to use literacy to understand and critically examine the world around them (Souto-Manning & Martell, 2016; Tatum, 2005, 2015). Yet, early literacy data have suggested that Black boys score between one-tenth to one-fifth of a standard deviations lower than White boys in reading before they leave kindergarten (Aratani et al., 2011). By the fourth grade, Black boys score 30 points lower than White boys in reading (Aratani et al., 2011; U.S. Department of Education, 2014). Similarly, by the eighth grade, the academic gaps in reading for Black boys remain at such levels, meaning that Black boys score 30 points lower in reading than their White boy counterparts (Aratani et al., 2011). As such, early childhood teachers must take responsibility for their complicity in either pedagogical success or pedagogical failure while teaching not only reading but the interconnected uses of languages and literacies to interact within, learn from, and contribute to the world around them.

The Consequences of Anti-Black Misandry in Early Literacy

Educational inequities in early literacy are part and parcel of a larger system of anti-Black misandry that leads to compounding problems and consequences for Black boys. For example, given the inequitable academic experiences Black boys face in early literacy, Black boys are disproportionately assigned to special education classes

(Robinson, 2016; Wright & Ford, 2016). In fact, they are between three and five times more likely to be misidentified for such programs, particularly in high incidence areas, such as learning disabilities, emotional and behavioral disorders, intellectual disabilities, developmental delays, and other health impairments (Wright & Ford, 2016). Teachers' stereotypes and biases about Black boys often inform their recommendations for their assignments to special education (Robinson, 2016; Wright & Ford, 2019), and many White teachers perceive Black boys as indolent, unintelligent, undisciplined, and unmotivated in schools (Moore et al., 2018). These anti-Black misandric misperceptions began as early as early childhood education, and contribute to teachers' low expectations for Black boys throughout their schooling years (Davis, 2003; Hopkins, 1997; Howard, 2014; Rashid, 2009; Toldson & Johns, 2016; Wright & Counsell, 2018).

Disproportionate assignments to special education have also limited Black boys' opportunities to be screened, referred, and selected for gifted education programs, which often occur in third grade (Wright & Counsell, 2018; Wright & Ford, 2016). As it currently stands, Ford (2013) has suggested that Black boys are underrepresented in gifted education by 55 percent; they are approximately 2.5 times less likely to be enrolled in such programs (Anderson, 2019; Ford, 2013). Gifted education identification begins in third grade, and when Black boys are rerouted to remedial learning classes and programs early in their education, they lose the opportunity to be enrolled in courses that could provide them with the rigor and critical thinking skills they need to successfully navigate schooling and, consequently, become upwardly mobile beyond their school years (Ford, 2013). The exclusion of Black boys (and girls) from such opportunities is a way to keep gifted education programs populated with White middle-class children, reifying the idea that "no Blacks" (and particularly no Black boys) are allowed (Ford & King, 2014).

Anti-Black Misandry in Early Literacy and The Preschool-to-Prison Pipeline

Some researchers note that, if Black boys are unable to read by the third or fourth grade, they will become among those who fill future prison-spatial needs, which identifies early childhood education as the start of the preschool/school-to-prison pipeline, or the disproportionate funneling of Black children from classrooms into the criminal justice system (Allen & Smith, 2014; Barbarin, 2009; Essien, 2017; Losen, 2013; Losen & Gillespie, 2012; Wright & Ford, 2019). This conjecture is supported by data showing that two-thirds of students in general who cannot read by the fourth grade are highly likely to be arrested at some point in their lives (National Assessment of Adult Literacy, 2016). While a range of factors across systems of our society deny success to Black boys, statistics also show the disproportional arrest of Black men who have been failed by schooling and, therefore, cannot read as adults serving longer prison sentences for similar crimes in comparison to their White male counterparts (Alexander, 2010; Allen & Smith, 2014).

In addition to contributing to the preschool/school-to-prison pipeline, early literacy education that does not capture the lived experiences, interests, and brilliance of Black boys and (as discussed earlier, inequitably disciplines Black boys) also contributes to a kind of labeling that follows students through schooling and thereby limits opportunities for Advanced Placement courses, counseling into college prep classes, graduation with honors, which in turn impact university and professional opportunities.

While early childhood educators must understand the links between the preschool/school-to-prison pipeline and denying academic and professional futures with literacy education influenced by anti-Black misandry, we must simultaneously understand the critiques of data that often uncover anti-Black misandric data. For example, Ivory Toldson, a professor at Howard University, an historically Black College and University (HBCU) in Washington, D.C., has openly critiqued the third-grade-reading-score prison nexus. He has argued that it has prompted well-meaning teachers and scholars to "spread fiction about [someone] planning prison construction based on second [or third, or fourth] grade reading" (Toldson, 2019, p. 11). He further contended that we need to more closely interrogate the methods by which we determine that Black children, and Black boys in this case, are not reading at their proper grade levels, because most of the determining measures we use are flawed. As he stated:

> Many students who are not reading on grade level have scores that are full of errors. They could [not] care less about the tests (and honestly, why should they), or they didn't sleep the night before, or they didn't like the educator, and see through the con (they know that you want them to do well because it helps the educator, not the student). (p. 11)

In other words, Toldson challenged us to consider the institutional and structural factors that may impact Black boys' (and girls') underperformance in reading. This leads to what he considers a "compassionate understanding" (p. 12) of those performances, which challenges educators not to believe every bad statistic in education about Black children without a deeper analysis of the factors that may negatively impact their performance outcomes. Compassionate understanding should also lead early childhood educators to consider the consequences of failing to address anti-Black misandry in early literacy education.

Academic Landscape in Early Mathematics

Similar to their early literacy practices, most teachers lack the appropriate skillset to effectively teach early mathematics (Jett, 2013; Martin, 2012; Wright et al., 2016). As such, Black boys experience challenges in early mathematics due to institutional inequities informed by anti-Black misandry in early childhood classrooms. For example, Black boys leave kindergarten scoring one-fifth standard deviation lower than their White counterparts (Aratani et al., 2011). By the fourth grade, Black boys score 30 points lower than their White boy counterparts in math. Sadly, by the eighth grade, the gap increases to 40 points (Aratani et al., 2011). To decrease such gaps, Baker (2014) found that foundational to Black boys' success in math in secondary grades is the infusion of home and community learning stimulation such as math games prior to the start of kindergarten (Baker, 2014). While the early mathematic experiences of Black boys are crucial, we know so little about those experiences, which is another form of anti-Black misandry in early childhood education.

Consequences of Anti-Black Misandry in Early Mathematics

It is noted in early childhood education that early mathematical thinking and reasoning is crucial for later development in math, reading, and science (Wright et al., 2016). Therefore, when Black boys do not have such experiences early on in their schooling and educational careers, they struggle in math and other content areas later on in school.

Given such "struggle" in math and the recent push for science, technology, engineering, and math education (STEM; Wright et al., 2016), Black boys may be excluded from entry in STEM programs, which prepare children for more rigorous and advanced careers in the STEM fields (Basile, 2020; Wright et al., 2016; Wright & Ford, 2016). As such, early childhood educators need to learn how to counteract anti-Black misandry in early childhood mathematics. Black-BoyCrit Pedagogy can serve as an essential pedagogical tool used to counter the consequences of anti-Black misandry in early mathematics.

Toward a BlackBoyCrit Pedagogy

The characteristics of anti-Black misandric teaching and the realities of the social and academic landscape for Black boys in early childhood education leave us no choice but to commit to pedagogical overhaul if we, indeed, care about the future of Black boys. Toward that end and building from the foundation laid in this chapter, in Chapter 2, I offer BlackBoyCrit Pedagogy growing out of the need for a critical look at current pedagogy and a framework in which we can anchor much-needed change.

References

Alexander, M. (2010). *The new jim crow: Mass incarceration in the age of colorblindness*. The New Press.

Allen, Q., & White-Smith, K. (2014). "Just as bad as prison": The challenge of dismantling the school-to-prison pipeline through teacher and community education. *Equity and Excellence, 47*(4), 445–460.

Allen, Q., & White-Smith, K. (2018). "That's why I say stay in school": Black mothers' parental involvement, cultural wealth, and exclusion in their son's schooling. *Urban Education, 53*(3), 409–435.

Anderson, J. (1988). *Education of blacks in the South, 1860–1935*. University of North Carolina Press.

Anderson, R. (2019). *Wassup with all the black boys sitting in the principal's office? An examination of detrimental teacher interactions and school practices*. Black Boy Wonder Publishing.

Aratani, Y., Wight, V. R., & Cooper, J. L. (2011, May). Racial gaps in early childhood: Socioemotional health, developmental, and educational outcomes among African- American boys. National Center for Children in Poverty. www.nccp.org/publications/../text_1014

Baker, C. E. (2014). Does parent involvement and neighborhood quality matter for African- American boys' kindergarten mathematics achievement? *Early Education and Development* , 3(1), 342–355.

Barbarin, O. (2009). Halting African-American boys' progression from preK-prison: What families, schools, and communities can do! *American Journal of Orthopsychiatry*, 80(1), 81–88.

Basile, V. (2020). Standin tall: Criminalization and acts of resistance among elementary boys of color. *Race, Ethnicity, and Education*, 23(1), 94–112.

Becker, J. Carr, B. L., Knapp, G. R., Giraldo, L. G. (2017). At the nexus of education and incarceration: Four voices from the field. *Harvard Educational Review*, 87(2), 260–277.

Bell, D. (1988). *And we are not saved: The elusive quest for racial justice*. Basic Books.

Bonner, F. (2003). To be young, gifted, African American, and male. *Gifted Child Today*, 26(2), 26–34.

Boutte, G. (2016). *Educating African American children: And how are the children?*Routledge.

Brown, A. L. (2012). On human kinds and role models: A critical discussion about the African American male teacher. *Educational Studies*, 48(3), 296–315.

Bryan, N. (2017). White teachers' role in sustaining the school-to-prison pipeline. *Urban Review*, 49(2), 326–345.

Bryan, N., & Wright, B. L. (2019). And how are the boys? Towards an African American male pedagogy to promote academic and social success among black boys in early childhood education. In B.Crawford, C.Newman, S.Platt & A. Hilton (Eds.), *Comprehensive education in the 21st century: Increasing access in the age of retrenchment* (pp. 99–124). Information Age Publishing.

Curry, T. (2017). *Man-not: Race, class, genre and the dilemmas of black manhood*. Temple University Press.

Dancy, T. E. (2014). (Un)Doing hegemony in education: Disrupting school-to-prison pipelines for black males. *Equity & Excellence*, 47(4), 476–493.

Davis, J. E. (2003). Early schooling and academic achievement of African American males. *Urban Education*, 38(5), 515–537.

Dumas, M., & Nelson, J. (2016). (Re)-imagining black boyhood. Toward a critical framework for educational research. *Harvard Educational Review*, 86(1), 27–47.

Duncan, G. (2002). Beyond love: A critical race ethnography of the schooling of adolescent black males. *Equity and Excellence in Education*, 35(2), 131–143.

Essien, I. (2019). Pathologizing culture in early childhood education: Illuminating microaggressions from the narratives of the parents of black children. *Western Journal of Black Studies*, 43(1/2), 9–21.

Essien, I. (2017). Teaching black boys in early childhood education: Promising practices from exemplar teachers. *Journal of African American Males in Education*, 8(2). http://journa lofafricanamericanmales.com/wp-content/uploads/2017/12/2-Essien- 2017- Teaching-Black-Boys-in-Early-Childhood-Education.pdf

Ferguson, A. A. (2000). *Bad boys: Public schools in the making of black masculinity*. University of Michigan Press.

Ford, D. (2013). *Recruiting and retaining culturally different students in gifted education.* Prufock Press.

Ford, D., & King, R. A. (2014). No blacks allowed: Segregated gifted education in the context of Brown vs. Board of Education . *Journal of Negro Education*, 83(3), 300–310.

Gilliam, W. S., Maupin, A., Reyes, C. R., Accavitti, M., & Frederick, S. (2016). *Do early educators' implicit biases regarding sex and race relate to behavior expectations and recommendations of preschool expulsions and suspensions?*Yale Childhood Study Center.

Goff, P., Jackson, M., & Di Leone, B. (2014). The essence of innocence: Consequences of dehumanizing black children. *Journal of Personality and Social Psychology*, 106(4), 526–545.

Hale, J. E., & Bocknek, E. (2016). Applying a cultural prism to the study of play behavior of black children. *The Negro Educational Review*, 67(1), 77–105.

Harper, S. R. (2010). An anti- deficit achievement framework for research on students of color in STEM. *New Directions for Institutional Research*, 2010(148), 63–74.

Hicks-Tafari, D. (2018). "Whose world is this?" A composite counterstory of black male elementary school teachers as hip-hop otherfathers. *Urban Review*, 50(5), 795–817.

Hilliard, A. (2003). No mystery: Closing the achievement gap between Africans and excellence. In T. Perry, C. Steele, & A. Hilliard (Eds.), *Young, gifted and black: Promoting high achievement among African American students.* Boston Press.

Hopkins, R. (1997). *Educating black males: Critical lessons in schooling, community, and power.* SUNY Press.

Hotchkins, B. (2016). African American males navigate racial microaggression. *Teacher College Record*, 118(0603013), 1–36.

Howard, T. (2014). *Black maled: Perils and promises in the education of African American males.* Teacher College Press.

Howard, T. C., & Reynolds, R. (2013). Examining Black male identity through a raced, classed, and gendered lens: Critical race theory and the intersectionalityof the black male experience. In M. Lynn & A. D. Dixson (Eds.). *Handbook of critical race theory in education: CRT and innovations in educational research methodologies.* Routledge.

Jett, C. C. (2013). HBCUS propel African American male mathematics majors. *Journal of African American Studies*, 17(2), 189–205.

Johnson, L. L., Bryan, N., & Boutte, G. (2019). Show us the love: Revolutionary teaching in (un)critical times. *Urban Review*, 51(1), 46–64.

Kirkland, D., & Jackson, A. (2009). Beyond the silence: Instructional approaches and students' attitudes. In J. C. Scott, D. Y. Straker, & L. Katz (Eds.), *Affirming students' right to their own language: Bridging language policies and pedagogical practices* (pp. 132–150). Routledge.

Kirwan Institute for the Study of Race and Ethnicity. (2015). Implicit bias: State of the science. http://kirwaninstitute.osu.edu/research/understanding-implicit-bias/.

Kunesh, C. E., & Noltemeyer, A. (2019). Understanding disciplinary disproportionality: Stereotypes shape preservice teachers' beliefs about black boys' behavior. *Urban Education*, 54(4), 471–498

Ladson-Billings, G. (2011). Boyz to men? Teaching to restore black boys' childhood. *Race, Ethnicity and Education*, 14(1), 7–15.

Ladson-Billings, G. (2006). From achievement gap to education debt: Understanding achievement in U.S. schools. *Educational Researcher*, 35(7), 3–12.

Ladson-Billings, G. (2002). I ain't writin nuttin: Permission to fail and demands to succeed in urban classrooms. In L. Delpit and J. K. Dowdy (Eds.) *The skin that we speak: Thoughts on language and culture in the classroom.* New Press.

Lewis, C. W., Butler, B. R., Bonner III, F. A., & Joubert, M. (2010). African American male discipline patterns and school district responses resulting impact on academic achievement: Implications for urban educators and policy makers. *Journal of African American Males in Education*, 1(1), 7–25.

Losen, D. J. (2013). Discipline policies, successful schools, racial justice, and the law. *Family Court Review*, 51, 388–400.

Losen, D. J., & Gillespie, J. (2012). *Opportunities suspended: The disparate impact of disciplinary exclusion from school*. Civil Rights Project.

Love, B. L. (2019). *We want to do more than survive: Abolitionist teaching and the pursuit of educational freedom*. Beacon Press.

Martin, D. (2012). Learning mathematics while black. *Educational Foundations*, 26(1), 47–66.

Milner, H. R. (2020). Disrupting punitive practices and policies: Rac(e)ing back to teaching, teacher preparation, and brown . *Educational Researcher*, 49(3), 147–160.

Milner, H. R. (2010). Start where you are, but don't stay there: Understanding diversity, opportunity gaps, and teaching in today's classrooms. Harvard Education Press.

Milner, H. R., Cunningham, H. B., Delale-O'Connor, L., & Kestenberg, E. G. (2019). *"These kids are out of control": Why we must reimagine "classroom management" for equity*. Corwin Press.

Minow, M., Shweder, R., & Markus, H. (2008). *Schools: Pursuing equality in societies of difference*. Russell Sage.

Moore, E., Michael, A., & Penick-Parks. (2018). *The guide for white women who teach black boys*. Corwin Press.

Morris, M. (2016). *Pushout: The criminalization of black girls in schools*. The New Press.

National Assessment of Adult Literacy. (2016). Program for the international assessment of adult competencies. https://nces.ed.gov/surveys/piaac/

National Association for the Education of Young Children (NAEYC). (2002). *Early learning standards: Creating the conditions for success*. State Departments of Education

Noguera, P. A. (2014). Urban school and the black male "challenge." In H. R. Milner & K. Lomotey (Eds.), *Handbook of urban education*. Routledge.

Parker, K. (2018). An open letter to black parents whose suns have been pushed out of preschools. https://singlemomsofar.wordpress.com/2018/08/03/an-open- letter-to-black- parents-whose-suns-have-been-pushed-out-of-preschool/

Patton-Davis, L., & Museus, S. D. (2019). What is deficit thinking? An analysis of conceptualizations of deficit thinking and implications for scholarly research. *Currents*, 1(1), 117–129

Perry. T., Steele, C., & Hilliard, A. III. (2004). *Young, gifted, and black: Promoting high achievement outcome among African-American students*. Beacon Press.

Polite, V., & Davis, J. E. (Eds.). (1999). *African American males in school and society: Policy and practice for effective education*. Teachers College Press.

Powell, T., & Coles, J. (2020). 'We still here': Black mothers' personal narratives of sense-making and resisting anti-blackness and the suspension of their children. *Race Ethnicity and Education*. 1–20. https://doi.org/10.1080/13613324.2020.1718076

Powell, T. (2014, July 24). My son has been suspended five times. He's only 3. www.washingtonpost.com/posteverything/wp/2014/07/24/my-sonhas-been-suspended-five-times-hes-3/

Rashid, H. (2009). From brilliant baby to child placed at risk: The perilous path of African American boys in early childhood education. *Journal of Negro, Education*, 78 (3), 347–358.

Robinson, S. A. (2016). Remediating the learning disabilities of black males: Implications for PK-12 teaching. *Journal of Education and Development in the Caribbean*, 15(1), 159–173.

Rodriquez, D. (2010). The disorientation of the teaching act: Abolition as pedagogical position. *The Radical Teacher*, 88, 7–19.

Schott Foundation for Public Education. (2015). *Black lives matter: The Schott 50 State Report on public education and black males*. Schott Foundation for Public Education.

Sealey-Ruiz, Y., & Greene, T. (2015). Popular visual images and the (mis) reading of black male youth: A case for racial literacy in urban pre-service teacher education. *Teaching Education*, 26(1), 55–76.

Shujaa, M. J. (1994). *Too much schooling, too little education: A paradox of black life in white societies*. Africa World Press.

Siddle-Walker, V. (1996). *Their highest potential: An African American school community in the segregated South*. University of North Carolina Press.

Skiba, R. J., Michael, R. S., Nardo, A. C., & Peterson, R. (2002). The color of discipline: Sources of racial and gender disproportionality in school punishment. *Urban Review*, 34(4), 317–342.

Souto-Manning, M., & Martell, J. (2016). *Reading, writing, and talk inclusive teaching strategies for diverse learners, K-2*. Teachers College Press.

Stovall, D. (2018). Are we ready for school abolition? Thoughts and practices of radical imaginary in education. *Taboo: The Journal of Culture and Education*, 17(1). https://doi.org/10.31390/taboo.17.1.06

Tatum, A. (2015). Engaging African American males in reading (reprint). *Journal of Education*, 195(2), 1–4.

Tatum, A. (2005). *Teaching reading to black adolescent males: Closing the achievement gap*. Stenhouse Publishers.

Thomas, A. (2017). *The hate u give*. Harper Collins Publishers.

Toldson, I. (2019). *No BS (bad stats): Black people need people who believe in black people enough not to believe every bad thing they hear about black people*. Brill Sense Publisher.

Toldson, I., & Johns, D. (2016). Erasing deficits. *Teachers College Record*, 118(6), 1–7.

Upchurch, C. (1997). *Convicted in the womb: One man's journey from prisoner to peacemaker*. Bantam Books.

U.S. Department of Education. (2014). *Civil Rights data collection: Data snapshot (school discipline)*. Office of Civil Rights.

Warren, C. (2017). *Urban preparation: Young black men Moving Chicago's South Side to success in higher education*. Harvard Education Press.

Warren, C., Douglas, T., & Howard, T. (2016). In their own words: Erasing deficits and exploring what works to improve K-12 and postsecondary black male school achievement. *Teachers College Record*, 118(6), 1–4.

Wesley, L., & Ellis, A. (2017). Exclusionary discipline in preschool: Young black boys' lives matter. *Journal of African American Males in Education*, 8(2), 22–29. http://journalofafricanamericanmales.com/wp-content/uploads/2017/12/3-Wesley-Ellis-2017-ExclusionaryDiscipline-in-PreSchool.pdf

Whiting, G. W. (2009). The Scholar Identity Institute: Guiding Darnel and other black males. *Gifted Child Today*, 32(4), 53–56.

Williams, H. (2005). *Self-taught: African American education in slavery and freedom*. University of North Carolina Press.

Wright, B., & Counsell, S. (2018). *The brilliance of black boys: Cultivating success in the early grades*. Teacher College Press.

Wright, B. L., Counsell, S., Goings, R., Freeman, & Peat. (2016). Creating access and opportunities: Preparing African American male students for STEM trajectories PreK-12. *Journal of Multicultural Education*, 10(3), 384–404.

Wright, B., & Ford, D. *(2016)*. "This little light of mine": Creating early childhood classroom experiences for African-American boys PreK-3. *Journal of African American Males in Education*, 7(1), 5–19.

Wright, B. L., & Ford, D. (2019). Re-mixing and re-imagining the early childhood school experiences of brilliant black boys. *Boyhood Studies: An interdisciplinary journal*, 12(1), 17–37.

Wynter-Hoyte, K., Bryan, N., Singleton, K., Grant, T., Goff, T., Green, D., & Rowe, I. (in press). A seat at the kitchen table: The lived experiences of black female preservice teachers in an urban education cohort. *Equity and Excellence in Education*.

X., M., & Haley, A. (1965). *The autobiography of Malcolm X.* Grove Press.

2

JUST WHAT ARE BLACK CRITICAL THEORY AND BLACK MALE STUDIES DOING IN THIS "NICE" FIELD OF EARLY CHILDHOOD EDUCATION?

Toward a BlackBoyCrit Pedagogy

Given that most teachers are well-meaning individuals who want to do what is right for *all* children, and especially Black children (Boutte, 2016), I know you will be interested in my concerns for Black boys. Reflecting on my own early childhood experiences and those of Black boys who presently enter the doors of early childhood classrooms, I am deeply concerned with the way Black boys are (mis)treated in schools. The anti-Black misandric mistreatment of Black boys is concretized in the fabric of the public schooling system (Warren, 2017) as Black boys continue to be positioned in negative ways. Much like COVID-19, the pandemic virus that, as I write this text, has disproportionately killed tens of thousands of Black people nationwide (Yancy, 2020), such mistreatment of Black boys is a virus that continues to spread throughout our schools and truncates Black boys' schooling and life opportunities. Currently, there is no cure in place or even widespread recognition of where the responsibility for change lies. However, I believe there is an antidote for this virus in the critical pedagogies, literacies, and schooling practices of teachers—especially those who are summoned to teach Black boys, like Black male teachers. I call these pedagogies and practices, *BlackBoyCrit Pedagogy*.

Over the past decades, scholars have introduced several compelling critical pedagogical frameworks that I believe have changed the field of education for Black children writ large. For example, culturally and racially-situated frameworks, including Ladson-Billings' (1994/2009) conception of *culturally relevant pedagogy*, Gay's (2010) *culturally responsive pedagogy*, Lynn and Jenning's (2009) *critical race pedagogy*, Paris's (2012) *culturally sustaining pedagogy*, and Bristol's (2015) *gender relevant pedagogy* have all sought to explain the consequences of white supremacy in schools, and have provided alternative culturally and racially-specific pedagogical pathways to support the academic and social success of Black children in schools. We, as scholars, are indebted to the work of these predecessors.

DOI: 10.4324/9780429287619-3

Despite the compelling nature of these pedagogical frameworks, I yearn for something more pedagogically empowering that centers anti-Black misandry for Black children, and especially for Black boys whose schooling experiences continue to be replete with what I call *pedagogical malfeasance*. Pedagogical malfeasance is a set of instructional practices intentionally designed to center White ways of knowing and being and that, simultaneously, dehumanize Black boys. This set of instructional practices is enacted daily (although unwittingly in some cases) by teachers who are sworn to *first* do no harm: an ethical commitment by which teachers are expected to perform their professional duties in classrooms (Boutte, 2016). According to Boutte (2016), teachers are given a moral and ethical obligation to meet the academic and social needs of all children. Primary among those needs is countering the impact of schooling that *spiritually murders* Black students through systems of white supremacy and racism. Love (2019) has proposed that spirit murder is the psychological harm done to Black children because they are Black in America. In 2017, Lamar Johnson and I named the bullets that commit spirit murdering in schools as bullets of disrespect; cultural, heritage, and community omission; silencing, and rejection. BlackBoyCrit Pedagogy insists on destroying those methods of spiritual murder and replacing them with spiritual and academic uplift.

At the time of writing this book, I was dealing with my own spirit murder. I witnessed online the public lynching of a 46-year-old Black man, George Floyd, who was slowly and brutally murdered at the hands of police officers. Several days after his tragic killing the video of Mr. Floyd's death continued to circulate in the media and popular press as well as on social media outlets like *Facebook*, where I first witnessed it. After being accused of using a counterfeit 20-dollar bill at a local convenience store in Minneapolis, Minnesota, Mr. Floyd was handcuffed, and arrested by four officers (three White men and one Asian man). During the arrest, Derek Chauvin, a White officer with whom Floyd was previously acquainted, pinned Floyd to the concrete by thrusting his knee onto Floyd's neck. Taken by eye-witnesses, video-recordings suggest that Chauvin's knee was on Mr. Floyd's neck for approximately 8 minutes and 46 seconds (Baker, 2020). Much like Mr. Eric Garner, a Black man who died in the choke hold of White police officers, Mr. Floyd cried out, "Please, please, I can't breathe" (Fernandez & Burch, 2020). George Floyd's death by asphyxiation led to massive protests across the nation.

Mr. Floyd's experience is not an anomaly. Many Black boys and men, including Philando Castile, Eric Garner, Tamir Rice, and Walter Scott, are victims of what Black Studies professor Robin D. G. Kelly (2018) labels as the "snuffing out of [B]lack lives in real time, looped over and over again" (p. 160). Black girls and women are equally vulnerable; Sandra Bland and Breonna Taylor have also been victims of such snuffing out, and have lost their lives at the hands of police officers. While sleeping in her home in Louisville, Kentucky, Ms. Breonna Taylor was killed by police officers a few weeks before Mr. Floyd (Oppel & Taylor, 2020). Following those murders were also those of Black transwomen including Riah Milton, Dominique Fells, and Tony McDade (Carlisle, 2020).

Despite my own spirit murder, I began thinking about the ways in which Black boys in early childhood classrooms are forced to endure the metaphorical *knees on their necks*—anti-Black misandric conditions that squeeze the life out them by stymieing their upward mobility in and beyond schools—by teachers who have sworn first to do no harm, yet do so much harm in classrooms (Boutte, 2016) when they mistreat, disrespect, and stereotype Black boys in classrooms. To that end, I offer this book and my conceptualization of BlackBoyCrit Pedagogy in massive protest against anti-Black misandry in early childhood education. This protest is necessary because we should do something about the conditions of Black boys' educational experiences in and beyond their early years. Drawing upon Black Critical theory (BlackCrit) and Black Male Studies (BMS), *Black-BoyCrit Pedagogy* is an inter-curricular framework that acknowledges and contests anti-Black misandry in the early childhood experiences of Black boys to provide them educational experiences that are grounded in their lived realities; their histories, literacies, and communities; and in the lived realities of their Black male teachers. I hope teachers will find utility in the application of this pedagogical framework to not only address the academic and social needs of Black boys in early childhood education, but to explore and address their own complicity in the maintenance of anti-Blackness, anti-Black misandry, and pedagogical malfeasance in early childhood classrooms.

Against this backdrop, and because BlackCrit and Black Male Studies have been birthed out of Critical Race Theory (CRT), I would like to briefly discuss the concept of CRT in education. Next, I explore BlackCrit, and a conceptualization of forms of anti-Black violence in schools, and Black Male Studies, the foundational frameworks in which I ground BlackBoyCrit Pedagogy. Finally, I introduce and describe BlackBoyCrit Pedagogy, which serves as the guiding pedagogical framework for this book.

Critical Race Theory (CRT) in Education

Drawn from critical legal studies, CRT became an important theorization of white supremacy and racism, and a direct challenge to multiculturalism (Dumas & ross, 2016), which undertheorized the psychological and material effects of white supremacy and racism in educational research and practice (Ladson-Billings & Tate, 1995). In the field of education, CRT became a more sophisticated way of understanding the persistency of educational inequities through a race lens (Lynn & Dixon, 2013). Although CRT has several tenets, I want to acknowledge a few that have been regularly applied in CRT in education studies, and to encourage readers to learn more about all the tenets through the growing body of scholarship in this one area. These tenets include: (a) understanding the permanence of race and racism; (b) understanding intersectionality; (c) acknowledging Whiteness as property; (d) valuing *counterstorytelling*; (e) seeing CRT as social justice-oriented; and (f) valuing the interdisciplinary nature of CRT.

Permanence of Racism

Critical race scholars (Bell, 1992; Cook, 2013; Ladson-Billings & Tate, 1995) believe that race and racism are endemic to American society, and they undergird every American institution, including the field of education. As such, people of Color are negatively impacted by being at the "bottom of the well" (Bell, 1992) or the lowest rungs in American society. Furthermore, the permanence of racism serves a counterargument to the notion of post-racialism, or the idea that America has transcended race (Stovall, 2013). Derrick Bell (1992) describes racism or white supremacy as permanent by emphasizing the ways that it is embedded/normalized in every institution and system including schools that guide our daily lives, and that while small victories toward racial justice will be made, the structural and institutional nature of racism will remain at the core of American society. As such, racism is invented and reinvented in new ways; thereby, negatively impacting people of Color.

Intersectionality

CRT scholars have suggested that race is not a stand-alone identity; it intersects with other forms of oppression, including gender, sexuality, class, and religion to complicate the lives of people of Color (Crenshaw, 1995). More pointedly, the notion of intersectionality proposes that people of Color who possess several marginalized identities experience race, racism, and racial discrimination differently in society and schools.

Whiteness as Property

Given the normalization of race and racism, CRT scholars put forward the concept of Whiteness as property; i.e., the privileges and benefits associated with being White are upheld by race and racism (Bell, 1992; Cook, 2013). These privileges are afforded in every American institution, including education, where the experiences of White children are the hallmark of what is considered "good" early childhood education—a presumption that marginalizes children of Color.

Counterstorytelling

CRT scholarship urgently and effectively challenges dominant ideologies, narratives, and perspectives about people of Color through *counterstorytelling*: using stories that center and elevate the voices of people of Color (Boutte et al., 2011; Cook, 2013). However, sometimes, CRT and, by extension, counterstorytelling, tend to be more adult-centric than child-centric (Bryan, 2020), though I would argue that using it to explore Black children's experiences is fruitful.

Social Justice

CRT is a social justice project that, according to some scholars (Chapman, 2013; Cook, 2013), challenges injustices impacting the lives of people of Color. Just as there is no separation between social justice and CRT, as CRT requires critical race praxis or the on-the-ground work essential to combating race-based social injustices (Stovall, 2013), there is no separation between social justice and BlackBoyCrit Pedagogy.

Interdisciplinary

Finally, it is also important to note that CRT is interdisciplinary, meaning that it draws on and is informed by several disciplines. These disciplines include, but are not limited to women and gender studies and race and ethnic studies with the goal of "challenging the boundaries of the analysis of and racism in education" (Solórzano, 2013, p. 55).

BlackCrit Theory

Following CRT, scholars have formulated a number of "crits," including *AsianCrit, LatCrit,* and *TribalCrit.* Additional "crits," including *ParentCrit* (Nishi & Motoya, 2017) are under development. Recently, Dumas and ross (2016) theorized Black Critical Theory, also known as *BlackCrit,* to unearth the specificity of anti-Blackness in the schooling experiences of Black children. BlackCrit acknowledges that CRT is a theorization of race in general, and includes Black examples and experiences, but does not theorize Blackness specifically (Caldera, 2020; Coles, 2019; Dumas & ross, 2016). Theorizing Blackness helps us arrive at the idea of anti-Blackness, or what Dumas and ross (2016) have called "a social construction, as the lived experience of social suffering and resistance, and perhaps most importantly, as an antagonism in which Black is a despised thing-in-itself in opposition to all that is pure, human(e) and White" (pp. 416–417). Similarly, theorizing Blackness and, more precisely, anti-Blackness moves us beyond a general race critique. According to Dumas and ross (2016), CRT assumes that it "accomplishes all that Black people need" (p. 417) and "Black people become situated as (just) race" (p. 417); however, it cannot adequately employ counterstories of Black people "because it does not, on its own, have language to richly capture how anti-Blackness constructs Black subjects, and positions them in and against law, policy, and everyday (civic) life" (Dumas & ross, 2016, p. 417). Similarly, counterstorytelling cannot adequately provide Black people with the language to speak out against the dark or to iterate how laws and policies reflect an historic cultural disdain for Blackness (Dumas & ross, 2016). Therefore, BlackCrit is essential for helping us understand that Blackness matters and will continue to matter "in more detailed ways" (Dumas & ross, 2016, p. 417).

Instead of tenets (more prevalent in CRT), BlackCrit has framing ideas. Dumas and ross (2016) have suggested that tenets are authoritative and inflexible, whereas framing ideas allow for ideological flexibility. Dumas and ross (2016) introduced three essential framing ideas for BlackCrit: (1) Anti-Blackness is endemic to American society, (2) Blackness exists in tension with neoliberal-multiculturalism, and (3) BlackCrit creates space for Black liberatory fantasy. The two framing ideas particularly important to BlackBoyCrit Pedagogy are that anti-Blackness is endemic to American society, and space is created for Black liberatory fantasy.

Framing Idea #1: Anti-Blackness is Endemic to American Society

Because one of the goals of this book is to highlight anti-Black misandry in the schooling experiences of Black boys, the framing idea of anti-Blackness is foundational. Otherwise stated, while CRT scholars contend that race and racism are endemic to the social, economic, political, and educational realities of people of Color (Bell, 1992; Lynn & Dixon, 2013), BlackCrit acknowledges that anti-Blackness is endemic to Black lives and to all institutions in which Black lives live (Coles, 2019; Dumas & ross, 2016). Making explicit the differences between the permanence of race, racism, and anti-Blackness, Dumas and ross (2016) explained

> But, antiblackness is not simply racism against Black people. Rather, anti-blackness refers to a broader antagonistic relationship between blackness and (the possibility of) humanity. The concept is most developed in an intellectual project called Afro-pessimism (although not everyone who writes in, or in relation to, this project would define themselves as Afropessimists). Afro-pessimism posits that Black people exist in the social imagination as (still) Slave, a thing to be possessed as property, and therefore with little right to live for herself, to move and breathe for himself. (p. 429)

In other words, anti-Blackness in its truest form does not imagine Blackness beyond being subjugated and entrapped within the institution of enslavement. Here, there is neither humanity nor life, which explains the existence of #AllLivesMatter (Dumas & ross, 2016), which connotes the hypervisibility of White lives and the invisibility and/or non-existence of Black ones (Curry, 2017). Hill (2016) noted that such invisibility of Black life renders Black people—and especially boys and men—*nobodies* who are deemed unworthy of basic human and civil rights.

Framing Idea #2: Blackness Exists in Tension with Neoliberal-Multiculturalism

Blackness existing in tension with neoliberal-multiculturalism is another vitally important framing idea. After World War II, the United States slowly began to embrace a multicultural society in which anti-discrimination policies became law (Coles, 2019; Dumas & ross, 2016). However, in the mid-1980s, anti-discrimination policies were rolled back due to neoliberalism: the idea that privatization and free market advancement (Dumas & ross, 2016) would take care of historical race-related issues and provide market opportunities to people of Color. Black people, falsely accused of not taking advantage of these market opportunities, were perceived as hindering themselves from progress, while other minoritized groups took advantage of those opportunities (Dumas & ross, 2016). This grand narrative perpetuated the myth that Black people refused to pull themselves up by their own bootstraps—an idea that exists outside the Black liberatory fantasy.

Framing Idea #3: The Creation of Space for Black Liberatory Fantasy

The idea of creating space for Black liberatory fantasy is another essential component of BlackCrit. Black liberatory fantasy enables Black people to create a world not yet for themselves, or to invoke a radical imagination in which the colonized becomes the colonizer and the colonizer the colonized (Dumas & ross, 2016; Stovall, 2018). Black liberatory fantasy also enables Black people to see Whiteness—the ideology of White dominance (Matias, 2013)—as dead in the Black mind. This Black radical imagination compels Black people to "resist a revisionist history that supports dangerous majoritarian stories" (Dumas & ross, 2016, p. 431) that often minimize the role White people continue to play in oppressing and dominating Black people (Dumas & ross, 2016). Collectively, these are the framing ideas of BlackCrit.

Anti-Black Violence in Schools

Building on Dumas and ross's (2016) notion of BlackCrit and more precisely anti-Blackness, Johnson et al. (2019) identified five types of anti-Black violence that occur and are enacted against Black boys (and children) in schools. They include *physical, symbolic, linguistic, curricular and pedagogical*, and *systemic school violence*. According to Johnson et al. (2019), physical violence entails school and state-sanctioned violence against the bodies of Black children. The examples are continually exposed in schools: For example, a White female teacher, Lisa Houston, at a high school in upstate South Carolina jumped on a desk and started to pull a Black male student's hair (locs, specifically) in an attempt to "wake him up" (Hyde, 2018). When I was in 2nd grade, I remember my White female teacher picked up a Black boy, Damion (pseudonym), to physically remove him from the classroom. Black teachers have also engaged in physical violence towards Black children. Kristen Haynes, a Black teacher in a Chicago school district, encouraged her friend, Juanita Taylor, who was also employed by the school district, to physically assault nine-year-old Jomaury Champ (Savini, 2019). Taylor led Champ into the school's restroom to assault him there.

Another form of anti-Black violence in schools is *symbolic violence* or "the metaphorical representation of violence that stems from racial abuse, pain, and suffering against the spirit and humanity of Black people" (Johnson et al., 2019, p. 52). For example, in my 2016 study out of which this book is born, I learned from a Black mother (who was also a teacher at one the schools in the study) that, as she stood in the hallway of the school, she overheard White teachers discussing Black boys whom they had labeled troublemakers and whom they did not want enrolled in their second-grade classrooms.

According to Johnson et al. (2019), *linguistic violence* is another type of anti-Black violence that Black boys and girls face in schools. Linguistic violence is the policing of language varieties, including Black language—a rule-governed language. As a young child, I recall how teachers discouraged my use of Black language in elementary classrooms. As such, they engaged in linguistic violence by using a correctionist approach, wherein teachers see Black language and other language varieties as broken English that needs to be corrected rather than recognizing students bilingual abilities as they speak a legitimate language rich in history, grammatical structure, and literacy and social use (Baker-Bell, 2020; Baines et al., 2018).

Curricular and pedagogical violence entails omitting or distorting the experiences of Black boys from the curriculum and pedagogies. Johnson et al. (2019) have argued that, when teachers use and overuse White-centric curricula and schooling practices, they engage in *curricular and pedagogical violence*. Interestingly, this particular kind of violence is inclusive of *Developmentally Appropriate Practices* (DAP), the hallmark of standards for early childhood teaching and schooling practices, grounded in developmental theories that drive instruction and practice in early childhood classrooms (Gestwicki, 2017). In DAP, we see three major components: (1) knowledge of child development and learning; (2) knowledge of the experiences of individual children; and (3) knowledge about young children's social and cultural contexts (Gestwicki, 2017). Knowledge of child development and learning entails a set of supposedly universal views of childhood development and the theories that are used to make curricular and pedagogical decisions for all young children. However, this knowledge and these theories are grounded in the experiences of individual White children, and White young children's social and cultural contexts. As a result, these three components continue to be informed by the cultural ways of knowing and being of White children, thereby marginalizing Black-centric learning theories and children's experiences (Boutte, 2016).

DAP is not the only example of racial curricular and pedagogical violence in early childhood education. Early childhood educators' dependency on what Pritchard (2017) terms literacy normativity is another form of curricular and pedagogical violence. Literacy normativity refers to conventional language and literacy practices that minimize the connections between language, race, and other identities (e.g., gender and sexuality; Pritchard, 2017) and ignores the vast literacies found in Black homes, communities and histories. Literacy normativity is also antithetical to critical literacy practices: an approach to teaching literacy that encourages what Vasquez (2017) has called "a critical perspective or way of being" (p. 3) in both the world and the early childhood classroom. In other words, critical literacy pushes young learners to not only *read* the word, but to read the *world* through lenses of equity (Cowhey, 2006; Freire, 1970; Nash et al., 2018). Literacy normativity also undoes the teaching of critical racial literacy, which focuses specifically on issues of race and racism in the literacy process (Nash et al., 2018). Chapter 5 further addresses the dangers of literacy normativity in early childhood classrooms.

Last, but certainly not the least egregious, *systemic school violence* deals with laws and policies (e.g., suspension and expulsion, tracking, etc.) that disproportionately disenfranchise Black and other young children in schools. For example, the preschool-to-prison pipeline—the disproportionate funneling of young Black children into the criminal justice system (Gilliam et al., 2016)—has recently become a concern, and is a quintessential example of systemic school violence. Table 2.1 provides a brief overview of the five types of anti-Black violence in which teachers and other educational professionals engage.

Unfortunately, given how they are stereotypically positioned in both schools and society (Curry, 2017; Howard, 2014), the schooling experiences of Black boys in and beyond early childhood education are replete with the aforementioned types of anti-Black violence. As such, it becomes the responsibilities of teachers to ensure they work to dismantle each form of anti-Black violence as a way to protest anti-Blackness and anti-Black misandry in classrooms. Teachers should use the chart in Table 2.1 to assess their pedagogies, literacy, and school practices to locate and confront anti-Black misandric violence in their classrooms and schools. In Chapter 4, I provide guiding questions teachers can use to self-assess to determine their complicity in upholding anti-Blackness and enacting anti-Black violence in classrooms.

Black Male Studies

Although some scholars may disagree with Curry's (2017) conception of Black Male Studies due to its critique of foundational scholarship on Black feminism including the notion of intersectionality,[1] I find Black Male Studies beneficial to my work because of its explicit focus on the racialized and gendered conditions and victimization of Black boys (and men). I agree with Curry's assertion that, although CRT adequately explains the racialized conditions of Black boys and men, it inadequately theorizes their gendered conditions. In other words, Black Male Studies provides an essential framework for exploring the ways in which Black boys are subjected to both racial and gendered violence. Constructed to critique both historical and contemporary gender scholarship on Black men and boys, Black Male Studies (BMS) is a new, developing Black boy/male-centric framework in the field of Black Philosophy that challenges anti-Black misandry; in other words, whereas CRT and BlackCrit centralize race and anti-Blackness, Black Male Studies centralizes anti-Black misandry. Curry (2017) describes racism and anti-Blackness as misandric phenomena based on deficit tropes and perceptions of Black men and boys: lazy, unintelligent, and hypersexual to name just a few.

Currently, both historical and contemporary gender scholarship (particularly in America) presumes that Black males are victimizers and perpetrators against Black (and White) women and children; such anti-Black misandric narratives, theories,

TABLE 2.1 Five Types of Anti-Black Violence in Schools

Types of Violence	Definition	Examples
Physical	The physical abuse and assault that stem from racial discrimination and prejudicial ideologies and beliefs.	• Hitting, pushing, beating, etc. • Lynching • Police brutality • Sexual abuse • Sexual assault
Symbolic	A metaphorical representation of violence that stems from racial abuse, pain, and suffering against the spirit and humanity of Black people.	• Racial epithets and slurs • Rejecting the experiences and lived realities of Black youth • Silencing the voices of Black youth • (Mis)reading Black youths' culture, race, gender, and language
Linguistic	This form of violence marginalizes and polices the language of Black youth (which is referred to as Black language, African American language, or African American Vernacular English) through privileging and promoting White mainstream English.	• Socializing Black youth to view Black language as "not good," "broken English," and "incorrect." • Devaluing the connection between language, race, and identity • Teaching Black students and students from other ethnic groups that code-switching is the best approach to "mastering" White mainstream English (Baker-Bell, 2017). • Teaching grammar and vocabulary in isolation from the texts being taught and pedagogy that is disconnected to the lived realities and experiences of youth from racially and linguistically diverse backgrounds.
Curricular and Pedagogical	This form of violence infiltrates schools' curricula through teaching texts, materials, and standards that center Eurocratic notions of existing and being in the world (Cridland-Hughes & King, 2015). In conjunction, the *conventional* curriculum provides a false narrative about Black people through promoting deficit-based ideologies which inform teachers' pedagogical and instructional practices in classrooms. In general, this is a form of epistemic violence which attacks Black ways of knowing.	• Enacting culturally irrelevant and unresponsive curricula • Selecting texts where Black youth do not see characters who look like them reflected in dynamic and positive ways. • Feeding Black youth inaccurate, distorted, diluted, incomplete, and sanitized versions of history • Presenting mathematicians and scientists who are predominately White, monolingual, and male, while mathematicians and scientists who identify as women and people from linguistically and racially diverse backgrounds are omitted • Omitting critical conversations from the curricula that explore the intersections of race, gender, religion, language, sexuality, etc. • Emphasizing and overemphasizing Developmentally Appropriate Practices (DAP). • Literacy Normativity

(Continued)

TABLE 2.1 (Cont.)

Types of Violence	Definition	Examples
Systemic School	This form of violence is deeply ingrained within schools' structures, processes, discourses, customs, policies, and laws, which oftentimes reflect racist and hegemonic ideologies.	• Underfunded and overcrowded schools • Inexperienced teachers and/or teachers who are not certified in the subject area (s) they teach • Overrepresentation of Black youth in special education courses • Tracking • Disproportionality of Black youth in gifted and talented courses • Zero-tolerance school discipline policies • Lack of educational and support services that promote a positive healthy development—physically, mentally, and emotionally.

Adapted from L. Johnson, N. Bryan, and G. Boutte, 2019, "Show Us the Love: Revolutionary Teaching in (Un)Critical Times," *Urban Review, 51*(1), pp. 46–64. Reprinted with permission.

and frameworks are, first, inaccurate, and second, ignore the ways Black males too are victimized (Curry, 2017; Curry & Utley, 2018). In addition, they position Black men and boys outside gender scholarship. Indeed, historical and contemporary gender theories undertheorize the lived realities and experiences of Black men and boys unless they are being socially constructed as threats, embodying a set of Black male privileges and a patriarchal status to which Black women and girls are subjected (Curry, 2017). As such, Black men and boys are placed in the category of *genre* instead of gender. The latter is "synonymous with female" (Curry, 2017, p. 5). Curry has argued that *genre* is different from *gender* because it reconciles the historical and contemporary presumptions that Black men share similar male privileges and patriarchal status as their White male counterparts. Within the category of genre, Curry (2017) refers to Black men and boys as "Man-not," (p. 6): individuals who are neither afforded rights to privileges, patriarchal statuses, humanity, masculinities, nor manhood. As Curry stated, "The Black male is negated not from an origin of (human) being, but from nihility" (p. 6). Consequently, the a priori focus of gender studies has "become discourses about women, where racialized men [Black in this case] are interpreted by the lack of power they have compared with (real) [W]hite men" (p. 5).

Black Male Studies theorists (Curry, 2017; Curry & Utley, 2018) have asserted that, given the historical and contemporary vulnerability and victimization, including death, sexual abuse, and rape of Black males, there is a need for "new theories to account for the particular vulnerability of Black males beyond the language of hypermasculinity" (Curry & Utley, 2018, p. 2010). Hypermasculinity deals with the socially constructed idea of what it means to be a man or boy

(Connell, 2005; Sumison, 1999). Within Black Male Studies, Curry and Curry (2018) encouraged a "Black Public philosophy" (p. 42)—a new paradigm that centers the anti-Black misandric violence Black boys and men confront in society. Black Public philosophy unapologetically allows Black males to share their stories and counterstories against the pathological backdrop that often shapes their lived realities and experiences, and can be used as a pedagogical tool to raise the critical consciousness of Black boys as well as a theoretical approach for analyzing the experiences of Black boys who also are vulnerable victims of racialized and gendered violence in the form of stereotypes applied to Black boys.

BlackCrit and Black Male Studies purport to center Blackness and maleness. They are foundational in my framework—BlackBoyCrit Pedagogy—to protest anti-Blackness, and anti-Black misandry in early childhood education in order to ensure, but also serve as a guide to examining pedagogical, literacy and schooling practices in early childhood classrooms. Because Black boys are not only "convicted in the womb" (Upchurch, 1997), guilty until proven innocent, and are taught to hate themselves through messages received societally, pedagogically, and curricularly (Curry, 2017), this pedagogy is essential for Black boys in early childhood classrooms. It ensures that teachers, administrators, and systems of education remove their knees from Black boys' necks so that they can breathe and offers a more just, humanizing, and loving early childhood experience. In the same manner Mr. George Floyd's life mattered, the lives of Black boys in early childhood education matter, and BlackBoyCrit Pedagogy is one way educators can ensure that Black boys matter in and beyond early childhood classrooms. In so doing, it is crucial that early childhood educators "check themselves, before they wreck themselves" (Matias, 2013, p. 68) and Black boys: examining their dispositions before they attempt to use and apply BlackBoyCrit Pedagogy.

However, as I offer a BlackBoyCrit Pedagogy, I must make one thing clear. Given the focus on Black boys and male teachers in this pedagogical framework, I am not ignoring the experiences of Black girls and female teachers in early childhood education. I am fully aware that, much like Black boys in early childhood education, Black girls' academic and social needs go egregiously unmet and that Black girls are also erroneously labeled and perceived through White perceptions of behavior, loud, and disrespectful (Love, 2019; Morris, 2016). Black female teachers, as do Black male teachers, also represent a small percentage of the teaching profession (Jackson & Kohli, 2016). Less than 10 percent of teachers are Black and female (Jackson & Kohli, 2016). Consequently, like Black male teachers, Black female teachers are still underrepresented in early childhood education; therefore, they are oftentimes unavailable as Role Models for Black girls. For this reason, I want early childhood teachers to understand that BlackBoyCrit Pedagogy is expansive enough to be framed and reframed to focus on young Black girls. In other words, BlackBoyCrit Pedagogy does not erase the experiences of Black girls, and is far from exclusionary, but is introduced in such a way to encourage the theorization of pedagogies that addresses the varying ways to be Black and girls (queer and gender non-conforming, for example) who are invisible in curricular, pedagogical, and literacy practices.

Toward a BlackBoyCrit Pedagogy

Guided by and grounded in BlackCrit and Black Male Studies, BlackBoyCrit Pedagogy is an inter-curricular framework that acknowledges Blackness and male-ness, and contests anti-Black misandry in the early childhood experiences of Black boys, and instead provides them educational experiences that are grounded in their lived realities and those of their Black male teachers. BlackBoyCrit Pedagogy responds to the call of several Black male scholars, including Brown (2009), who called for a relevant pedagogy that supports Black boys in classrooms. Drawing on the framing ideas of BlackCrit and Black Male Studies, I theorize what I call *developing ideas of BlackBoyCrit Pedagogy*, as these ideas, thoughts, and framings, as should be all theories and pedagogies, are always under construction. I also call them *developing ideas* because they stand on the foundations of Dumas's and ross's (2016) BlackCrit framing ideas, which are described as flexible. The thought of developing ideas not only suggests the flexibility of BlackBoyCrit Pedagogy, but also signifies my openness to others' critique of the framework for both personal and professional development and growth. Consequently, I suggest four developing ideas for Black-BoyCrit as a Pedagogy that:

1. Acknowledges the inter-curricular nature of anti-Black misandry in ECE and underscores the necessity to work collaboratively with Black boys to confront and dismantle this social construction, and to develop anti-Black misandric consciousness in teaching, learning, and literacy practices.
2. Centers teaching, learning, and literacy practices that are simultaneously influenced by Blackness, maleness, and diverse expressions of Black mascu-linity as well as the experiences of boys and male teachers that move beyond the language of hypermasculinity, thereby creating a symbiotic relationship between Black boys and male teachers in and beyond early childhood classrooms.
3. Humanizes and heals the wounded spirits of Black boys (as committed by anti-Black misandry) as a way to contest the consequences of anti-Black misandric violence in early childhood schooling, curricular, and literacy practices.
4. Positions Black families and communities as informants and integral partners in the academic and social enterprise of Black boys in early childhood education.

Below I parse out each of the aforementioned developing ideas of Black-BoyCrit Pedagogy so that teachers can carry forward the framework as they read the perceptions and insights of Black boys on the pedagogies, literacy, and schooling practices of their male teachers presented in this book. This parsing is also important in helping teachers better understand how they too can implement BlackBoyCrit Pedagogy in early childhood classrooms.

Developing Idea # 1: The Inter-curricular Nature of Anti-Black Misandry

It is important to note that the first developing idea of BlackBoyCrit Pedagogy—acknowledging the inter-curricular nature of anti-Black misandry in ECE—recognized that, much like the interdisciplinary nature of CRT as described earlier, I propose BlackBoyCrit Pedagogy as *inter-curricular*, meaning that it is expansive, interdisciplinary, and draws on a multiplicity of early childhood education curricula. In so doing, it recognizes that anti-Black misandry is evident in all curricular aspects of early childhood education, including literacies, math, science, social studies, and play. More pointedly, like schools and society writ large (Curry, 2017; Dumas & ross, 2016), early childhood curricula are anti-Black misandric in nature. With this in mind, BlackBoyCrit Pedagogy can be transformed into BlackBoy (Math)Crit Pedagogy, BlackBoy (Science)Crit Pedagogy, BlackBoy (Play)Crit, and so forth and so on. This means that, when any of the aforementioned curricula are topics of focus in curriculum planning (much like what will happen in Chapter 8) or further theory development, it is then possible to place the subject matter in parentheses to demonstrate the expansiveness and the particular focus as the framework is considered across all elements of teaching and learning in early childhood education.

To that end, BlackBoyCrit Pedagogy is no different than what has already been done in critical pedagogical work. That is, it allows for expansion. Take, for example, critical race pedagogy: a pedagogical framework that centers on addressing race, racism, and white supremacy in teaching and learning (Lynn & Jennings, 2009). Building on and expanding critical pedagogy, which ignores and decenters race (Kincheloe, 2006) and CRT, Lynn and Jennings (2009) theorize critical race pedagogy by centering issues of race and racism at the heart of the pedagogical framework.

Acknowledging the inter-curricular nature of anti-Black misandry is crucial; it allows early childhood educators who engage in integrated curriculum (teaching and learning that make connections across the curricula; Drake & Burns, 2004), to do so. For example, some early childhood educators may avoid teaching content areas including math, literacy, science, and social studies in isolation, but rather find themes across the aforementioned content areas to engage young learners in the teaching and learning process (Vasquez, 2017).

Once early childhood educators acknowledge the inter-curricular nature of anti-Black misandry in early childhood education, they must work collaboratively with Black boys to combat and protest anti-Black misandry in early childhood curricula. In other words, early childhood educators must arm Black boys with the tools to identify anti-Black misandry in the teaching and learning process. Early childhood educators must be aware that this can be accomplished in a multiplicity of ways. In other words, there is no one-size-fits-all process to address anti-Black misandry. In each of the portraits that will be later presented throughout this book, early childhood educators will see how the Black male teachers uniquely and courageously assist Black boys in identifying anti-Black misandry through their personal lives, pedagogies, literacy, and schooling practices in their classrooms.

Developing Idea # 2: Centering Teaching, Learning, and Literacy Practices that are Influenced by Blackness, Maleness, and Diverse Expressions of Black Masculinity

The second developing idea—centering teaching and learning and literacy practices that are simultaneously influenced by diverse Black masculine experiences of Black boys and male teachers—addresses how teaching and learning processes and literacy practices can be grounded in Blackness, maleness, and the diverse masculine experiences of Black boys and men. Guided by BlackCrit theorists who remind us that "only a critical theorization of Blackness confronts the specificity of anti-Blackness" (Dumas & ross, 2016, p. 416), and Black Male Studies scholars who insist that only a critical theorization of Black maleness confronts anti-Black misandry, I suggest a critical look at the ways that Black manhood is constructed. By diverse Black masculine expressions and experiences, I mean a type of Black masculinity that values all the ways in which one can be boy and man, or express multiple gender identities and sexualities (Connell, 2005; Curry, 2017; Givens et al., 2016; Major & Billson, 1992; McCready, 2004, 2010; McCune, 2014). Connell (2005) has termed such expressions as *multiple masculinities*. This type of Black masculinity includes both cisgender and non-cisgender expressions thereof (Connell, 2005; McCready, 2004; McCune, 2014). Curry (2017) has proposed that, whereas White boys and men are able to express multiple masculinities, Black boys and men are oftentimes inhibited from doing so. This means that, guided by BlackBoyCrit Pedagogy, Black male teachers can use their own diverse Black masculine, multiple masculinities, and anti-Black misandric experiences to develop a Black masculine and anti-Black misandric consciousness among young boys—an awareness of not only positive aspects of Black boy and manhood and masculinities, but also of the anti-Black misandric violence that shapes the lives of Black boys and male teachers. According to Curry (2017), Black boys and men are rarely able to see themselves beyond pathological assumptions about them; however, by centering those experiences, Black boys and male teachers can engage in a paradigm shift (Howard, 2014)—a renewed and refreshing outlook on and perception of themselves. This paradigm shift is also consistent with what Curry (2017) refers to as a "Black public philosophy," which aims to dismantle gender-based stereotypes and biases about Black boys and men.

It is important to note that White males, females, and other women teachers of Color should not be intimidated by this focus on centering Black masculine and anti-Black misandric experiences in the teaching and learning process and literacy practices; they too can draw on the experiences of Black boys and men to inform their pedagogical, schooling, and literacy practices through stories about Black men and boys in the media and popular press, among other sources.

When Black male teachers center their lived diverse Black masculine expressions and experiences, they become 'mirrors' in which Black boys see themselves and 'windows' (Sims-Bishop, 1990) through which Black boys see the world. This symbiotic relationship positions Black male teachers as Role Models (as described in the introduction) instead of mere role models in the lives of young Black boys. Similarly, they become pedagogues of experiences; drawing and centering their own racialized and gendered experiences in the teaching and learning process (Brown, 2011). And, because teaching is relational (Nelson, 2016) and Black boys' diverse masculine identities are often bound up in those of their Black male teachers, educators must normalize curricular experiences and literacy practices that prioritize Black masculinity in early childhood classrooms (Kirkland & Jackson, 2019). Black Masculine Literacies (Kirkland & Jackson, 2019), which I will further introduce in Chapter 5, can serve as an adequate literacy practice that prioritizes the diverse masculine expressions of Black boys. It is also central to BlackBoyCrit Pedagogy.

Developing Idea # 3: Humanizing and Healing Black boys

The third developing idea—the act of humanizing and healing Black boys—requires teachers to acknowledge that anti-Black misandric and dehumanizing schooling practices are endemic to schooling and that they not only disenfranchise Black boys in early childhood education (Basile, 2020) but inflict trauma and do lasting harm. These dehumanizing schooling practices include, but are not limited to, the removal of Black boys from classrooms for minor and subjective behavioral infractions such as talking too much, failing to comply with school dress codes, and being "off-task" (Wright & Counsell, 2018). As such, given the growing body of work on the pedagogies of healing (Boutte et al., 2017), it is imperative that early childhood educators work collaboratively with Black boys to humanize and heal them from the wounds committed by the anti-Black misandric violence that is present in most classrooms. Teachers should note that no early childhood classroom, not even their own, is exempt from the effects and consequences of anti-Black misandry. Humanizing and healing Black boys require teachers to listen, hear, and understand them, and to create co-generative dialogic spaces (Emdin, 2016) where Black boys and teachers can engage in ongoing conversations to shift classroom dynamics for the personal and collective empowerment of Black boys therein (Basile, 2020; Emdin, 2016). In other words, the voices of and insights from Black boys can reframe the daily operations of early childhood classrooms.

Developing Idea # 4: Black Families and Communities as Informants in the Academic and Social Enterprise

The fourth and final developing idea—seeing Black families and communities as informants and integral partners in the academic and social enterprise of Black boys—serves to contest dominant narratives about Black family involvement in the educational experiences of young children. Dominant narratives suggest that Black

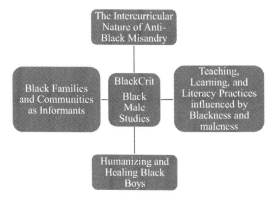

FIGURE 2.1 A Glimpse of BlackBoyCrit Pedagogy

families are not actively involved in their children's educational lives (Boutte & Johnson, 2014; Braden et al., 2020; Reynolds, 2010). However, we know this myth is far from the truth. Black families *are* actively involved; however, most early childhood educators do not *see* Black families as active partners in the lives of Black children, and fail to acknowledge and value the wisdom, insights, and experiences of Black families to support the academic and social outcomes in early childhood classrooms. The wisdom, insights, and experiences of Black families can inform teachers' pedagogical and schooling practices, particularly regarding the ways in which anti-Black misandry impacts their sons in and beyond early childhood classrooms (Braden et al., 2020; Reynolds, 2010). Furthermore, Black communities are replete with expertise and resources (human and material) that can support Black boys in early childhood education. Figure 2.1 provides a glimpse of BlackBoyCrit Pedagogy and how it is anchored in both BlackCrit and Black Male Studies.

All in all, BlackBoyCrit Pedagogy purports to bring attention to the anti-Black misandric nature of early childhood education, as reflected in pedagogies, literacy, and schooling practices, to ensure better academic and social outcomes among Black boys. I hope this pedagogical framework offers us a new way forward in the field of early childhood education. We owe it to Black boys.

Note

1 While intersectionality is an important tenet of CRT, I have found that most Black masculinist scholars committed to it have harshly critiqued intersectionality, drawing instead on thinking in Black Male Studies to address the victimization of Black boys in institutional spaces such as schools. Curry (2017) has argued that intersectionality is built on deficit assumptions of Black men and boys because it socially constructs them in pathological (i.e., dangerous) ways, and should not be used to explain their lived social realities. He further added that there is no empiricism beyond qualitative anecdotal accounts to confirm that Black people experience life in America differently based on intersections; consequently, Blackness overrides any other form of oppression.

References

Baines, J., Tisdale, C., & Long, S. (2018). "We've been doing it your way long enough": Choosing the culturally relevant classroom. Teachers College Press.

Baker, K. (2020, June 27). The black officer who detained George Floyd has pledged to fix the police. *The New York Times*. http://newyorktimes.com

Baker-Bell, A. (2020). *Linguistic justice: Black language, literacy, identity, and pedagogy*. Routledge.

Baker-Bell, A. (2017). I can switch my language, but I can't switch my skin: What teachers must understand about linguistic racism. In E. Moore, Jr., A.Michael, & M. W. Penick-Parks (Eds.), *The guide for white women who teach black Boys* (pp. 97–107). Corwin Press.

Basile, V. (2020). Standin tall: Criminalization and acts of resistance among elementary boys of color. *Race, Ethnicity, and Education*, 23(1), 94–112.

Bell, D. (1992). *Faces at the bottom of the well*. Basic Books.

Boutte, G. (2016). *Educating African-American students: And how are the children?*Routledge Press.

Boutte, G., & Johnson, G. (2014). Community and family involvement in urban schools. In H. R. Milner and K. Lomotey (Eds.), *Handbook on urban education* (pp. 167–182). Routledge.

Boutte, G. S., Johnson, G. L., Wynter-Hoyte, K., & Uyoata, U. E. (2017). Using African diaspora literacy to heal and restore the souls of black folks. *International Critical Childhood Policy Studies Journal*, 6(1), 66–79.

Boutte, G., López-Robertson, J., & Powers-Costello, E. (2011). Moving beyond colorblindness in early childhood classrooms. *Early Childhood Education Journal*, 39(5), 335–342.

Braden, E., Gibson, V., Gillete, R. (2020). Everything black is not bad! Families and teachers engaging in critical discussions about race. *Talking Points*, 31(2), 2–11.

Bristol, T. (2015). Teaching boys: Toward a gender-relevant pedagogy. *Gender Education*, 27(1), 53–68.

Brown, A. L. (2009). "Brothers gonna work it out": Understanding the pedagogic performance of African American male teachers working with African American male students. *Urban Review*, 41(5), 416–435.

Brown, A. L. (2011). Pedagogies of experience. A case study of the African American male teacher. *Teaching Education*, 22(4), 363–376.

Bryan, N. (2020). Shaking the bad boys: Troubling the criminalization of black boys' childhood play, white hegemonic masculinity and femininity, and 'the school playground-to-prison pipeline.' *Race, Ethnicity, and Education*, 23(5), 673–692. https://doi.org/10.1080/13613324.2018.1512483 (Original work published 2018).

Caldera, A. (2020). Eradicating anti-Blackness in U.S. schools: A call-to-action for school leaders. *Diversity, Social Justice, and the Educational Leader*, 4(1), 12–25.

Carlisle, M. (2020, June 13). Two black trans women were killed in the U.S. in the past week as Trump revokes discrimination protections for trans people. *Time*. http://time.com/5853325/blacktrans

Chapman, T. (2013). Origins of and connections to social justice in critical race theory in education. In M. Lynn, & A. D. Dixson (Eds.), *Handbook of critical race theory in education* (pp. 101–112). Routledge.

Connell, R. W. (2005). *Masculinities*. University of California Press.

Coles, J. (2019). The Black literacies of urban high school youth centering antiBlackness in the context of neoliberal multiculturalism. *Journal of Language and Literacy Education*, 15(2), 1–35.

Cook, D. A. (2013). Blurring the boundaries: The mechanics of creating composite characters. In M. Lynn & A. D. Dixson (Eds.), *Handbook of critical race theory in education* (pp. 181–194). Routledge.

Cowhey, M. (2006). *Black ants and Buddhists: Thinking critically and teaching differently in the primary grades.* Stenhouse Publisher.

Crenshaw, K. (1995). Retrenchment: Transformation and legitimation. In antidiscrimination law. In K. Crenshaw, N. Gotanda, G. Peller & K. Thomas (Eds.), *Critical race theory: The key writings that formed the movement* (pp. 103–122). The New Press.

Cridland-Hughes, S. A., & King, L. J. (2015). Killing me softly: How violence comes from the curriculum we teach. In K. Fasching-Varner and N. D. Hartlep (Eds.), *The assault on communities of color* (pp. 67–71). Rowman & Littlefield.

Curry, T., & Curry, G. (2018). Taking it to the people: Translating empirical findings about black men and black families through a black public philosophy. *Dewey Studies*, 2 (1), 42–71.

Curry, T. (2017). *Man-not: Race, class, genre and the dilemmas of black manhood.* Temple University Press.

Curry, T., & Utley, E. (2018). She touched me: Five snapshots of adult sexual violation of black boys. *Kennedy Institute of Ethics Journal*, 28(2), 205–241.

Drake, S., & Burns, R. (2004). *Meeting standards through integrated curriculum.* Association for Supervision and Curriculum Development.

Dumas, M., & ross, k. (2016). "Be real black for me": Imagining BlackCrit in education. Urban. *Education*, 51(4), 415–442.

Emdin, C. (2016). *For white folks who teach in the hood … and the rest of y'all too: Reality pedagogy and urban education.* Beacon Press.

Fernandez, M., & Burch, D. (2020, June 18). George Floyd, From 'I want to touch the world' to 'I can't breathe.' *The New York Times*. https://www.nytimes.com/article/george-floyd-who-is.html

Freire, P. (1970). *Pedagogy of the oppressed.* Continuum.

Gay, G. (2010). *Culturally responsive teaching: Theory, research, and practice.* Teacher College Press.

Gestwicki, C. (2017). *Developmentally appropriate practices: Curriculum and development in early childhood education.* Cengage Learning.

Gilliam, W. S., Maupin, A., Reyes, C. R., Accavitti, M. and Frederick, S. (2016). *Do early educators' implicit biases regarding sex and race relate to behavior expectations and recommendations of preschool expulsions and suspensions?* Yale Childhood Study Center.

Givens, J. R., Nasir, N., ross, k., & de Royston, M. M. (2016). Modeling manhood: Reimagining black male identities in school: Modeling manhood. *Anthropology & Education Quarterly*, 47(2), 167–185.

Hill, M. L. (2016). *Nobody: Casualties of America's war on the vulnerable, from Ferguson to Flint and beyond.* Atria Books.

Howard, T. (2014). *Black male(d): Perils and promises in the education of African American males.* Teacher College Press.

Hyde, P. (2018, May 25). Lisa Houston, teacher seen pulling student's hair in video will return to Palmetto High. *Greenville News*. https://www.greenvilleonline.com/story/news/education/2018/05/25/teacher-video- return-palmetto-high/646159002/

Jackson, T., & Kohli, R. (2016). Guest editors' introduction: The state of teachers of color. *Equity and Excellence in Education*, 49(1), 1–8

Johnson, L. L., & Bryan, N. (2017). Using our voices, losing our bodies: Michael Brown, Trayvon, and the spirit murders of black male professor. *Race, Ethnicity, and Education*, 20(2), 163–177.

Johnson, L. L., Bryan, N., & Boutte, G. (2019). Show us the love: Revolutionary teaching in (un)critical times. *Urban Review*, 51(1), 46–64.

Kelly, R. D. G. (2018). Black study, black struggle. *Ufahamu: A Journal of African Studies*, 40 (2), 153–168.

Kincheloe, J. L. (2006). *Critical pedagogy: Primer*. Peter Lang.

Kirkland, D., & Jackson, A. (2019). Toward a theory of black masculine literacies. In T. Ransaw, C. P. Gause, & R. Majors (Eds.), *The handbook of research on black males: Quantitative, qualitative, and multidisciplinary* (pp. 367–396). Michigan State Press.

Ladson-Billings, G. (1994). *The dreamkeepers/Successful teachers of African American children*. Jossey-Bass.

Ladson-Billings, G. (2009). *The dreamkeepers: Successful teachers of African American children* (2nd ed.). Jossey-Bass.

Ladson-Billings, G., & Tate, W. (1995). Towards a critical race theory in education . *Teachers College Record*, 97(1), 47–68.

Love, B. L. (2019). *We want to do more than survive: Abolitionist teaching and the pursuit of educational freedom*. Beacon Press.

Lynn, M., & Dixon, A. (2013). *Handbook of critical race theory in education*. Routledge.

Lynn, M., & Jennings, M. (2009). Power, politics and critical race pedagogy: A critical race analysis of black male teacher pedagogy. *Race, Ethnicity and Education*, 12(2), 173–196.

Major, R., & Billson, J. M. (1992). *Cool Pose: The dilemmas of black manhood in America*. Touchstone.

Matias, C. (2013). Check yo' self before you wreck yo 'self and our kids: Counterstories from culturally responsive White teachers? … to culturally responsive White teachers! *Interdisciplinary Journal of Teaching and Learning*, 3(2), 68–81.

McCready, L. (2010). *Making space for diverse masculinities: Difference, intersectionality, and engagement in an urban high school* (Adolescent Cultures, School and Society). Peter Lang.

McCready, L. (2004). Understanding the marginalization of gay and gender non-conforming black male students. *Theory Into Practice*, 43(2), 136–143.

McCune, J. (2014). *Sexual discretion: Black masculinity and the politics of passing*. University of Chicago Press.

Morris, M. (2016). *Pushout: The criminalization of black girls in schools*. The New Press.

Nash, K., Howard, J., Miller, E., Boutte, G. S., Johnson, G., & Reid, L. (2018). Critical racial literacy in homes, schools, and communities: Propositions for early childhood contexts. *Contemporary Issues in Early Childhood*, 19(3), 256–273.

Nelson, J. (2016). Relational teaching with black boys: Strategies for learning at a single-sex middle school for boys of color. *Teachers College Record*, 118(6), 1–30.

Nishi, N. W., & Montoya, R. (2017). ParentCrit: Critical race parenting for our children's lives and humanity introduction. *International Journal of Qualitative Studies in Education*, 31(1), 1–2.

Oppel, R., & Taylor, D. R. (2020, June 28). Here's what you need to know about Breonna Taylor's death. *The New York Times*. https://www.nytimes.com/article/breonna-taylor-police.html

Paris, D. (2012). Culturally sustaining pedagogy: A needed change in stance, terminology, and practice. *Educational Researcher*, 4(3), 93–97

Pritchard, D. E. (2017). *Fashioning lives: Black queers and the politics of literacy*. Illinois University Press.

Reynolds, R. (2010). "They think you're lazy," and other messages black parents send their black sons: An exploration of critical race theory in the examination of educational outcomes for black males. *Journal of African American Males in Education*, 1(2), 145–163.

Savini, D. (2019, February 6). George Tilton Elementary students: "I was beaten with a belt". *CBS Chicago.* https://chicago.cbslocal.com/2019/02/06/george-tilton-elementary-school-student-beaten-belt/

Sims-Bishop, R. (1990). Mirrors, windows, and sliding glass doors. *Perspectives: Choosing and Using Books for the Classroom,* 6(3), ix–xi.

Solórzano, D. (2013). Critical race theory's intellectual roots: My email epistolary with Derrick Bell. In M. Lynn & A. D. Dixson (Eds.), *Handbook of critical race theory in education* (pp. 48–68). Routledge.

Stovall, D. (2018). Are we ready for 'school abolition'? Thoughts and practices of radical imaginary in education. *Taboo: The Journal of Cultural and Education,* 17(1), 51–61. https://doi.org/10.31390/taboo.17.1.06

Stovall, D. (2013). Fightin the devil 24/7: Context, community, and critical race praxis in education. In M. Lynn & A. D. Dixson (Eds.), *Handbook of critical race theory in education* (pp. 287–301). Routledge.

Sumison, J. (1999). Critical reflections on the experiences of male early childhood workers. *Gender and Education,* 11(4), 455–468.

Upchurch, C. (1997). *Convicted in the womb: One man's journey from prisoner to peacemaker.* Bantam Books.

Vasquez, V. (2017). *Critical literacy across the K-6 curriculum.* Routledge.

Warren, C. (2017). *Urban preparation: Young black men moving Chicago's South Side to success in higher education.* Harvard Education Press.

Wright, B., & Counsell, S. (2018). *The brilliance of black boys: Cultivating success in the early grades.* Teacher College Press.

Yancy, C. W. (2020). COVID-19 and African Americans. *American Medical Association.* http://jamanetwork.com

3

ANTI-BLACK MISANDRY AND THE RECRUITMENT AND RETENTION NARRATIVE

Seeing Black Male Teachers as Pedagogues in the Lives of Black Boys

Any discussion of BlackBoyCrit Pedagogy has to start with the role of Black male teachers in the lives of Black boys. While I fully believe that every teacher can and must adopt this pedagogical stance, my early childhood experiences with my teacher, Mr. C., have helped me intimately understand the power of having a Black male teacher in the classroom. Thus, I offer this chapter as a foundational element in supporting Black boys: examining the need for Black male teachers and other teachers who understand how to counter anti-Black misandry. Guided by the four developing ideas introduced in Chapter 2, educators will see BlackBoyCrit Pedagogy operationalized by the Black male teachers in three distinct ways. They include: (1) Black males demonstrate characteristics of BlackBoyCrit Pedagogues; (2) Black male teachers apply Black Masculine Literacies as a praxis of BlackBoyCrit Pedagogy; and (3) Black male teachers infuse BlackBoy (Play)Crit Literacies into the early childhood curriculum. Figure 3.1 provides a brief overview of each of the idiosyncratic ways the Black male teachers highlighted in this book applied BlackBoyCrit Pedagogy in their early childhood classrooms. However, Chapters Four, Six, and Eight will provide more detailed accounts of how each teacher operationalized BlackBoyCrit Pedagogy in his early childhood classroom.

Black boys have long depended on the guidance and mentorship of Black male teachers who "love on" Blackness and Black children (Lynn, 2006; Lynn et al., 1999; McKinney de Royston et al., 2017; Williams, 2005). Even so, some Black male teachers themselves underestimate the impact of their Role Modeling presence in classrooms, particularly in early childhood spaces. Other Black male teachers (and administrators) may not even see the importance of their roles, and reinstitute anti-Black misandry because of their own internalized anti-Black misandry. Mr. C., however, understood his Role, and brought out the best in us as he encouraged my classmates and me to always do our best in schools and paired that expectation with

DOI: 10.4324/9780429287619-4

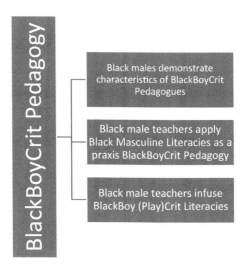

FIGURE 3.1 BlackBoyCrit Pedagogy

what I now describe as BlackBoyCrit Pedagogy. Through my personal and professional experiences, I have learned that Black boys need Black male teachers who support them curricularly and pedagogically in oppressive, anti-Black misandric schooling systems where neither the lives of Black boys nor male teachers matter.

While most of what we know about the need for Black male teachers focuses on the recruitment and retention of Black males as a solution to curtail the so-called "underperformance" of Black boys in and beyond early childhood education (Bryan & Williams, 2017; Brown & Butty, 1999; Bristol & Goings, 2019; Chmelynski, 2006; Jones & Jenkins, 2012; Lewis & Toldson, 2013; Meidl, 2019; Scott & Alexander, 2019), such recruitment and retention initiatives have promulgated one-dimensional and hegemonic masculine views of Black male teachers (e.g. disciplinarians, role models, father-figures) and have overshadowed the pedagogical expertise of Black male teachers. This overshadowing is anti-Black misandric in nature.

The goal of this chapter is to shift the conversation by pointing to the fact that recruitment and retention efforts are oftentimes informed by anti-Black misandric discourses, and turn the focus to learning from Black male teachers as pedagogues who are able to support the academic and social needs of Black boys. In other words, the pedagogies and schooling practices of most Black male teachers have always confronted anti-Black misandry, and have served to humanize, heal, and empower Black boys in and beyond early childhood education (Brown, 2009). In this regard, we must acknowledge that to ignore the pedagogical acumen of Black male teachers is to engage in anti-Black misandry and to ignore important learning opportunities for all teachers.

With such considerations, in this chapter, I briefly discuss the overwhelming White teaching force, and current calls for recruiting and retaining Black male teachers in early childhood education as anti-Black misandric phenomena. These discourses are followed by conversations on the need to focus on the pedagogical practices of Black male teachers of Black boys, and the benefits of those pedagogies and schooling practices.

The Overwhelmingly White Teaching Force

Educational discourses have notoriously focused primarily on White teachers. These are the examples we see in most of the texts used in preservice teacher education and inservice professional development with the exception of a few authors (Bristol, 2018; Foster, 1997; Jackson & Kohli, 2016; Lynn, 2006) and the tokenized inclusion of teachers of Color here and there. Consequently, I do not want to spend much time discussing White teachers which would constitute yet another instance of centering Whiteness and is another example of anti-Black misandry in teacher education. However, in this chapter that looks at the importance of Black male Role Models, it is important to mention that the teaching profession is overwhelming White and female; it has been this way for an extremely long time. As it currently stands, more than 80 percent of teachers in the United States are White, middle-class, and female, and the percentage of White teachers has been increasing since school desegregation (Cook & Dixon, 2013; Sleeter & Milner, 2011; Picower, 2021), when many Black teachers lost their teaching jobs and were replaced by White teachers. The teaching profession has yet to recover from this loss (Siddle-Walker, 2018), and anti-Black systems including culturally biased national teacher licensure exams including *PRAXIS I and II*, and the pipeline of aspiring White female teachers who enroll in preservice teacher education programs remain in place to maintain an overwhelmingly White female teaching force (Goings & Bianco, 2016; Wynter-Hoyte et al., 2019).

National teacher licensure exams including *PRAXIS I and II* have become gatekeepers to the profession. By that, I mean that, much like most national assessments, *PRAXIS I and II* are culturally biased exams based on White ways of knowing. Such cultural bias disproportionately impacts the number of Black teachers who will enter the teaching profession (Goings & Bianco, 2016; Wynter-Hoyte et al., 2020). Even so, national recruitment and retention efforts and initiatives including *Call Me Mister* and *Black Men to the BlackBoard* are presently underway to recruit and retain a more diverse teaching force; despite the under-representation of Black woman teachers, these efforts have focused on the recruitment and retention of Black men to classrooms (Brown & Butty, 1999; Lewis & Toldson, 2013). Similarly, preservice teacher education programs continue to produce a pipeline for White female teachers to enter the profession because Black preservice teachers often leave teacher education programs. Structural and institutional inequities including racially hostile environments and the underrepresentation of Black preservice teacher educators who can guide, mentor, and support them often push Black preservice teachers out of teacher education programs (Sleeter & Milner, 2011). Few efforts are underway in pre-service teacher education programs to address anti-Blackness and to diversify those programs and, subsequently, inservice teaching programs (Sleeter & Milner, 2011).

The Call to Classrooms: Positive and Negative Trends in Recruiting and Retaining Black Male Teachers in Early Childhood Education

In response to the overwhelmingly White teaching force, for more than two decades, there have been calls to increase the paltry 2 percent of Black male teachers in classrooms across all grade levels (Bristol, 2018; Bristol & Mentor, 2018; Jones & Jenkins, 2012; Lewis & Toldson, 2013). Efforts including *Call Me Mister*, a Black male teacher diversity initiative started in the early 2000s at Clemson University in South Carolina, have been actively recruiting Black males to classroom teaching (Bristol, 2018; Jones & Jenkins, 2012). Since then, other Black male recruitment and retention initiatives have emerged. The Obama Administration's former Secretary of Education, Arne Duncan, introduced *Black Men to the Blackboard*, an initiative that promised to increase the percentage of Black male teachers from 2 to 5 percent by 2020 (Bristol, 2018). Other recruitment and retention programs including *Profound Gentlemen* have been equally instrumental in responding to the call. *Pathways2-Teaching* has been introduced at the high school level to encourage Black males and other students of Color to consider pursuing teaching as a profession (Bianco et al., 2011; Goings & Bianco, 2016). Each of these programs has made noble attempts to confront the challenges (i.e., finance, systemic barriers) Black males face entering the teaching profession and to increase the underrepresentation of Black male teachers in the early childhood/elementary classroom (Meidl, 2019). Yet, despite the efforts of Black male teacher recruitment and retention initiatives like these and the need to increase the low percentage of Black male teachers in classrooms, the overwhelming focus on the recruitment and retention of Black male teachers is influenced by anti-Black misandric narratives that are important to understand (Brockenbrough, 2012; Meidl, 2019; Pabon, 2016; Woodson & Pabon, 2016).

These narratives are in response to the myth surrounding the dismal academic and social outcomes of Black boys who are socially constructed as being disinterested in learning (Pabon, 2016). As such, Black male teachers become what Brown (2012) refers to as *pedagogical kinds*, those whose professional roles are defined for them before they enter classrooms. These Black male teachers are expected to serve as role models, father-figures, and disciplinarians who will discipline and control Black boys, a role that not only stereotypes but diminishes the role of Black male teachers as intellectuals and academic experts.

In addition, gender and sexuality play a role in the recruitment and retention of Black males to classrooms. Whereas cisgender heterosexual Black male teachers are perceived to be the right kind of men for the teaching profession because they model hegemonic masculine norms for Black boys (Warren, 2020), nongender-conforming and queer Black men are then constructed as not being the right kind of men for Black boys and the teaching profession (Brockenbrough, 2012; Pabon, 2016; Warren, 2020; Woodson & Pabon, 2016). Given that there are a myriad ways to be Black and male as discussed in the Introduction, this unfortunate mistreatment of and discrimination against nongender-conforming and queer men is also anti-Black misandric in nature. As such, our calls to recruit and retain Black male teachers must be examined for perpetuating the notion that Black male Role Models can only be heterosexual and cisgender and must not just include but normalize those men who defy hegemonic masculine norms and expectations (Brockenbrough, 2012). Consistent with BlackBoyCrit Pedagogy, understanding Black maleness as broadly defined provides opportunities for Black boys to understand and appreciate diverse and multiple expressions of Black masculinity as early as early childhood education (Brockenbrough, 2012; Warren, 2020; Woodson & Pabon, 2016).

Seeing Black Male Teachers as Pedagogues in Early Childhood Education

Much of the work on the pedagogical practices of Black male teachers has been conducted at middle and secondary school levels (Brown, 2012, Lynn, 2006). Little has been explored in the teaching of young children. The majority of the work on culturally relevant Black male teacher pedagogy in early childhood is informed by Gloria Ladson-Billings' conception of culturally relevant pedagogy. Gloria Ladson-Billings (1994) conducted a three-year study on successful teachers of Black children, out of which she coined the term *culturally relevant pedagogy* (CRP). CRP seeks to empower Black students "intellectually, socially, emotionally, and politically" (pp. 17–18) by drawing on cultural knowledge that is familiar to them. Boutte (2016) asserted that, given its implementation over two decades ago, Ladson-Billings' conception of culturally relevant pedagogy has stood the test of time, and scholars have demonstrated its effectiveness in educational research and practice in PreK-12 classrooms. More pointedly, culturally relevant pedagogy has demonstrated student success when teaching and learning mirror aspects of their cultural ways of knowing and being (Brown, 2012; Milner, 2010).

We are also indebted to the scholarship of Marvin Lynn (2006), the first scholar to bring attention to the pedagogies and schooling practices of culturally relevant Black male teachers (Lynn, 2006). Lynn helped us to understand that Black male teachers in early childhood education also center the teaching of race and racism in pedagogical practices to deepen the critical consciousness of young learners. His work has influenced that of many scholars (Bristol, 2018; Bristol & Goings, 2019; Brown, 2009; Woodson & Pabon, 2016) who desired to socially construct Black male teachers beyond the one-dimensional constructions and narratives of role models and father-figures. Inspired by Lynn's (2006) initial work on the pedagogies and schooling practices of Black male teachers, many scholars have defined those pedagogies and schooling practices as those that: (a) confront race and racism; (b) teach for liberation /freedom; (c) uplift the Black community; (d) center Black cultural ways of knowing and being including hip-hop; and (e) address the issues of gender relevance (Bristol, 2015; Brown, 2009). However, because the teachers in these studies were mainly teaching Black students, and especially boys, I would also add that these Black male teachers were also confronting not only race, racism, and white supremacy, but also anti-Black misandry through pedagogies and practices. These pedagogies and schooling practices that counter anti-Black misandry are not solely reserved for Black boys; however, White children can also benefit from not only the explicit teaching of race, racism, and white supremacy, but also anti-Black misandry in early childhood classrooms.

The pedagogies and schooling practices of Black male teachers have demonstrated the power to move Black boys (and girls) academically and socially from what Ladson-Billings (2009) has referred to as the "junk drawer" (p. 121) to the "china cabinet" (p. 121). She meant that teachers who center the experiences of Black students—in this case, Black boys—can and do help them navigate anti-Blackness and Black suffering in schools so that they can be humanized, healed, empowered, and uplifted (Ladson-Billings, 2009). In other studies, Black boys have suggested that the presence of Black male teachers has motivated them to attend school, shielded them from anti-Black misandric schooling practices, and inspired them to attend and complete post-secondary education (Warren, 2017). Furthermore, research that focuses on Black families illuminates their acknowledgement of the benefits of the pedagogies and schooling practices of Black male teachers, which they perceive as grounded in the experiences of Black boys (Bryan, 2020). They also believe that Black male teachers teach Black boys in ways that honor them, serve as mentors positive Role Models for them, and are more likely to protect Black boys from anti-Black misandric violence as enacted by White teachers, administrators, and other educational professionals in schools and classrooms (Bryan, 2020).

Conclusion

In conclusion, although it is clear that we need more Black male teachers in classrooms, we also need to be careful about the anti-Black misandric narratives that surround the recruitment and retention of Black male teachers to classrooms. As such, we should promote Black male teachers as those who confront not only race, racism, and white supremacy, but also anti-Black misandry through their pedagogies and schooling practices. These pedagogies and practices are designed to inspire Black boys in and beyond the classroom, provide them mirrors in which they see themselves, and offer them windows through which they can see the world.

References

Bianco, M., Leech, N., & Mitchell, K. (2011). Pathways to teaching: African American teens explore teaching as a career. *Journal of Negro Education*, 80(3), 368–383.

Boutte, G. (2016). *Educating African-American students: And how are the children?* Routledge.

Bristol, T. (2015). Teaching boys: Towards a theory of gender-relevant pedagogy. *Gender Education*, 27(1), 53–68.

Bristol, T. (2018). To be alone or in a group: An exploration into how the school-based experiences differ for black male teachers across one urban school district. *Urban Education*, 53(3), 334–354.

Bristol, T., & Goings, R. (2019). Exploring the boundary-heightening experiences of black male teachers: Lessons for teacher education program. *Journal of Teacher Education*, 70(1), 51–64.

Bristol, T., & Mentor, M. (2018). Policing and teaching: The positioning of black male teachers as agents in the universal carceral apparatus. *The Urban Review*, 50(2), 218–234.

Brockenbrough, E. (2012). "You ain't my daddy": Black male teachers and the politics of surrogate fatherhood. *Teacher College Record*, 114(5), 1–43.

Brown, A. L. (2009). "Brotha gonna work it out": Understanding the pedagogic performance of African American male teachers working with African American male students. *Urban Review*, 41(5), 416–435.

Brown, A. L. (2012). On human kinds and role models: A critical discussion about the African American male teacher. *Educational Studies*, 48(3), 296–315.

Brown, J. W., & Butty, J. L. (1999). Factors that influence African American male teachers' educational and career aspirations: Implications for school district recruitment and retention efforts. *Journal of Negro Education*, 68(3), 280–292.

Bryan, N. (2020). Remembering Tamir Rice and other black boy victims: Imagining black PlayCrit literacies inside and outside urban literacy education. *Urban Education*. https://doi.org/10.1177/0042085920902250

Bryan, N., & Williams, T. M. (2017). We need more than just male bodies in classrooms: Recruiting and retaining culturally relevant black male teachers in early childhood education. *Journal of Early Childhood Teacher Education*, 38(3), 209–222.

Chmelynski, C. (2006). Getting more men and black into teaching. *Education Digest*, 7(5), 40–42.

Cook, D. A., & Dixson, A. (2013). Expanding critical race theory and method: A composite counter story on school reform and the experiences of black teachers in New Orleans post Katrina. *International Journal of Qualitative Studies in Education*, 26(10), 1238–1258.

Foster, M. (1997). *Black teachers on teaching*. The New Press.

Goings, R., & Bianco, M. (2016). It's hard to be who you don't see: An exploration of black male high school students' perspectives on becoming teachers. *The Urban Review*, 48(1), 628–646.

Jackson, T., & Kohli, R. (2016). Guest editors' introduction: The state of teachers of color. *Equity and Excellence in Education*, 49(1), 1–8.

Jones, R., & Jenkins, A. (2012). *Call me mister: The reemergence of African American male teachers in South Carolina*. Advantage Media Group.

Ladson-Billings, G. (1994). *The dreamkeepers: Successful teachers of African American children*. Jossey-Bass.

Ladson-Billings, G. (2009). *The dreamkeepers: Successful teachers of African American children* (2nd ed.). Jossey-Bass.

Lynn, M. (2006). Education for the community: Exploring the culturally relevant practice of black male teachers. *Teachers College Record*, 108(12), 2497–2522.

Lynn, M., Johnson, C., & Hassan, K. (1999). Raising the critical consciousness of African American students in Baldwin Hills: A portrait of an exemplary African American male teacher. *Journal of Negro Education*, 68(1), 42–51.

Lewis, C., & Toldson, I. (Eds.). (2013). *Black male teachers: Diversifying the United States' teacher workforce*. Emerald Publishing.

McKinney de Royston, M., Vakil, S., Ross, K. M., Givens, J., & Holman, A. (2017). "He's more like a brother than a teacher": Politicized caring in a program for African American males. *Teacher College Record*, 119(4), 1–40.

Meidl, C. (2019). Challenges to recruiting black males into early childhood education. *Urban Education*, 54(4), 564–591.

Milner, H. R. (2010). *Start where you are, but don't stay there: Understanding diversity, opportunity gaps, and teaching in today's classrooms*. Harvard Education Press.

Pabon, A. (2016). Waiting for black supermen: A look at a problematic assumption. *Urban Education*, 51(8), 915–939.

Picower, B. (2021). *Reading, writing, and racism: Disrupting whiteness in teacher education and in the classroom*. Beacon Press.

Scott, L., & Alexander, Q. (2019). Strategies for recruiting and retaining black male special education teachers. *Remedial and Special Education*, 40(4), 236–247.

Siddle-Walker, V. (2018). *The lost education of Horace Tate*. The New Press.

Sleeter, C., & Milner, R. (2011). Researching successful efforts in teacher education to diversify teachers. In A. F.Ball, & C. Tyson (Eds.), *Studying diversity in teacher education* (pp. 81–103). Rowman & Littlefield.

Sumison, J. (1999). Critical reflections on the experiences of male early childhood workers. *Gender and Education*, 11(4), 455–468.

Warren, C. (2020). Meeting myself: Race-gender oppression and a genre study of black men teachers' interaction with black boys. *Race, Ethnicity, and Education*, 23(3), 367–391.

Warren, C. (2017). *Urban preparation: Young black men moving Chicago's South Side to success in higher education*. Harvard Education.

Williams, H. (2005). *Self-taught: African American education in slavery and freedom*University of North Carolina Press.

Woodson, A., & Pabon, A. (2016). "I'm none of the above": Exploring themes of heteropatriarchy in the life histories of black male educators. *Equity and Excellence in Education*, 49(1), 57–71.

Wynter-Hoyte, K., Long, S., McAdoo, T. M., & Strickland, J. D. (2020). "Losing one African American teacher is one too many": A critical race analysis of support for praxis core as African American students speak out. *Teachers College Record*, 122(11).

Wynter-Hoyte, K., Muller, M., Bryan, N., Boutte, G. S., & Long, S. (2019). Dismantling eurocratic practices in teacher education: A preservice teacher program focused on culturally revelant, humanizing, and decolonizing pedagogies. In T. Hodges & A. Baum (Eds), *Handbook of research on field-based teacher education* (pp. 300–320). IGI Global.

4

BLACK MALES AS *BLACKBOYCRIT PEDAGOGUES* IN EARLY CHILDHOOD CLASSROOMS

Black Boys' Portraits of Mr. Javien, Mr. Tal, and Mr. Henry

BlackBoyCrit Pedagogy requires that early childhood teachers see literacy as a social, critical, multiliterate practice that allows us to produce and consume texts in many forms and to read texts in many ways. I, along with other scholars (Baker-Bell, 2020; Husband, 2012; Johnson et al., 2017; Kinloch, 2010; Kinloch et al., 2017; Kirkland & Jackson, 2009; Kirkland & Jackson, 2019; Morrell, 2015; Sealey-Ruiz & Greene, 2015; Smith, 2016; Tatum, 2005) invite you to see literacy in many forms including in non-print (e.g., body, clothes, music, dance, signs, gesture, expression, etc.) and print (e.g., books, magazines, digital texts, and so forth). Seeing literacy in such a way helps all of us to move beyond literacy normativity as briefly discussed in Chapter 2 and as will be further addressed in Chapter 5. As such, the bodies of White and Black teachers, male and female, in early childhood classrooms are texts that young children read. Because of strong messaging in and out of school, the White body is typically read favorably (e.g., pure, beautiful, intelligent); and the Black body can be simultaneously read unfavorably (e.g., as less beautiful, less intelligent, nonhuman/nonexistent) by White people (Smith, 2016; Yancy, 2017). For Black boys and families like those introduced in this chapter, however, the Black male body in the early childhood education classroom was read as a positive text. Their experiences are not unlike my own: I read the presence of Mr. C., my kindergarten teacher, as a positive and humanizing text that provided me a mirror in which to see myself, and a window through which to see the world.

Because the body is indeed "a tablet that [renders] the self textually" (Kirkland & Jackson, 2019, p. 367), the overwhelming presence of White female bodies in early childhood education can serve as a dangerously narrow text for Black boys (Milner, 2010; Moore et al., 2018). This is particularly damaging when White teachers are unable to appreciate and respond to both the individual and collective strengths and needs of Black boys. Bryan and Jett (2018) have argued that the abundance of White

DOI: 10.4324/9780429287619-5

female teachers in early childhood classrooms also sends messages to children about who can (i.e., White females) and who cannot (i.e., Black males and other people of Color and White males) become teachers. In other words, the White female teacher body becomes a recruitment tool for young White children—especially girls who, given current teacher demographics, are more likely to become teachers in the future—while sending messages to Black boys, other children of Color, and White boys that they cannot become teachers. Thus, the recruitment and retention of teachers to the early childhood classroom can implicitly begin as early as early childhood education (Bryan & Jett, 2018).

The physical presence of teachers in classrooms does more than serve as teacher recruitment tools for the profession; it also serves as language and literacy practices for Black boys who are able to read the texts of early childhood classrooms for various social cues. We know that, when Black male teachers are absent, they cannot provide Black boys and other children of Color mirrors in which to see themselves, or windows through which they can see the world and their own possibilities of teaching professionally in the future. That being said, one might ask: What is possible when Black male teachers are present in these same spaces? What does such a presence mean for Black boys who rarely see positive public images of Black men, particularly of those in the teaching profession? And, as I deepen this exploration of BlackBoyCrit Pedagogy, what are the characteristics of Black male teachers who embody this kind of teaching – BlackBoyCrit Pedagogues?

Based on W. E. B. Du Bois' (1903) assertion that "children learn more from what you are than what you teach (p. 20)," I use this chapter to introduce three Black male kindergarten teachers—Mr. Tal, Mr. Henry, and Mr. Javien— through the eyes of Black boys who were students in their early childhood classrooms and how the teachers enacted BlackBoyCrit Pedagogy. Table 4.1 below provides an overview of the characteristics of BlackBoyCrit Pedagogues. Although Table 4.1 provides such an overview, readers should note that the "Zoom Out" sections of the chapter are also sub-headed (italicized through the

TABLE 4.1 Characteristics of BlackBoyCrit Pedagogues

- Demonstrating love and caring for Black boys
- Being appreciated, valued, and respected by Black families
- Building relationships with Black boys as foundations
- Giving Black boys multiple opportunities to be their better selves
- Seeing the importance of decriminalizing practices
- Letting Black boys know they are valued
- Helping Black boys see possible futures
- Providing positive Black male images
- Positioning Black families as partners
- Serving as role models
- Building Black boys' anti-Black misandric consciousness
- Uplifting Black boys

chapter) with characteristics of male teachers who embrace BlackBoyCrit Pedagogy.

I begin by introducing the teachers themselves. Next, I briefly introduce the three kindergartners—Maurice, Roland, and Ameer—and their maternal caregivers, Mrs. Aretha, Mrs. Boins, and Mrs. Martha (because two of the boys were not being raised by biological mothers, I use the term *maternal caregivers* to describe adopted mothers, grandmothers, and fictive kin whose roles were to take care of the boys). From there, I share each of the three boys' portraits of their teachers: Maurice on Mr. Tal, Roland on Mr. Henry, and Ameer on Mr. Javien, and in each of those sections, I draw from those portraits, characteristics that help to define BlackBoyCrit Pedagogues. Collectively, these portraits demonstrate how Black male teachers serve as texts as well as "mirrors and windows" (Sims-Bishop, 1990) for the Black boys and, in the process, support them academically, emotionally, and socially.

Introduction of Key Players

The key players in these stories about Black male teachers include three kindergarten-age boys, their teachers, and their maternal primary caregivers. Table 4.2 provides a brief summary of these teachers.

The Teachers

Black male teachers represent only 2 percent of our nation's teaching force across all grade levels (Lewis & Toldson, 2013). However, they are far more underrepresented at the early childhood education level, comprising less than 1 percent of all early childhood teachers (Bureau of Labor Statistic, 2014). Despite these challenges, there are Black male teachers in such classrooms, and particularly in kindergarten classrooms, who are supporting Black boys and other students in critical ways. They work in elementary schools in varying geographic areas (e.g., urban, suburban, and rural), and have varying degrees of experience teaching at the early childhood education level. The next few sections provide detailed information about each of the teachers.

TABLE 4.2 Black Male Early Childhood Teachers

Teachers	Ages	Years of Experience	Elementary Schools	Teacher Preparation Program
Mr. Tal	24	3	Tillers Plain	PWI
Mr. Henry	26	4	Ponce De Leon	PWI
Mr. Javien	35	4	Simon	HBCU/PWI

Mr. Tal, Tillers Plain Elementary School

During the time of my study, Mr. Tal was 24 years old and had been teaching for three years. He stated that he had always wanted to be a teacher. As a young child, he found himself playing school or imitating the pedagogical and schooling practices of his own teachers. He loved and was genuinely committed to the children who attended Tillers Plain. In fact, he grew up in the nearby Tillers Plain community and attended the elementary school himself as a young boy. Mr. Tal suggested that he wanted to teach at Tillers Plain Elementary because the teachers there shaped him into the consummate professional he currently is, and he wanted to "return what he learned to the people" (King, 2017, p. 95), giving back to the same community that had given so much to him. He also saw it as an opportunity to uplift and empower students like Maurice, whose perceptions I will share later in this chapter.

Given the institutional inequities faced by the residents of Tillers Plain, Mr. Tal was never supposed to graduate high school or attend college. However, he beat the odds. Once he graduated high school, he attended a Predominantly White Institution (PWI) in the Lowcountry[1] of South Carolina, where he majored in elementary education. There, he was a participant in the *Call Me Mister* Program, a "grow-your-own" initiative designed to recruit and retain Black male teachers to classrooms (Jones & Jenkins, 2012). In his teacher education program, he was not trained to teach Black boys, but through building relationships with them in classrooms and his own willingness to learn, he learned how to better support Black boys in classrooms.

In spite of his ultimate success, Mr. Tal admitted that he feared his dream to teach might not be realized; he struggled to successfully pass his *PRAXIS* I and II exams, the required licensure assessments for becoming a teacher. Mr. Tal's struggle to pass is not an anomaly. Many aspiring Black teachers face similar challenges. According to Goings and Bianco (2016), because these exams are culturally biased, Black preservice teachers fail these exams at three to five times the rate of their White preservice counterparts. Some scholars (Bianco et al., 2011) suggest that, for Black preservice teachers, these exams create a leaky pipeline to the teaching profession that may cause it to lose a number of future teachers. According to Wynter-Hoyte et al. (2020), losing any number of Black teachers is simply too many. Nevertheless, Mr. Tal persisted, and was finally able to pursue his dream job at the elementary school he once attended.

Tillers Plain Elementary School is a Prek–5th grade Title One school located in an urban area of the Lowcountry of South Carolina. Title One schools are identified by the federal government as K–12 schools wherein 40 percent or more of the students live below the poverty line (Boyle & Lee, 2015). According to the South Carolina School Report Card, Tillers Plain Elementary has consistently maintained an "average" school rating since 2012. At the time of this study, there were 622 students who attended the school. Ninety-eight percent of those students were Black and 2 percent were Latinx. Ninety-seven percent of the students qualified for free and/or reduced lunches. The principal of the school was a White woman who had served in that capacity for seven years. There were 45 teachers on staff. Twenty-three teachers were White. Eighteen were Black. There were also three Latinx teachers and one Asian teacher. Tillers Plain Elementary was tucked away in the historically neglected community of Mr. Tal's childhood and youth, Tillers Plain, which is predominantly Black and Brown. Tillers Plain has a negative reputation, and most people considered it a "dangerous" neighborhood without considering the ways White Flight depleted the area's financial and municipal resources. White Flight occurs when White people move from communities to distance themselves from Black and Brown people whom they believe will bring down the quality of their neighborhoods (Rothstein, 2017). Therefore, the majority of the students who attended Tillers Plain were Black and Latinx; these were the students Mr. Tal was committed to teaching.

Mr. Henry, Ponce De Leon Elementary School

When I met Mr. Henry, a 26-year-old Black male kindergarten teacher, he was in his fourth year of teaching at the early childhood level. Prior to taking a teaching position in Riley School District Two at Ponce De Leon Elementary School (pseudonyms), where he worked during the time of the study, Mr. Henry taught for three years in Riley School District One (pseudonym). He decided to change districts because he bought a new home in the District Two area. To that end, Mr. Henry was new to both the area and the school.

Mr. Henry grew up in the Lowcountry of South Carolina, and attended public K-12 schools there. After graduating high school, he attended a PWI in the Lowcountry and received a bachelor's degree in early childhood education. Mr. Henry had received a football scholarship to attend college; however, a severe injury ended his football career, so he shifted his passion for sports to supporting students on and off the football field. At the PWI, Mr. Henry did not learn how to teach Black boys, and much of what he learned about teaching Black boys came from his own experiences working with them in early childhood classrooms.

During the day, Mr. Henry was a kindergarten teacher; at night, he was a football coach. Mr. Henry is approximately 6 feet 3 inches tall and athletically built, and he admitted that, when people asked about his profession, they were shocked to learn he was a kindergarten teacher. He was neither offended nor surprised by people's responses, but saw them as an opportunity to challenge people to think beyond gender stereotypes and biases.

Similar to Mr. Tal, Mr. Henry faced challenges on his journey to becoming a teacher. Although he did not have issues successfully passing the *PRAXIS* I and II exams, he almost failed his practicum experience, a component of preservice teacher education wherein aspiring teachers are assigned to schools to practice the craft of teaching. Mr. Henry suggested that his host teacher, a White woman to whose classroom he was assigned, was extremely hostile toward him, and did not provide him the kind of assistance he needed to be successful. At the midpoint of his practicum experiences, he received low scores on his evaluation, which meant that he was in danger of failing. However, he worked closely with his supervising professor, another White woman, who provided strategies for his success despite the challenges he faced. While scholars have underscored how *PRAXIS* I and II exams create a leaky pipeline to classrooms for Black students, few scholars have investigated the ways in which White female teachers who dominate early childhood classrooms also contribute to the challenges Black preservice teachers— and a Black male in this case—face to become inservice teachers. Fortunately, Mr. Henry was able to overcome this hurdle and pursue his career as a teacher. Ponce De Leon was fortunate to have Mr. Henry as its first and only Black male kindergarten teacher on the faculty.

Ponce De Leon is a predominantly White school, which is located in a suburban community in Riley County School District Two. It consists of two campuses— Lower and Upper. The Lower Campus of Ponce De Leon Elementary, where Mr. Henry taught, housed grades PreK-2, and the Upper Campus housed grades 3–5. According to the South Carolina Department of Education, the school was considered an academically high-performing school, and has consistently maintained an "excellent" school rating since 2012. According to the South Carolina School Report Card, the school exceeds expectations for meeting the 2020 South Carolina Performance Vision, which states that, by 2020, "all students will graduate with the knowledge and skills necessary to compete successfully in the global economy, participate in a democratic society and contribute positively as members of families and communities" (South Carolina Department of Education, 2014, n.p.). At the time of this study, there were 797 students who attended Ponce De Leon's Upper and Lower campuses. Ninety-seven percent of the students were White, 1 percent African-American, and 1 percent Latinx and Asian. Additionally, less than 30 percent of the students qualified for free and/or reduced lunches. The principal of the school was a White woman who had served in this capacity for four years. There were 50 teachers on staff, 30 of whom held National Board Certification, a highly respected teacher endorsement given to the nation's top teachers (Cowan & Goldhaber, 2016). Forty-two teachers were White; and five were Black. There were also three Latinx teachers.

Mr. Javien, Simon Elementary School

Although he was born in Nassau, Bahamas, Mr. Javien, a 35-year-old Black male kindergartner teacher, grew up in the Lowcountry of South Carolina and attended public schools there. After graduating from high school, he attended a Historically Black College (HBCU) located in the Lowcountry, where he received a bachelor's degree in sociology. Mr. Javien originally wanted to become a social worker, but after completing his undergraduate program, he was unable to find a job in his field of study. During one of our interviews, Mr. Javien revealed that he came from a lineage of public-school educators, and, quite naturally, several family members expected him to become a teacher as well. His maternal grandmother taught during segregated schooling; she was a teacher and a school administrator; and Mr. Javien's own mother taught and served as a media specialist for more than 20 years. However, despite such lineage, he admitted that he never wanted to enter the profession, even after his mother and grandmother recommended it as a professional option. According to Mr. Javien, he was not interested "in tying shoes and wiping runny noses." Indeed, Mr. Javien resisted the notion until he had no other choice, and needed a job. He took a position as a teacher's assistant in a special education classroom in an elementary school in the Lowcountry, and soon developed a love for teaching, which led him to pursue a master's degree in education. As he stated, "What drove me into the classroom was what I saw in that classroom as a teacher's assistant. Anything that could have happened in there happened, I wanted to be a part of it." Once Mr. Javien completed graduate school, he sought certification to teach in his home state, and landed a job at Simon Elementary in rural South Carolina. Mr. Javien had taught four years at Simon. Like Mr. Henry, he was the first and only Black male kindergarten teacher both at his school and in his district.

Simon Elementary is a Title One school, and based on South Carolina's School Report Card Data, it received an "average" rating for student academic performance in 2014, after having been identified as "below average" for three consecutive years. An average rating meant that "the school['s] performance meets the standards for progress towards the 2020 South Carolina Performance Vision" (South Carolina Department of Education, 2014). Below average meant that the school was in jeopardy of not meeting the Vision. At the time of this study, there were 317 students in Child Development-6th grade who attended the school. Ninety-eight percent of the students were African-American, while 2 percent were White. Additionally, 90 percent of the students qualified for free and/or reduced lunch. The principal of the school was a Black woman who had served in this capacity for three years. There were 25 teachers on staff. Twelve were Black and 13 were White.

Black Boy Kindergartners and Caregivers

In this section, I introduce the boys and their caregivers. Table 4.3 highlights the Black boys, caregivers, and their relationships to each other and to local schools.

TABLE 4.3 Black Boy Kindergartners and Caregivers

Black Boys	Ages	Teachers	Elementary Schools	Family Members	Familial Relationship
Maurice	6	Mr. Tal	Tillers Plain	Mrs. Aretha	Grandmother
Roland	6	Mr. Henry	Ponce De Leon	Mrs. Boins	Mother
Ameer	6	Mr. Javien	Simon	Mrs. Martha	Grandmother

Maurice and His Grandmother, Mrs. Aretha

When I met 6-year-old Maurice, he was a kindergarten student in Mr. Tal's class at Tillers Plain Elementary School in an urban city in South Carolina. Maurice made huge academic gains in reading and math under Mr. Tal's tutelage. He loved writing and drawing pictures that he often shared with Mr. Tal; each picture was created to express Maurice's appreciation for his teacher. During my visits to Mr. Tal's classroom, Maurice frequently engaged in conversations with me. He was excited to show me his pictures and his writing, of which he was most proud.

During the time of this study, Maurice's mother was in the military and was deployed in the Middle East, so his grandmother, Mrs. Aretha, decided that she would raise him in the Tillers Plain community to create a stable living environment for him. Because of erroneous assumptions about children raised by family members other than parents, most White teachers, presumed that Maurice's parents were uninvolved in his life; however, Maurice's parental arrangement was intentional so that he would not be transient and living with a series of relatives during his mother's deployment. Oftentimes, the diverse construction of Black families is disregarded when measured against a White familial structure (Boutte & Johnson, 2014; Johnson et al., 2017), and Black families are vilified when they are structured in ways that are different from many middle-class White families. However, the concept of family is often much broader in Black communities than in White communities, and includes extended family members who take on the responsibilities of raising relatives as well as fictive kin, individuals who may not be biologically related, but who still give and receive support, love, and care (Fordham, 1996; Cook, 2010).

True to this concept, Mrs. Aretha was actively involved in Maurice's educational life and had developed a strong professional relationship with Mr. Tal, whom she greatly admired and respected. On several occasions, she expressed that Mr. Tal was the perfect teacher to support Maurice both academically and socially, because he was extremely patient with students. Such patience was necessary according to Mrs. Aretha, who described Maurice as "having a temper," a fact which concerned her, particularly because Black men and boys were being executed by White police officers in and beyond Black communities. Her fears were not unfounded. In 2015, Officer Michael Slager shot and killed Walter Scott in North Charleston, South Carolina, the area of the city in which Mrs. Aretha lived and where Maurice attended school. It is important to note that, when she described Maurice as having a temper, Mrs. Aretha was not viewing him from a deficit perspective; as do most Black mothers (Perry, 2019), she was genuinely concerned about how people, mainly police officers and teachers, would perceive Maurice's interactions with them which, while no different from the actions of young White boys, could mean life or death for Maurice. Most Black mothers (and fathers) have such concerns for their children, especially their sons (Perry, 2019).

Roland and His Mother, Mrs. Boins

A brilliant student, Roland was a 6-year-old Black boy kindergartener in Mr. Henry's class at Ponce De Leon Elementary School (Lower Campus). Roland enjoyed playing with his friends at school, as well as playing sports. He also loved the fact that Mr. Henry played football as a young child and in college, a connection that strengthened their relationship. Roland deeply admired Mr. Henry, and spent time in his classroom before and after school, where they engaged in sports-related conversations.

Roland grew up in a two-parent home in the Ponce De Leon community. His mother, Mrs. Boins, was a local Black attorney and served as the president of Ponce De Leon's Parent Teacher Association (PTA). Although she recognized Roland's brilliance, she admitted that he did not like attending school. She admitted that she even had to motivate him to attend preschool. However, everything changed when he became a student in Mr. Henry's kindergarten classroom. As Mrs. Boins explained:

> My son [Roland] isn't very interested in school, and because he doesn't like school, Mr. Henry was a motivator for him to go there. Like, I would say: 'You are going to school to see Mr. Henry.' Then, he'll say, 'Ok, I'll go.' I like that [Mr. Henry] has a good relationship like with all the students. I've heard that from other parents too. Overall, it's been a positive experience.

In other words, Mrs. Boins suggested that Roland only became interested in school because Mr. Henry motivated him to come, and Mr. Henry's ability to motivate Roland is consistent with research studies that suggest that Black students who have at least one Black teacher during their PreK-12 experience are more likely to do well in school and attend college (Easton-Brooks, 2019).

Given her position on the school's PTA, Mrs. Boins was instrumental in hiring Mr. Henry to teach at Ponce De Leon. She recalled how impressed she was with him during the interview process. According to her, she knew he would be a perfect fit, and he did not fail to disappoint, as he was always the talk of the school in positive ways. Mr. Henry was actively involved in both the school and the community, and Mrs. Boins spoke highly of the mentoring program he established for Black boys at the school.

Ameer and His Grandmother, Mrs. Martha

Ameer was a student in Mr. Javien's kindergartner class at Simon Elementary. Due to autism, he was shy, but always actively engaged in the learning process. He would raise his hands to answer the questions Mr. Javien asked during lessons, but would often ignore my questions when I asked him about Mr. Javien's teaching style during our discussions. However, when he did answer, he had a lot to say. According to Mrs. Martha, his grandmother, Ameer has autism, which causes him to be anti-social at times. However, she noticed that Ameer became more social under Mr. Javien's tutelage, and declared jokingly that Ameer is now so talkative that he "doesn't know when to shut up." As she stated, "Mr. Javien has done too good of a job with mine [referring to Ameer, her grandson]." She also acknowledged that one of the characteristics she liked most about Mr. Javien was that he encouraged the Black boys who were enrolled in his class to talk: "He tells them, 'you are not going to bow your head and cover your mouth.'" Ameer always did his best to work hard on his assignments, but he required additional support from Mr. Javien, who was willing to give it as often as possible.

As his grandmother, Mrs. Martha played an active role in Ameer's life. After Ameer's mother faced several life challenges, Mrs. Martha took on the responsibility of raising Ameer. She admitted that, given Ameer's condition, taking care of him is not always easy, but she is excited to see the kind of progress Ameer is making in school. In her spare time, Mrs. Martha also served as a substitute teacher at Simon Elementary, so she knew many of the teachers, including Mr. Javien, on a personal level, and she knew how they positively (or negatively) interacted with the children they taught.

Portraits of Black Male Kindergarten Teachers

In this section, I highlight Black boys' perceptions of their Black male kindergarten teachers as told through my lens as an observer, listener, and often a participant in their classrooms. To tell their stories, I apply portraiture methodology (Lawrence-Lightfoot & Hoffman-Davis, 1997) which means that I position myself as a photographer who captures important moments during various events. In this case, I captured moments that I saw as celebrations, namely the pedagogies, literacy, and schooling practices of Black male kindergarten teachers who I refer to as BlackBoyCrit Pedagogues and their influence on Black boys as exemplars of BlackBoyCrit Pedagogy. As I positioned myself as a photographer, I engaged in the act of "zooming in" to share snapshots of the data I collected and the stories I tell, however, I am not an outsider looking into each event. Rather, I am an insider who simultaneously understand what it means to be a Black boy and male teacher and share in the moments of pedagogical celebration, which had a particular impact on me as I "zoomed out" to provide a detailed analysis of the collected data.

Zoom In

> "I wanna be a teacher like Mr. Tal."
>
> —*Maurice*

It was never a boring day in Mr. Tal's kindergarten classroom. In fact, it was always a highly energetic space. Teachers who are committed to Whitecentric classroom management practices may erroneously perceive Mr. Tal's classroom as one in disarray. However, such was not the case. Children would often be seen moving around the classroom as they were actively engaged in the activities planned by Mr. Tal. Activities included learning stations that allowed young learners to build academic skills. Maurice was always a part of the action. He took advantage of the flexibility of movement Mr. Tal provided his students, and constantly floated back and forth between his seat and the classroom cubby where his bookbag was located. He often secured the bookbag to pull out markers, crayons, and other supplies located therein. Mr. Tal could sometimes be heard in his calm and smooth voice telling Maurice to return to his seat. During several classroom observations, Maurice often talked to me so much that Mr. Tal had to redirect his attention to completing the classroom assignments. Maurice was extremely inquisitive, always asking questions about me and my purpose for visiting his room. At times, I felt guilty for being more of a distraction than a participant-observer. However, I enjoyed engaging with Maurice and his classmates, as I had the opportunity to learn more about them and Mr. Tal.

Based on my own observations, and unlike his grandmother, I did not believe Maurice had a bad temper. Like most boys, he was an active 6-year-old kindergartner who wanted the love, care, attention, and patience that all children deserve from their teachers and other adults. Like many young boys, Black and White, Maurice was extremely energetic, needed space to move around the classroom, and responded best when he was involved in high-energy activities and lessons that kept him interested in the teaching and learning process. Otherwise, he would grow bored and disengaged. Maurice also responded to opportunities to express himself; for a child his age, he had a great deal to say. Mr. Tal knew how to accommodate Maurice; he listened, understood, and took Maurice's ideas and recommendations into consideration. "Sure, Maurice," Mr. Tal often responded to his requests to move freely throughout the classroom during moments where he needed a break from class assignments. On other occasions, Mr. Tal held Maurice's hands to engage and redirect him during moments where he needed it. Everything Mr. Tal did was done in love, care, and with much patience.

In response, Maurice often expressed his appreciation for Mr. Tal through notes and pictures, for which Mr. Tal created a special folder for safekeeping. In one picture he shared with me, Maurice had drawn an image of a heart and attempted to write the words "I love you." Maurice always asked Mr. Tal and me how to correctly spell words so that he could write them on the pictures he drew for Mr. Tal. On one occasion, rather than spell the words, Mr. Tal grabbed Maurice's pencil, and invited Maurice to grab his hands so they could write the words together.

Mr. Tal was extremely patient with active students like Maurice, perhaps more patient than any teacher I have seen in action. Even Maurice knew this. During an informal conversation in Mr. Tal's classroom, Maurice stated that "[Mr. Tal] gives children one more chance." Mrs. Aretha, Maurice's grandmother, also appreciated Mr. Tal's patience and positive interactions with Maurice; she found that such characteristics encouraged Maurice to come to school, because, like Roland, he previously hated doing so. As she explained:

> It's like you don't often get children who look forward to coming to school … and they have that … To me it's priceless because I raised three others and they were smart, but it was like pulling teeth … 'It's time to get up to go to school' … you know? And with him it doesn't take much now. 'Maurice, it's time to get up for school' [and] he's up! You know, he is ready to go. And you know you just don't get that.

Mrs. Aretha had previously experienced teachers who were less patient with boys like Maurice, but, when she first met Mr. Tal, Mrs. Aretha felt he was the kind of teacher Maurice needed. During Tillers Plain's Open House, where children and families met with teachers at the beginning of the school year, she noticed that Mr. Tal was more relatable to the children: he knelt down to look Maurice in the eye and to shake his hand. Mrs. Aretha's previous experiences with preschool teachers, who were mostly White, were significantly different. They often seemed unrelatable. In contrast, she believed Mr. Tal was a positive role model who was greatly influencing Maurice during school, which was most apparent when, one day, unprompted and unsolicited, Maurice blurted out in class, "I wanna be a teacher like Mr. Tal." Later, when I asked him why, he replied with a statement similar to the one I quoted above: "Because Mr. Tal give kids many, many chances."

Zoom Out

Research studies (Foster, 1997; Lynn, 2006) have long suggested that Black male teachers possess the kind of positive attributes and characteristics—most of which far too often go unnoticed– needed to support Black boys in classrooms. In other words, Black male teachers have always been BlackBoyCrit Pedagogues in the lives of Black boys. Mr. Tal has several positive attributes that provide exemplars for teachers employing BlackBoyCrit Pedagogy. However, I believe the level of support he provided Maurice is the most significant; it serves as a counternarrative to what traditionally happens to and for Black boys in classrooms. Most teachers have far less patience with Black boys, particularly those who are highly active like Maurice; they negatively stereotype them even before they enter classrooms (Hotchkins, 2016). Such teachers simply see Black boys as what Duncan (2002) has described as "beyond love" (p. 131): undeserving of the love and patience teachers should naturally provide all children. Such mistreatment contributes to the ways Black boys are pushed out of schools as early as third and fourth grade (Kunjufu, 2005; Noguera, 2014).

Demonstrating Love and Caring

Mr. Tal displayed deep levels of love and care for his young students. This defied the stereotypes often projected onto Black men who are rarely constructed as loving and caring, particularly Black teachers hired with the expectation that they will discipline and control Black children's bodies rather than teach, heal, and protect them from the wounds that schooling and society have already inflicted on them (Brown, 2012). However, Mr. Tal's behavior in his early childhood classroom contradicts such portrayals of Black male teachers as "pedagogical kinds," (Brown, 2012) only expected to be disciplinarians and father figures described in the Introduction of the book. Mr. Tal's displays of affection toward Maurice, and his expression of diverse and multiple masculinities challenges notions of hegemonic and hyper masculinities that are expected of Black male teachers in classrooms. BlackBoyCrit Pedagogues embrace and display diverse expressions of Black masculinity in early childhood education. Displaying such diverse expressions is an excellent lesson for Maurice, who, like most Black boys, are supposedly socialized into hegemonic masculine ways of knowing and being (hooks, 2004; Warren, 2020). Similarly, BlackBoyCrit Pedagogues engage in humanizing and healing practices that protest the anti-Black misandry most Black boys face in early childhood classrooms. Interestingly, accounts of White men in early childhood education who are negatively stereotyped dominate early childhood literature (Sumison, 1999). When attempting to provide love and care for young children, most of these men were treated with suspicion, and some had their sexuality questioned as if sexual orientation made a difference in terms of their abilities to teach. Though their experience shed important light on narrow definitions of masculinity in the teaching profession, these studies also demonstrated a marginalization and exclusion of the varied orientations of men of Color—and particularly Black men—who teach young children.

Being Appreciated, Valued, and Respected by Black Families

Because, like the other BlackBoyCrit Pedagogues in this book, Mr. Tal sees Black families as partners in the academic enterprise of Black boys, he was well-received and respected by parents. They appreciated him and knew that he had their children's best interest at heart. In fact, Mrs. Aretha noted that she "feels better knowing that Mr. Tal is [Maurice's] teacher." According to her, he protected, humanized, and healed Maurice from negative interactions she had witnessed between students and other teachers, which have been described by scholars (Boutte & Bryan, 2019; Curry, 2017; Johnson et al., 2019) as anti-Black misandric symbolic violence that Black boys and other children of Color face in many classrooms. The ways in which parents like Mrs. Aretha viewed and respected Mr. Tal demonstrates the importance of what Curry (2017) has referred to as a *Black Public philosophy*, or a reframing of the way we view and perceive men in and beyond early childhood education, thus challenging old stereotypes and biases. It also confirms the importance of seeing Black mothers as informants who know what Black boys like Maurice need from Black male teachers.

Building Relationships as Foundations

Mr. Tal's classroom management practices provide further examples of those of BlackBoyCrit Pedagogues. They are similar to the practices of Black teachers during segregated schooling. During the pre-Brown v. Board of Education era, Black teachers used classroom management practices that "[kept] students in the classroom" (Milner, 2010, p. 90). For example, they refused to send students to the principal's office to be disciplined; rather, they often visited students' homes to build relationships and have conversations with parents (Milner, 2020; Siddle-Walker, 2000). Given his understanding regarding how anti-Black misandry informs school disciplinary practices, Mr. Tal also recognized the inappropriateness of sending Maurice to the principal's office for behaviors that were merely indications that he needed support in negotiating life in school. In this way, Mr. Tal pushed back against anti-Black misandric schooling practices that push active boys like Maurice out of classrooms and into the principals' offices and ultimately into the criminal justice system. Mr. Tal refused to allow school to cease to be a place of learning for Maurice; he rejected schooling as an anti-Black misandric punishment hub (Wright & Counsell, 2018; Milner, 2020).

In these ways, Mr. Tal created what Bean-Folkes and Lewis Ellison (2018) have called a "culture of love" (p. 214). BlackBoyCrit Pedagogues understand the importance of building relationships, creating a culture of love in their classrooms, and establishing communities of learning that value Black boys by creating a loving community grounded in Black cultural ways of knowing and being.

Giving Black Boys Multiple Opportunities to be Their Better Selves

Maurice's pictures and notes of appreciation illustrate that Maurice understood that Mr. Tal was extremely patient with him, giving him chances to perform better academically and socially—chances that other teachers may not have offered. Through the lens of BlackBoyCrit Pedagogy, when there is a symbiotic relationship between Black boys and male teachers, mutual appreciation and respect abound. This is atypical in some classrooms and in schools where Black boys may not appreciate and respect Black male teachers who they perceive as authoritative in their approaches (Howard, 2012).

Similarly, because young children are astutely aware of social injustices, including issues of race, racism, and anti-Black misandry in and beyond the classroom (Anderson, 2019; Boutte et al., 2011; Braden et al., 2020), it is highly possible that Maurice understood that Black boys like him are not always given multiple chances. Black male victims of police brutality, including Tamir Rice, Eric Gardner, Michael Brown, and others were never given second chances. They were physically murdered within seconds of meeting White police officers and vigilantes. Another group of Black boy victims, widely known as the Central Park Five, were falsely accused of raping a White woman jogger in New York in

1989, and were also not given second chances (Burns, 2012). Though they were later exonerated, all were unjustly convicted and sent to prison for a rape they did not commit. Rather than receiving second chances, they were spiritually murdered. BlackBoyCrit Pedagogues, like Mr. Tal, understand that giving Black boys second and/or multiple chances is a way to protect them from anti-Black misandry in early childhood classrooms.

Seeing the Importance of Decriminalizing Practices

Maurice understood that Mr. Tal did not value criminalizing, punishing, and excluding students from the classroom environment, which is customary in most early childhood classrooms. Such exclusion from schools often leads to the preschool-to-prison pipeline. When asked about why he was so patient with students like Maurice, Mr. Tal acknowledged that the schooling system was already constructed to target and criminalize Black boys, and he wanted to interrupt such anti-Black misandric targeting, which he also experienced in school. He fully understood how teachers damaged him as a Black boy in his own schooling experience, and therefore drew on his own anti-Black misandric experiences and consciousness (as required by BlackBoyCrit Pedagogy) to support Black boys in classrooms and schools. Consequently, he was not only patient with Maurice and other boys, but also understood the importance of reflecting on his own practices so he could improve them, and in engaging students in lessons that counter anti-Black misandry and kept Black boys interested in the teaching and learning process. In an effort to avoid the limited praise and appreciation he once received in PreK-12 schools, Mr. Tal constantly provided positive instead of negative reinforcement to his students, reassuring them of their intelligence, and finding opportunities to let students demonstrate their brilliance. According to Mr. Tal, he saw positive feedback as a way to dispel some of the anti-Black misandric myths about Black boys in schools and in society writ large. Although he felt he did an exceptional job working against anti-Black misandry in his classroom, he also sought critical resources, including books and professional conferences about Black boys, in order to continue growing and developing into the teacher for whom his Black boys longed.

Letting Black Boys Know They are Valued

The positive attributes and the interactional style Mr. Tal used to support Maurice and the other students left a lasting impression on Maurice. Given Mr. Tal's ability to counteract anti-Black misandric practices, Maurice felt acknowledged, valued, and appreciated, which led to his desire to consider teaching as a future professional option. In other words, BlackBoyCrit Pedagogues provide windows and mirrors for Black boys, and counter anti-Black misandry in classrooms. This approach can serve as recruitment tools for the teaching profession, and it can occur as early as early childhood education. Although we do not know what profession Maurice will pursue in the future, Mr. Tal planted a positive seed about teaching—a seed that might struggle to germinate because of the anti-Black misandric mistreatment Black boys face in schools, but could blossom into a torch passed from Mr. Tal, who decided to teach as a way to counter anti-Black misandry and to give back, to Maurice. As Goings and Bianco (2016) found while investigating the perceptions of Black male high school students about the teaching profession, many became disinterested in teaching because of the ways in which teachers mistreated them in schools. However, a few—like Mr. Tal and the other male teachers presented in this book—answer the call.

Helping Black Boys See Possible Futures

Whatever the outcome may be, it is important to note that Mr. Tal's physical presence in the early childhood classroom became a mirror in which Maurice could see himself, and a window through which he could see possibilities for becoming a teacher. As I mentioned above, Black boys rarely see and experience the pedagogical and schooling practices of Black male teachers in classrooms, and particularly in early childhood classrooms. However, we know that, when Black male teachers are present, they benefit Black boys like Maurice in ways that are not always highlighted in educational research, media, or popular press. As Mr. Tal himself made clear, the absence of Black male teachers in classrooms have dire anti-Black misandric consequences for Black boys, who may never learn to respect Black men in pedagogical capacities. He further added that, not only are Black men missing from classrooms; they are also missing in literacy resources, including the children's literature used in early childhood classrooms. This socializes Black boys into perspectives regarding who can and cannot become teachers, which perpetuates anti-Black misandric constructions of Black men in society. Nevertheless, for Maurice, Mr. Tal's presence became a living text that provided him a mirror in which to see himself and windows through which to see the world. This is consistent with BlackBoyCrit Pedagogy, and is a characteristic of BlackBoyCrit Pedagogues.

Given Maurice's desire to become a teacher, it is important to note that Mr. Tal enacted the kinds of pedagogical and schooling practices that counter anti-Black misandry and that are not simply beneficial to Maurice's education; Maurice himself could reenact these same BlackBoyCrit pedagogical practices as a future teacher. Indeed, if Maurice chooses teaching as a professional option, he could understand the need to counter anti-Black misandry, and draw on the Black cultural wealth of his students, and particularly Black boys, to support them while interrupting the preschool/school-to-prison nexus that could annihilate them.

At the same time, however, it is important to note that, although Maurice experienced a Black male teacher who counters anti-Black misandry in early childhood education, it is highly unlikely this trend will continue throughout his schooling experiences. Teaching against anti-Black misandry is still relegated to the margins in early childhood and other classrooms. As it currently stands, most teachers remain White, female, middle-class, and monolingual (Baker-Bell, 2020). They are far more likely to engage in cultural conflict with Maurice and other Black boys than they are to support and nurture them through the use and application of pedagogies and school practices that counter anti-Black misandry, such as BlackBoyCrit Pedagogy. Milner (2010, 2020) described cultural conflict as teachers' inability to draw on cultural ways of knowing to support Black boys and other children. As a result, this forces boys like Maurice to adopt anti-Black misandric, Eurocentric, and historically harmful pedagogical and schooling practices for Black children, should they decide to enter preservice and inservice teaching in earnest (Boutte & Bryan, 2019). It remains clear that most teacher education programs are still not preparing teachers to address the needs of Black children in classrooms, thus forcing teachers to enter inservice teaching with the same old anti-Black misandric pedagogies and schooling practices as their White counterparts (Johnson et al., 2019). As such, although Mr. Tal planted a fertile seed for BlackBoyCrit Pedagogy in Maurice's consciousness, it is unclear who will water it in the future.

Zoom In

"I'm glad I have a Brown teacher."

—Roland

One day, as he prepared for school, Roland told his mother, "I'm glad I have a Brown teacher." Mrs. Boins explained that Roland had White teachers in pre-school and, like him, she was excited that he had a Black male teacher, Mr. Henry, because it was good for him to be provided an image of a positive Black men in that capacity. Although Roland had a residential father at home who was actively involved in his life, it was important that he also saw positive images of other Black men, since society has constructed the entire group inaccurately in grossly negative and anti-Black misandric ways.

In addition to motivating Roland to attend school, Mr. Henry also motivated Roland in the classroom. During one observation, Roland raised his hands in an attempt to get Mr. Henry's attention and request permission to go to the restroom. At the time, Roland and his classmates were working on a math activity called Numbers, Operations, Work, and Answer (NOWA). NOWA is a math technique Mr. Henry taught his students in order to help them better solve math problems. Roland started to briskly wave his hand in a manner he was sure would get Mr. Henry's attention. However, Mr. Henry, who was working with another student, did not notice; the student with whom Mr. Henry was working was having a hard time solving the math problems, and Mr. Henry was engrossed in supporting him. Suddenly, Roland shouted, "Daddy, can I use the bathroom?" Without hesitation, Mr. Henry responded, "Yea, go quickly!" not even realizing that Roland had referred to him as "Daddy." Later that day, I asked Roland why he called out, "Daddy," and he said, "[Mr. Henry] kinda reminded me of my daddy," even though he understood they were not one in the same. Similarly, I asked Mr. Henry about his response to Roland, and he revealed that his Black boys constantly called him "daddy." He explained:

> You have to accept the fact that you are looked upon as a role model or some father figure. I don't mind that. The kids just see something in you they like. Because plenty of times the children say, 'Daddy or I mean Mr. Henry' … and the kid says 'I don't know why I keep calling you daddy.' But I understand. This is the person you see and you are around all the time: a person who talks and listens to you like your daddy, so I understand. Actually, the boys … the girls usually hug me more and stuff, but the boys will be like 'Daddy or I mean Mr. Henry …' I tell them, 'No, you gotta a dad, and I have met him, and he is cool.' I tell them, 'Don't go home saying that!'[laughs]. It is just funny that they do that, but I just feel like … you know … they see you as somebody who could be a part of their family … somebody they like.

Zoom Out

Some scholars have suggested that young children are what Annamma et al. (2017) refer to as color evasive, meaning they do not see people's skin color. This is not the dominant narrative in most early childhood classrooms, even though most early childhood teachers attempt to uphold these ideologies and beliefs. Many researchers (Boutte et al., 2011; Souto-Manning, 2013; Souto-Manning & Martell, 2016) have countered that young children in fact do see color.

Like most Black boys, Roland is far more color conscious than color evasive. He understood that Mr. Henry was different from teachers with whom he had previous experiences in early childhood education, most of whom were White. Unlike his other teachers, Mr. Henry humanized and healed Roland by motivating him to attend school for several reasons. BlackBoyCrit Pedagogues motivate Black boys to come to school through their humanizing and healing approaches. While this is not only attributed to Black male teachers, Mr. Henry's skin color was important; it provided Roland a mirror in which to see himself, and windows through which he could see the world.

Providing Positive Black Male Images

Mrs. Boins also appreciated having Mr. Henry as Roland's teacher, and the positive relationship between them. Although she made it clear that Roland had a positive role model in his father, she also appreciated that, at school, he could see positive images of other professional Black men. As an important characteristic of

BlackBoyCrit Pedagogues, Mr. Henry portrayed a positive image in his classroom that countered erroneous anti-Black misandric constructions of Black men as responsible for the destruction of their communities (Curry, 2017). He also showed Roland his future potential.

I agree with Mrs. Boins that, regardless of Black boys' having residential and/or non-residential fathers, they need many positive images of Black men and Black manhood in all of its iterations, to fight against ways that media and popular press continually and inaccurately concretize anti-Black misandric images of Black males in society. One of those images commonly perpetuated is of Black men as absent fathers. Clearly, this is not the case for Roland, as his father is actively involved in his life and, in fact, research shows that, of all racial and ethnic groups, Black men are most involved in the lives of their children (Center for Disease Control and Prevention, 2013).

Positioning Black Families as Partners

There is also a dominant, anti-Black narrative suggesting that only Black boys from single-parent homes need Black men to serve as mentors to guide them in making appropriate life decisions (Brown, 2012). Mrs. Boins suggested that Roland, who has a residential and active father in his life, also needed a Black male mentor to serve as his teacher. Mrs. Boins' perception of Mr. Henry helps us shift our mindsets about who needs (or does not need) positive images of Black men in their lives. Typically, books on male mentoring construct Black boys who live below the poverty line with single mothers as those who need mentors, and Black male teachers are expected to fill those roles (Floyd, 2019). BlackBoyCrit Pedagogues, on the other hand, position Black families and communities as informants and partners. With this developing idea in mind, when Black families are positioned as partners in the academic and social enterprise, their insights (e.g., all Black boys need positive images of Black men) inform us about the best ways to support Black boys in and beyond early childhood education (Braden et al., 2020; Reynolds, 2010).

Serving as Role Models

Mr. Henry was what I refer to as a Role Model (as described in the Introduction). For Black boys, a role model, unlike the Role Model, lacks anti-Black misandric consciousness, and works to merely discipline and control Black boys in classrooms. This was not the case with Mr. Henry. Instead, he was a Role Model and Black-BoyCrit Pedagogue who possessed an anti-Black misandric consciousness, worked against deficit constructions of Black boys, and superseded the one-dimensional role of serving as a disciplinarian in school. Perceiving Mr. Henry as an important Role Model in his life, Roland often referred to him as "Daddy" acknowledging the importance of that positive interaction and symbiotic relationship, which reminded him of the same kinds of interactions and relationship with his biological father. This idea counters Brockenbrough's (2012) work, in which he argued that Black boys may not want Black male teachers to serve as father figures. Although such may be the case in some instances (Brockenbrough, 2012), much of Brockenbrough's work was conducted with Black male teachers who worked in middle and high school settings. There is still a limited understanding of how Black male kindergarteners perceive Black male teachers in early childhood spaces, or how Black male teachers feel regarding such construction. Mr. Henry did not have any issues with Roland's calling him "Daddy." However, he did want Roland to understand the importance of valuing his students' fathers at home, men whom he often called "cool." As such, Mr. Henry helped the children, and particularly Roland, to not only see the importance of admiring him as a teacher, but also admiring their biological fathers. Based on my own personal and professional experiences, I would argue that Black boys are sometimes taught to despise their fathers, who are mostly positioned in anti-Black misandric ways (e.g., uninvolved in their children's lives). To that end, based on Mr. Henry's response, one could argue that Black male teachers may *want* to be seen as father figures in the lives of Black boys, and in so doing, counteract children's negative identifications with fatherhood. Similarly, Black boys like Roland may want Black male teachers to be seen as quasi-father figures in their young lives, because they remind them of their own biological fathers, whom they admire. With BlackBoyCrit Pedagogy in mind, when BlackBoyCrit Pedagogues humanize and heal Black boys in such a way, Black boys may see them as fathers.

Zoom In

"He tell us to be good."

—Ameer

Sitting quietly during the focus group discussion with three other Black boys who actively shared their perceptions of Mr. Javien, Ameer struggled to have his voice heard. To alleviate this, I often interrupted the other boys to ensure they were providing Ameer an opportunity to share his perspectives. When he finally spoke, Ameer did not limit his responses; he not only shared how much he enjoyed his teacher's selection of children's books," but also identified Mr. Javien's other characteristics that he found appealing. When asked about those characteristics, Ameer, in a quiet voice, explained that "He tell us to be good." I wanted to know more about his comment, but Ameer hesitated to explain further. However, as I continued to probe during future classroom visits, I gained a deeper understanding of Ameer's declaration. I soon discovered that, when Ameer recounted Mr. Javien telling him and his classmates "to be good," he was not suggesting that they were bad. Rather, he was trying to help them understand that, given their positionality as Black boys, they had to make wise decisions to protect themselves from anti-Black misandry that even impacted them in their own school. In this way, Mr. Javien gave the Black boys life lessons. I often observed as he gave wise advice to help them understand what it means to be a Black boy in an anti-Black misandric world. During one such observation, Mr. Javien spoke to a group of Black boys about the importance of staying on task and avoiding behaviors that could be misinterpreted by others. When I asked Mr. Javien why he felt it important to have such conversations, he explained:

> I tell them society has certain preconceived stereotypes about Black males. So, I kinda tell stories about my personal experiences and I hope my stories help them per se to understand what's going on in the world. You don't want them to be caught off guard because it's so easy to do … So, I'll tell them that everybody won't judge you by the content of your character just as a sidebar conversation, or when something in the lesson leads us to talk about [it] … I mean … I bring that consciousness because it's true.

He further added that, given the tension between police officers and Black males, his Black boys needed to understand that everyone does not value their lives and continued:

> Being a Black male, it's hard … kinda like the situation where most people wouldn't ask Black males questions, but shoot, or other things can happen. I don't want [them] to be in a situation where they don't necessarily have the right to tell their story, [and] instead someone['s] telling it for [them].

Thus, Ameer's description of Mr. Javien telling him and others to "be good" also reflected Mr. Javien's way of building their self-esteem. Mr. Javien also shared his wisdom to humanize, heal, motivate, and encourage them. As Mr. Javien himself stated,

> No one ever told me I was going to be a kindergarten teacher. No one ever told me I was going to be doing a Master's (degree). I had struggles in school, so, if I can do it, and I had struggles, I tell them 'you can too. So, if Mr. Javien wasn't the best reader or speller and he did it, you can do it too.

Even Ameer's grandmother, Mrs. Martha, perceived Mrs. Javien's encouraging and motivating conversations as building pride in Black boys like her grandson. Mrs. Martha admitted that schools are structured in such a way to discourage the promotion of Black pride among children, but especially among young Black boys.

Zoom Out

Much of the research literature on Black male teachers underscore the importance of their Roles and Role Modeling in the lives of Black boys and how such Roles and Role Modeling inspire Black boys to see positive images of their past, present, and futures (Lynn, 2006; Lynn et al., 1999; McKinney et al., 2017). Similar to BlackBoyCrit Pedagogues such as Mr. Tal and Mr. Henry, Mr. Javien's ways of being in the classroom inspired and provided windows and mirrors for the Black boys therein, as he used his wisdom and his own anti-Black misandric experiences to advise them. Mr. Javien was intentional about centering issues of anti-Black misandry to forewarn his Black boys about their own vulnerability, and he helped his students understand that they do not live in a color evasive world, but rather in one that is built on Black male stereotypes that can lead to dire consequences in their personal lives.

Building Black Boys' Anti-Black Misandric Consciousness

BlackBoyCrit Pedagogues draw on their personal lived anti-Black misandric experiences, and center anti-Black misandry in their teaching to protect Black children from anti-Blackness in society writ large, and in schools in particular. In other words, Black male teachers, like Mr. Javien, who employ BlackBoyCrit Pedagogy are not afraid to position themselves in the teaching and learning process and to share their personal and professional stories to help Black boys develop deeper levels of anti-Black misandric consciousness. Such consciousness development is far too often omitted from teachers' pedagogies and schooling practices because most teachers are White, middle-class, and female, and their privileged experiences do not allow them to relate to the lived realities and experiences of Black boys.

Mr. Javien's conversations with his Black boys are also akin to what many scholars (and parents) have called "the talk" (Coates, 2015; Perry, 2019). Theorized often as a conversation between Black parents and children, "the talk" serves to protect Black children, and particularly boys, from anti-Black misandry in the form of police brutality, and to help develop their consciousness about the ways in which anti-Black misandry works in society. Scholars (Lynn, 2006; Lynn et al., 1999) have focused on the ways in which Black teachers engage in "the talk" with Black students, and particularly boys, in order to build on their consciousness about what it means to live while Black and male in America.

Uplifting Black Boys

Mr. Javien's conversations with his Black boys were also important because they uplifted rather than destroyed the Black boys in his classroom. "The talk" was not only a way to develop Black boys' consciousness about the existence of anti-Black misandry and how to protect themselves from it but was also a way to uplift, humanize, and heal them in and beyond early childhood classrooms. By sharing his struggles, Mr. Javien provided his Black boys the opportunities to see and understand that they too can be resilient, and overcome the adversities and anti-Black misandry they will one day face and often have already faced in their lives.

Mr. Javien also uplifted his students by revealing his own struggles with reading and how he overcame them. This was critical given the anti-Black misandric ways reading is typically taught and assessed in early childhood education (Husband, 2012; Tatum, 2005, 2015) leading to the construction of many Black boys as illiterate which, in turn, informs their views of themselves. However, with BlackBoyCrit Pedagogues like Mr. Javien, Black boys can work against their own internalized anti-Black misandric beliefs, understand the intergenerational inequities that both Black male teachers and boys experience in school (particularly in literacy), and overcome them. To this end, Mr. Javien's counterstorytelling was a hallmark of BlackBoyCrit Pedagogy and served as one way to dismantle the pedagogical and curricular structures that fails to expose the inequities that anti-Black misandry produces in and beyond early childhood education.

Practical Recommendations for Early Childhood Educators

Maurice, Roland, and Ameer have provided compelling insights of the pedagogies, literacy, and schooling practices of their Black male teachers. Through the boys' eyes we see three teachers who embody characteristics of BlackBoyCrit Pedagogues; they demonstrated love and caring, built relationships as foundational to teaching, let Black boys know they were valued, helped Black boys see possible futures, provided positive Black male images, positioned Black families as partners, served as Role Models, developed Black boys' anti-Black misandric consciousness, and provided counterstories to uplift Black boys. Those characteristics and insights inform the following recommendations provided in Table 4.4 as other teachers consider employing BlackBoyCrit Pedagogy.

Self-Examine, but also Transform Yourself

The teachers described in this chapter had clearly engaged in self- and institutional examination throughout their lives to be able to understand the anti-Black misandry they experienced and how to counter it. This allowed them to successfully support Black boys in their classrooms. However, they came to their teaching positions having been victims of anti-Black misandry so their familiarity with what it means to be a Black boy and Black male adult in an anti-Black

TABLE 4.4 Practical Recommendations for Early Childhood Educators

- Self-examine, but also transform yourself
- Listen, hear, and understand Black boys
- Listen to Black families
- Employ Empathy and Decriminalizing Schooling Practices to Interrupt the School-to-Prison Pipeline/Nexus
- Seek critical resources for professional development

misandric society were very real. This means that, for White teachers, the need to listen to and hear anti-Black misandric realities is all the more critical to being able to employ BlackBoyCrit Pedagogy. Because, as we learned in the discussions above, teachers must be concerned with how they are viewed by Black boys, it is essential that they examine themselves before engaging in the much-needed critical work to support the academic and social needs of Black boys. Such is non-negotiable. This kind of self-examination, involves consideration of the systemic benefits of being White and the consequent and equally systemic oppression of being Black. "White teachers [cannot continue] to [deny] and [evade] the significance of race and White privilege in their lives and work" (Jupp & Lensmire, 2016, p. 985). This may be difficult as it is not something that is typically explored in preservice and inservice teacher education and because self-examination is hindered by White entitlement, which influences some White educators' sociocultural awareness, even in equity work. Instead, I am asking White teachers to examine themselves by centering their complicity in anti-Black misandry, the particular disdain and hate for Black boys (and men) which is reflected in the school laws, policies, and practices (Curry, 2017). I believe that, because the schooling system has always been anti-Black misandric, and continues to be built on it (Anderson, 1998; Siddle-Walker, 2000), teachers should begin by determining how anti-Black misandry informs their lives, their pedagogies, and their literacy and schooling practices. As described in Chapter 2, teachers should revisit the five types of anti-Black violence to engage in self-examination. The following questions may be helpful in determining one's complicity in the maintenance of anti-Black misandry in schools:

1. What is anti-Black misandry? What are some ways I recognize it in society?
2. In what ways am I anti-Black misandric? What are the sources of my anti-Black misandry? What am I doing on an ongoing basis to interrupt anti-Black misandric violence in my life and in the lives of those around me?
3. How is anti-Black misandric violence reflected in my curricula, pedagogies, and schooling and literacy practices?
4. How am I working with school administrators and other colleagues to address anti-Black misandric violence in schools and classrooms as well as in school laws, policies, and practices?
5. How is anti-Black misandric violence reflected in the ways I engage and interact with Black boys in and beyond early childhood classrooms?

While it is important for teachers to examine their anti-Black misandry, it is equally important for them to change. As a teacher educator, I have come to a place in my professional career where I am tired of pleading with White preservice and inservice teachers to solely engage in self-examination; I now demand that they change. Change and transformation are the logical consequences of self-examination. I would argue that most White teachers already know they are racist, anti-Black, and anti-Black misandric; they have been socialized into these ideologies by simply living in a white supremacist society (Miller, 2015). Indeed, many, many research studies have pointed out these characteristics (Coates, 2015; DiAngelo, 2018), and we do not need any more studies to confirm them. However, if White teachers themselves cannot change, they should not sign up for a profession wherein they will interact with and be charged with the responsibility of educating Black children, and especially boys, whose lives can be easily and irrevocably altered in classrooms.

Listen, Hear, and Understand Black Boys

The voices and perspectives of Black boys like Maurice, Roland, and Ameer are silent in educational research, and those voices are also silenced in early childhood classrooms, as the majority of teachers either intentionally or unintentionally refuse to hear and understand Black boys (Dumas & Nelson, 2016). It amazes me the number of times I have conducted observations in early childhood classrooms, and witnessed teachers' refusals to listen to Black boys. For example, they ignore Black boys, and especially those they stereotype as "discipline problems" when they attempt to speak and to be actively involved in the classroom activities and lessons. In most cases, it seems that, much like Black people in general (Jay, 2009), Black boys are simultaneously invisible (e.g., ignored when attempting to be heard) and hyper-visible (e.g., stereotyped and positioned as problems). Boutte and Bryan (2019) documented an account of two Black boys (who were the only two Black boys assigned to their classrooms) and how they decided to make a bet that, after hiding from their White teachers and classmates, neither the teachers nor the students would miss them. The boys' assumptions were correct: no one noticed their disappearance until the end of the lunch and recess period. Such narratives reify the notion that Black boys are not only physically invisible in classrooms, but also verbally invisible therein. However, it is clear that, based on the perspectives of the boys outlined in this book, Black boys want to be heard, and teachers should make every effort to ensure that they are—to their teachers as well as to their peers.

Listen to Black Families

Much like the voices of Black boys, the voices, insights, and perceptions of Black families are deafeningly silent in early childhood education (Boutte & Johnson, 2014). As aforementioned, they are often described as uninvolved in the educational lives of Black boys. However, based on the insights, wisdom, and perspectives of Mrs. Aretha, Mrs. Boins, and Mrs. Martha, we know that Black mothers (and fathers) are involved in the educational lives of their sons, and they often know what it is best for them in early childhood classrooms. In other words, their insights can inform pedagogical and school practices, provided they are treated as informants and partners in the educational lives of Black boys.

Employ Empathy and Decriminalizing Schooling Practices to Interrupt the Preschool-to-Prison Pipeline/Nexus

Many Black boys like Maurice, Roland, and Ameer are being disproportionately removed from early childhood classrooms, and scholars have labeled this phenomenon as the preschool-to-prison pipeline (Gilliam et al., 2016). To that end, early childhood educators have a responsibility to interrupt the flow of the disproportionate number of Black boys who become trapped therein, and decrease the number of negative and anti-Black misandric schooling outcomes they are more likely to face because of that pipeline. White teachers should learn empathy toward Black boys, and may find the works of Chezare Warren useful in their quest (Warren, 2013, 2018). Similarly, early childhood educators can apply Vincent Basile's (2020) six categories of decriminalizing practices, which are classroom management practices that "disrupt punitive-based [anti-Black misandric] oppression of Black (and Latino) boys in schools" (p. 1). They include: (1) structural and procedural practices; (2) honoring space; (3) assuming brilliance; (4) highly respectful interactions; (5) positive reframing; and (6) repair. According to Basile, the *structural and procedural* category includes teachers' abilities to contest school rules, policies, and procedures that may be designed to minimize "impetus[es] for criminalization" (p. 7). *Honoring space* entails teachers' abilities to hold space for Black (and Latino) boys to resist school and classroom rules with impunity. The *assuming brilliance* category acknowledges teachers' abilities to see the beauty in what Black (and Latino) boys *can do* academically rather than what they *cannot do*; whereas, the *highly respectful* category ensures that all teacher interactions with Black (and Latino) boys are grounded in respect and in the teachers' abilities to humanize rather than dehumanize the boys. The *positive reframing* category consists of teachers' abilities to use oral communication to reframe negative actions and outcomes. Finally, the *repair* category includes teachers' abilities to "purposefully [engage] in any or all of the practices listed above after recognizing that criminalization has taken place—the criminalization could come from another adult, systemic practices, or the same adult engaging in the repair" (p. 7).

Seek Critical Resources for Professional Development

Much like Mr. Tal, teachers are always seeking resources to support their growth and development in classrooms. However, they must understand that not every resource is applicable to the lives and experiences of Black boys. There are many people including Black male educators promoting books, conferences, professional development sessions, and other resources plastered with images of Black boys, and argue that each is uniquely designed to support the academic and social needs of those boys. However, these resources neither counter anti-Black misandry nor are applicable to Black boys' lives, in spite of promoters' insistence.

True resources that counter anti-Black misandry honor the lived realities of Black boys from asset-based perspectives. They do not socialize Black boys into Whiteness via respectability politics, or force Black boys into believing they must be White in order to be humanized, healed, loved, honored, and celebrated. Oftentimes, the rhetoric surrounding such anti–Black misandric resources promotes these ideologies by treating Black boys—and not systemic inequities—as problems, purporting to save Black boys instead of empowering them to successfully navigate those inequities. In their most recent book titled *The Brilliance of Black Boys: Cultivating School Success in the Early Grades*, Wright and Counsell (2018) have provided a plethora of vetted resources that genuinely counter anti–Black misandry and support Black boys in early childhood classrooms. Teachers may find helpful these books and other texts in unlearning anti–Black misandry.

Conclusion

In summary, the three portraits collectively demonstrate the importance of Black male teachers in the lives of Black boys. According to E. L. Blackshear (1902/1969),

> [The Black teacher's] superior culture and character has acted as a powerful stimulus to the easily roused imagination of the colored youth, and the Black boy feels, in the presence of the Black 'professah' to him the embodiment of learning, that he too can become 'something'
>
> *(p. 337).*

Because bodies are texts, it should be our goal to also provide Black boys mirrors in which to see themselves, and windows through which they can see the world (Sims-Bishop, 1990). The presence of Black male teachers who center Black-BoyCrit Pedagogy in classrooms can do just that. For Maurice, Mr. Tal was a mirror in which he saw a positive reflection of himself, which encouraged him to imagine himself as a teacher in the future. For Roland, Mr. Henry was also a mirror; Roland was proud to have a Black male teacher—someone who looked like him in the classroom. This provided him motivation to come to school. Finally, for Ameer, Mr. Javien was a mirror in which he saw the possibility of becoming something good, and dismantling the anti-Black misandry, stereotypes, and biases that might hinder his life. All in all, BlackBoyCrit Pedagogues like Mr. Tal, Mr. Henry, and Mr. Javien are admired by Black boys because they care deeply for the students with whom they work and teach (Brown, 2012; Lynn, 2006). They are not merely those who have sworn to do no harm to children, but those who are intentional about doing what is right to support them.

Note

1 The Lowcountry is the coastal region of South Carolina including the Sea Islands, known for its rich history and connection to the enslavement of African people; The Lowcountry is where many enslaved Africans first entered the United States and cultivated both indigo dye and rice there.

References

Anderson, J. (1998). *Education of blacks in the South, 1860–1935.* University of North Carolina Press.

Anderson, R. (2019). *Wassup with all the black boys sitting in the principal's office? An examination of detrimental teacher interactions and school practices.* Black Boy Wonder Publishing.

Annamma, S., Jackson, D., & Morrison, D. (2017). Conceptualizing color-evasiveness: Using dis/ability critical race theory to expand a color-blind racial ideology in education and society. *Race, Ethnicity, and Education,* 20(2), 147–162.

Baker-Bell, A. (2020). *Linguistic Justice: Black language, literacy, identity, and pedagogy.* Routledge.

Basile, V. (2020). Standin tall: Criminalization and acts of resistance among elementary boys of color. *Race, Ethnicity, and Education,* 23(1), 94–112.

Bean-Folkes, J., & Lewis-Ellison, T. (2018). Teaching in a culture of love: An open dialogue about African American student learning. *School Community Journal,* 28(2), 213–228.

Bianco, M., Leech, N., & Mitchell, K. (2011). Pathways to teaching: African American teens explore teaching as a career. *Journal of Negro Education,* 80(3), 368–383.

Blackshear, E. (1969). "What is the negro teacher doing in the matter of uplifting the race?" In D. W. Kulp (Ed.), *Twentieth century negro literature* (pp. 334–338). Arno Press. (Original work published1902).

Boutte, G., & Bryan, N. (2019). When will black children be well? Interrupting anti-black violence in early childhood classrooms and schools. *Contemporary Issues in Early Childhood.* https://journals.sagepub.com/doi/10.1177/1463949119890598

Boutte, G., & Johnson, G. (2014). Community and family involvement in urban schools. In H. R. Milner and K. Lomotey (Eds.), *Handbook on urban education* (pp. 167–182). Routledge.

Boutte, G., López-Robertson, J., & Powers-Costello, E. (2011). Moving beyond colorblindness in early childhood classrooms. *Early Childhood Education, Journal,* 39(5), 335–342.

Boyle, A., & Lee K. (2015). Title I at 50: A retrospective. American Institutes for Research. www.air.org/sites/default/files/downloads/report/Title-I-at-50-rev.pdf

Braden, E., Gibson, V., Gillete, R. (2020). Everything black is not bad! Families and teachers engaging in critical discussions about race. *Talking Points,* 31(2), 2–11.

Brockenbrough, E. (2012). "You ain't my daddy: Black male teachers and the politics of surrogate fatherhood. *Teacher College Record,* 114(5), 1–43.

Brown, A. L. (2012). On human kinds and role models: A critical discussion about the African American male teacher. *Educational Studies,* 48(3), 296–315.

Bryan, N., & Jett, C. (2018). Playing school: Creating possibilities to inspire future black male teachers through culturally relevant play. *Journal of Multicultural Education,* 12(2), 99–110.

Bureau of Labor Statistics, U. S. Department of Labor. (2014). *Occupational outlook handbook.* www.bls.gov/ooh.

Burns, S. (2012). *The Central Park Five: The untold story behind one of New York's most infamous crime.* Vintage Books.

Center for Disease Control and Prevention. (2013). Fathers' involvement with their children: United States, 2006–2010. *National Health Statistics Report,* 71, 1–21.

Coates, T. (2015). *Between the world and me.* Spiegel & Grau.

Cook, D. A. (2010). Disrupted but not destroyed: Fictive kinship networks among black educators in post Katrina New Orleans. *Southern Anthropologist,* 35(2), 1–25.

Cowan, J, & Goldhaber, D. (2016). National Board certification and teacher effectiveness: Evidence from Washington State. *Journal of Research on Educational Effectiveness*, 9(3), 233–258.

Curry, T. (2017). *Man-not: Race, class, genre and the dilemmas of black manhood.* Temple University Press.

DiAngelo, R. (2018). *White fragility: Why it's so hard for white people to talk about racism.* Beacon Press.

Du Bois, W. E. B. (1903). *The souls of black folks.* Dovers Publication.

Dumas, M. and Nelson, J. (2016). Reimagining black boyhood: Toward a critical framework for educational research. *Harvard Educational Review*, 86(1), 27–47.

Duncan, G. (2002). Beyond love: A critical race ethnography of the schooling of adolescent black males. *Equity and Excellence in Education*, 35(2), 131–143.

Easton-Brooks, (2019). *Ethnic matching: Academic success of students of color.* Rowman & Littelfield.

Floyd, D. (2019). *Mentoring and rites of passage: Adolescence to manhood.* BookBaby Publishing.

Fordham, S. (1996). *Blacked out: Dilemmas of race, identity, and success at capital high.* University of Chicago Press.

Foster, M. (1997). *Black teachers on teaching.* The New Press.

Gay, G. (2010). *Culturally responsive teaching: Theory, research, and practice.* Teachers College Press.

Gilliam, W. S., Maupin, A., Reyes, C. R., Accavitti, M. and Frederick, S. (2016). *Do early educators' implicit biases regarding sex and race relate to behavior expectations and recommendations of preschool expulsions and suspensions?* Yale Childhood Study Center.

Goings, R., & Bianco, M. (2016). It's hard to be who you don't see: An exploration of black male high school students' perspectives on becoming teachers. *The Urban Review*, 48(1), 628–646.

hooks, b. (2004). *Skin again.* Jump in the Sun.

Hotchkins, B. (2016). African American males navigate racial microaggression. *Teacher College Record*, 118(0603013), 1–36.

Howard, L. (2012). The schooling of African-American male students: The role of male teachers and school administrators. *International Journal of Inclusive Education*, 16(4), 373–389.

Husband, T. (2012). Why can't Jamal read? There's no simple answer why black males struggle with reading, but part of the problem stems from correctable factors that tend to lead to an early disconnect. *Phi Delta Kappan*, 93(5), 23.

Jay, M. (2009). Race-ing through the school day: African American educators' experiences with race and racism in schools. *International Journal of Qualitative, Studies in Education*, 22 (6), 671–685.

Johnson, L. L., Bryan, N., & Boutte, G. (2019). Show us the love: Revolutionary teaching in (un)critical times. *Urban Review*, 51, 46–64.

Johnson, L., Jackson, J., Stovall, D., & Baszile, D. (2017). "Loving blackness to death": (Re)imagining ELA classrooms in a time of racial chaos. *English Journal*, 106(4), 60.

Jones, R., & Jenkins, A. (2012). *Call me mister: The reemergence of African American male teachers in South Carolina.* Advantage Media Group.

Jupp, J. C., & Lensmire, T. J. (2016). Second-wave white teacher identity studies: Toward complexity and reflexivity in the racial conscientization of white teachers. *International Journal of Qualitative Studies in Education*, (QSE,) 29(8), 985–988.

King, J. (2017). Education research in the black liberation tradition: Return what you learn to the people. *The Journal of Negro Education*, 86(2), 95–114.

Kinloch, V. (2010). *Harlem on our minds: Place, race, and the literacies of urban youth.* Teachers College Press.

Kinloch, V., Burkhard, T., & Penn, C. (2017). When school is not enough: Understanding the lives and literacies of black youth. *Research in the Teaching of English*, 52(1), 34–54.

Kirkland, D. (2011). Books like clothes: Engaging young black men with reading. *Journal of Adolescent and Adult Literacy*, 55(3), 199–208.

Kirkland, D., & Jackson, A. (2019). Toward a theory of black masculine literacies. In T. Ransaw, C. P. Gause, & R. Majors (Eds.), *The handbook of research on black males: Quantitative, qualitative, and multidisciplinary* (pp. 367–396). Michigan State Press.

Kirkland, D., & Jackson, A. (2009). Beyond the silence: Instructional approaches and students' attitudes. In J. C. Scott, D. Y. Straker, & L. Katz (Eds.), *Affirming students' right to their own language. Bridging language policies and pedagogical practices* (pp. 132–150). Routledge.

Kunjufu, J. (2005). *Keeping black boys out of special education.* African American Images.

Lawrence-Lightfoot, S., & Hoffman-Davis, J. (1997). *The art and science of portraiture.* Jossey-Bass.

Lewis, C., & Toldson, I. (Eds.). (2013). *Black male teachers: Diversifying the United States' teacher workforce.* Emerald Group.

Lynn, M. (2006). Education for the community: Exploring the culturally relevant practice of black male teachers. *Teachers College Record*, 108(12), 2497–2522.

Lynn, M., Johnson, C., & Hassan, K. (1999). Raising the critical consciousness of African American students in Baldwin Hills: A portrait of an exemplary African American male teacher. *Journal of Negro Education*, 68(1), 42–51.

McKinney de Royston, M., Vakil, S. Nasir, N., Givens, J., ross, k. m., & Holman, A. (2017). "He's more like a brother than a teacher": Politicized caring in a program for African American males. *Teachers College Record*, 119(4), 1–40.

Miller, E. (2015). Race as the Benu: A reborn consciousness for teachers of our youngest children. *Journal of Curriculum Theorizing*, 30(30), 28–244.

Milner, H. R. (2020). Fifteenth Annual AERA Brown Lecture in education research: Disrupting punitive practices and policies: Rac(e)ing back to teaching, teacher preparation, and Brown. *Educational Researcher*, 49(3), 147–160.

Milner, H. R. (2010). *Start where you are, but don't stay there: Understanding diversity, opportunity gaps, and teaching in today's classrooms.* Harvard Education Press.

Moore, E., Michael, A., & Penick-Parks, M. (2018). *A guide for white women who teach black boys.* Corwin.

Morrell, E. (2015). *Critical literacy and urban youth: Pedagogies of access, dissent, and liberation.* Routledge.

Noguera, P. (2014). Urban schools and the black male challenge. In H. R. Milner & K. Lomotey (Eds.), *Handbook of urban education* (pp. 114–127). Routledge.

Perry, I. (2019). *Breathe: A letter to my sons.* Beacon Press.

Reynolds, R. (2010). "They think you're lazy," and other messages black parents send their black sons: An exploration of critical race theory in the examination of educational outcomes for black males. *Journal of African American Males in, Education*, 1(2), 145–163.

Rothstein, R. (2017). *The color line: A forgotten history of how our government segregated America.* Liveright Publishing.

Sealey-Ruiz, Y., & Greene, T. (2015). Popular visual images and the (mis) reading of black male youth: A case for racial literacy in urban pre-service teacher education. *Teaching Education*, 26(1), 55–76.

Siddle-Walker, V. (2000). Valued segregated schools for African American children in the South, 1935–1969: A review of common themes and characteristics. *Review of, Educational Research*, 70(3), 253–285.

Sims-Bishop, R. (1990). Mirrors, windows, and sliding glass doors. *Perspectives: Choosing and using books for the classroom*, 6(3), ix–xi.

Smith, D. (2016). *Finding sanctuary in sisterhood: A middle school literacy group critically analyze race, gender, and size* [Doctoral dissertation, University of South Carolina]. Unpublished dissertation. https://scholarcommons.sc.edu/etd/3960

South Carolina Department of Education. (2014). *School report card data*. http://ed.sc.gov/data/report-cards/

Souto-Manning, M. (2013). *Multicultural teaching in the early childhood classroom*. Teachers College Press.

Souto-Manning, M., & Martell, J. (2016). *Reading, writing, and talk inclusive teaching strategies for diverse learners, K-2*. Teachers College Press.

Sumison, J. (1999). Critical reflections on the experiences of male early childhood workers. *Gender and Education*, 11(4), 455–468.

Tatum, A. (2015). Engaging African American males in reading (reprint). *Journal of Education*, 195(2), 1–4.

Tatum, A. (2005). *Teaching reading to black adolescent males: Closing the achievement gap*. Stenhouse Publishers.

Warren, C. (2020). Meeting myself: Race-gender oppression and a genre study of black men teachers' interactions with black boys. *Race, Ethnicity, and Education*, 23(3), 367–391.

Warren, C. (2018). Empathy, teacher dispositions, and preparation for culturally responsive pedagogy. *Journal of Teacher Education*, 69(2), 169–183.

Warren, C. (2013). The utility of empathy for white female teachers' culturally responsive interactions with black male students. *Interdisciplinary Journal of Teaching and Learning*, 3 (3), 175–200.

Wynter-Hoyte, K., Long, S., McAdoo, T.M., Strickland, J.D. (2020). "Losing one African American Teacher is one too many": A critical race analysis of support for Praxis Core as African American students speak out. *Teachers College Record*, 122(11).

Wright, B., & Counsell, S. (2018). *The brilliance of black boys: Cultivating success in the early grades*. Teachers College Press.

Yancy, G. (2017). *Black bodies, white gazes: The continuing significance of race in America* (2nd ed.). Rowman & Littlefield.

5

MOVING BEYOND LITERACY NORMATIVITY

Toward Black Masculine Literacies in Early Childhood Education

BlackBoyCrit Pedagogy requires teachers to understand how adhering to literacy practices that disregard the experiences of Black boys can be traumatic for them in early childhood classrooms. It is true that some children never forget the traumas that occur in the early years of their lives. Childhood trauma imposed by schooling is a different kind of remembering, perhaps the kind one should forget, but cannot. Such is certainly the case for me. In the fourth grade, I clearly remember being labeled a "struggling reader." I was embarrassed each time my name was called by the lab manager, calling me to leave the classroom to attend the computer lab to supposedly improve my skills. I never wanted to go. It was clear, at that point, that I had already been wounded by school (Olsen, 2009). However, my "struggle for literacy" was not an anomaly. Both historically and contemporarily, many Black boys in early childhood education are forced to endure such trauma. Furthermore, national and state-level reading assessments which typically use texts removed from the worlds of Black boys and rarely assess the reading skills they *do* possess, deem them as non-readers, reinforcing that trauma and pain. According to a compendium of research studies (Aratani et al., 2011; Husband, 2012), due to institutional and systemic school inequities, many Black boys in early childhood education leave these spaces without the basic skills that would allow them to successfully navigate the schooling process.

It is out of my personal history, trauma, and pain, as well as what I have learned through my own research about the experiences of Black boys in early childhood education, that I want to encourage early childhood educators to understand and challenge literacy normativity, and to acknowledge which books, texts, and literacy practices can either humanize or dehumanize Black boys in classrooms. Books and literacy practices that dehumanize Black boys have negative schooling implications in and beyond early childhood education. However, to address this issue, educators must be able to recognize what those assaulting

DOI: 10.4324/9780429287619-6

and dehumanizing texts and practices look, sound, and feel like. To provide those insights, I begin this chapter by revisiting the dangers of narrowly defined literacy normativity in early childhood classrooms and the reason early childhood teachers should counter them. Next, I define Black Masculine Literacies in early childhood education.

"So, what are you going to do about it?" The Dangers of Literacy Normativity in Early Childhood Education

Literacy normativity is described as "uses of literacy practices that inflict harm" (Richardson & Ragland, 2018, p. 24) on marginalized groups—in this case, Black boys. Harm is inflicted because what is normalized as literacy—e.g., what counts as literacy—in texts and assessments used in early childhood classrooms is not only divorced from non-White cultures, but because it is authenticated as "literacy," it causes marginalized students "to divorce themselves from their cultures and to learn according to European cultural norms" (Gay, 2010, p. 114). It also upholds the idea that "literacy is something [people] have or do not have, or sets of skills according to hegemonic literacy" (Richardson & Ragland, 2018, p. 31). Stated more pointedly, literacy normativity as it is narrowly envisioned in most classrooms is the result of centuries of white supremacist ideologies and indoctrination, and is therefore simply the normalization of Whiteness reflected in school literacy practices (Pritchard, 2017). This is extremely dangerous because young Black boys are forced to sacrifice their own Black cultural ways of knowing and being in order to see Whiteness as the norm in the learning of literacy, and teachers must work laboriously to dismantle literacy normativity by centering practices that counter literacy normativity in early childhood classrooms. In Chapter 6, you will see Black male teachers who courageously confront literacy normativity by developing a broad understanding of Black boy interests and male masculinity when selecting books and other texts to use in early childhood classrooms.

Examples of literacy normativity abound in early childhood literacy practice. One example is the teaching of phonics, phonemic awareness, vocabulary, and grammar (which has also been promoted as the hallmark of early childhood education) in isolation from meaningful texts that reflect students' cultures and identities. Another example is heavy reliance on ethnocentric language assessments (e.g., Dynamic Indicators of Basic Early Literacy Skills or DIBELS) that ignore the language and literacy practices Black boys bring to classrooms. As you will see in Chapter 6, Black male teachers will overhaul such ethnocentric language assessments and use Black boys' engagement with motivating texts to assess them as readers. Literacy normativity is also seen in the overwhelming number of children's books that reflect White cultural ways of knowing, histories, and communities rather than those of Black children (Sims-Bishop, 1990). Finally, literacy normativity is evidenced when classrooms value only so-called standardized English rather than also valuing the historically-grounded, rule-governed African-American Language (AAL; also termed Black

Language). Collectively, the omission and marginalization of Blackness and Black linguistic expressions in these practices produce curricula and pedagogies that constitute anti-Black misandry, are violent towards Black boys, and are antithetical to BlackBoyCrit Pedagogy.

The dangers of literacy normativity are not only inclusive of the types of anti-Black violence introduced and discussed in Chapter 2, but other consequences of which early childhood teachers should be aware. Literacy normativity can exacerbate the psychological erosion and problems produced by anti-Black misandry. Due to the wide usage of literacy normative practices in early childhood education that do not support positive views of Black boys, it is essential that we think deeply about how those practices omit, misrepresent, and tokenize Black boys' cultural ways of knowing and being (Baines et al., 2018). Literacy normativity also promotes stereotypes and biases about Black boys, oppressing and dehumanizing them. It disregards the collective and individual identities of Black children and upholds anti-Black misandry in Black boyhood. If early childhood educators do not intervene by protesting literacy normativity in classrooms, Black boys will internalize anti-Black misandry, which is inconsistent with BlackBoyCrit Pedagogy.

So, how does literacy normativity negativity impact White children? For White children, one of the major problems with literacy normativity is that they, too, will learn to internalize anti-Black misandry through teacher pedagogy and practices, especially when White families are also teaching anti-Black misandry at home (Miller, 2015). For example, I recently saw a Facebook video of a White woman who gave each of her young daughters a gift: Black dolls (MrLilmar, 2015). When her mother presented her with the Black doll, one of the daughters immediately began to frown, cry, and express her disdain. Instead of encouraging her to play with the doll as a way to shift her consciousness about both the Black doll and Black people, the White mother burst into laughter in a way that reinforced the young girl's white supremacy and anti-Blackness. White children are bombarded with similar messages that encourage them to love Whiteness and hate others (Baines et al., 2018; Miller, 2015).

Similarly, I recall standing in an elevator at a hotel with a White girl and her mother. The girl stared at me and ran behind her mother, an illustration of how young children learn early to see Black men as reprehensible. These messages come through the normalization of literacy normativity which foregrounds anti-Black misandric messages, stereotypes, and biases about Black boys and men in and beyond early childhood classrooms. For these and other reasons, early childhood educators must dismantle literacy normativity and have explicit, ongoing conversations with young children about anti-Black misandry. Young White children as early as three months old recognize racial differences, and prefer to interact with people of the same race because they have been carefully taught through interactions with their parents (Kelly et al., 2005). By the time White children reach five years of age, they are adamant about maintaining same-race friendships (Dunham et al., 2008).

TABLE 5.1 Practices Centering vs. Decentering Literacy Normativity

Practices Centering Literacy Normativity	Practices Decentering Literacy Normativity
Omit, misrepresent, or tokenize Black boys' cultural ways of knowing and being	Reflect Black cultural ways of knowing and being
Promote stereotypes and biases about Black boys	Promote the strengths and possibilities of Black boys
Harm, oppress, and dehumanize Black boys	Heal, restore, and uplift Black boys
Disregard the collective and individual identities of Black boys	Account for the collective and individual identities of Black boys
Uphold the anti-Black misandry of boyhood	Contests the anti-Black misandric violence towards Black boyhood

As such, literacy normativity produces what Joyce King (1991) terms dysconscious racism: an uncritical habit of mind that produces the obliviousness of race, racism, white supremacy, and anti-Black misandry. Nevertheless, we can interrupt such anti-Black misandry, and hate by eliminating the literacy normativity that sends uninterrupted messages of anti-Black misandry in early childhood classrooms. So, what are we going to do about it? Remain silent is not an option, as Bishop Desmond Tutu points out that remaining silent takes the side of the oppressor—or, in this case, the side of those who work to sustain systems of anti-Black misandry that hurt us all. The late Paulo Freire (1970) has warned us that the oppressor not only dehumanizes those he oppresses, but also dehumanizes himself. For this reason, Colin Kaepernick, a football player, took a knee on the football field to bring attention to not only the social injustices against Black people, but also the anti-Black misandry that are the catalysts of those injustices (Watson et al., 2018). In a similar fashion, early childhood educators can take a knee against literacy normativity in order to ensure the mattering of Black lives, and particularly those of Black boys in classrooms. Table 5.1 provides an overview of how teachers can center and decenter literacy normativity in early childhood education.

Black Masculine Literacies in Early Childhood Education

Unlike literacy normativity, Black Masculine Literacies is a practice grounded in everyday lived realities and experiences of Black boys, and account for the ways in which Black boys engage in literacy practices in homes and communities that are neither acknowledged, valued, nor tested in schools (Kirkland & Jackson, 2019; Kinloch, 2010; Wright, 2017). Because it centers the lived realities and experiences of Black boys to counter anti-Black misandry, it is not set apart from, but is consistent with and a praxis of what I term BlackBoyCrit Pedagogy (introduced in Chapter 2). Using examples like the work of Kirkland and Jackson (2019), we can initiate change for Black boys in early literacy and childhood classrooms. By studying the Black masculine literacy practices of 11–14-year-old Black boys who were participants in a

My Brother Keeper's mentoring program in Detroit, Michigan, Kirkland and Jackson learned that Black boys felt validated along the lines of race and gender when their hip-hop and sports-influenced identities were infused into the teaching and learning of literacy. Collectively, these identities enabled the boys to self-identify as "cool," moving in and out of literacy practices informed by African-American Language, *hegemonic masculinity* (dominant ways of being boys and men), and popular culture, which simultaneously allowed them to create strong friendships among each other and set themselves apart from other mentees in the program.

Black Language and Black Masculine Literacies

To better understand Black Masculine Literacies, early childhood educators must commit to unlearning literacy normativity as described above, and instead learn about language and literacy practices such as AAL or, better yet, Black Language. Like Baker-Bell (2020a), I prefer to use the term Black Language rather than AAL "to foreground the relationship between language, race, anti-Back racism …" (p. 2). Black Language is a rule-governed and legitimate language used by most Black people in the United States, including children (Alim & Smitherman, 2012; Baker-Bell, 2017; Perry & Delpit, 1998; Richardson & Ragland, 2018; Rickford & Rickford, 2000; Smitherman, 1999; Kinloch, 2010). In 1979, James Baldwin poignantly asked, "If Black English [or African-American Language] isn't a language, then tell me, what is?" Black children who are Black Language speakers are both bilingual (if not multilingual) and biliterate, which means they speak and read two or more languages (Boutte, 2016; Smitherman, 1999) when they speak Black Language and so-called White Mainstream English (or another language; Baker-Bell, 2020a,b). As bilingual speakers, they demonstrate cognitive abilities and the dexterity to choose and move across languages that monolingual speakers do not possess. However, rather than be valued for this linguistic prowess, they are typically shamed for it, another element in the anti-Black misandry and dehumanization of Black boys. Indeed, because children have the rights to their own languages, teachers should perceive Black boys as bilingual and/or multilingual, and should employ culturally appropriate strategies to embrace Black boys' linguistic and literate abilities in early childhood classrooms (Perry & Delpit, 1998).

Over the years, code-switching has been socially constructed as a dominant and appropriate strategy for teaching Black students to translate from their heritage languages to White Mainstream American English. Wheeler and Swords (2010), two White women scholars, have led the charge (Baker-Bell, 2020a). However, that widely-used practice has been contested and problematized as serving only White Mainstream English proficiency while not considering the ways language users draw from multiple language proficiencies (Baker-Bell, 2020a, b; Young et al., 2014). As Baker-Bell (2020b) has argued,

> any approach that does not interrogate why students of color are required to code-switch, and only acknowledges their native tongues as a bridge to learn

WME [White Mainstream English] perpetuates linguistic racism and upholds white linguistic and cultural hegemony.

(p. 9)

As an alternative, Baker-Bell (2020a, b) has recommended an *Anti-Racist Black Language Education and Pedagogy*: a pedagogical approach that centers Black linguistic forms to dismantle White linguistic hegemony. Also critiquing code-switching as a pedagogical practice, Young et al. (2014) has recommended a strategy called *code-meshing*, a blending of Black linguistic styles with WME, to support Black Language speakers.

Hegemonic Masculinity and Black Masculine Literacies

Much can also be learned about hegemonic masculinity as defined by Connell (2005) as the dominant ways of being boys and men. Despite its prevalence in the notion of Black Masculine Literacies as defined by Kirkland and Jackson (2019), I, along with Curry (2017) and Connell (2005), find problematic the use of the term hegemonic masculinity to describe the masculinities of Black boys and men. As mentioned in Chapter 2, the notion of hegemonic masculinity is grounded in Whiteness, meaning that Black boys and men do not benefit from displaying such masculinities in the same ways White boys and men do (Curry, 2017; McCready, 2010). In other words, to suggest that Black boys engage in literacy practices as informed solely by hegemonic masculinity is to ignore the anti-Black misandric history of Black boys (and men) who were and still are considered what Curry (2017) has called "Man-Not" (p. 6): neither human nor man, and lacking the rights and privileges afforded to White boys and men who have historically been granted their humanity and masculinity.

Examples of how Black boys do not benefit from hegemonic masculinities are highlighted in the works of Steven and Ross (2015). When they examined the language and literacy practices of 7–9-year-old Black boys over the course of four weeks in a summer program, Stevenson and Ross (2015) cited that young Black boys in the study demonstrated two modes of Black masculine identity as literacy practices: hegemonic Black masculinity and alternative forms of Black masculinity. Daniel, who participated in the study, engaged in hegemonic masculinity, or a type of masculinity that asserted male authority as he participated in a literacy circle, while Joshua engaged in what the authors termed an "alternative form of Black masculinity" (p. 82), a type of masculinity that "ran counter to hegemonic masculinity" (p. 82). Both of these young boys were able to draw from rap and hip-hop as Black Masculine Literacies when they were unable to provide expected written responses to literary assignments.

Stevenson and Ross (2015) further concluded that each mode of Black masculine expression produced different levels of academic success/literacy outcomes among the boys. Daniel, who participated in the study, exhibited hegemonic masculinities as he engaged in literacy, and experienced less success in the program. As such, Black boys have absolutely nothing to gain from being described as hegemonic masculine. It is a

TABLE 5.2 Black Masculine Literacies: Children's Books Positively Representing Black Boys

- Andrews, T. (2015). *Trombone Shorty*
- Arthur, G.A. (2017). *Brown Boy Brown Boy What Can You Be?*
- Barnes, D. (2019). *The King of Kindergarten*
- Barnes, D. (2017). *Crown: An Ode to the Fresh Cut*
- Beaty, D. (2013). *Knock Knock: My Dad's Dream for Me*
- Blue, R. & Naden, C. J. (2009). *Ron's Big Mission*
- Diggs, T. (2011). *Chocolate Me*
- Grimes, N. (2006). *Welcome Precious*
- Hughes, L. (2012). *Lullaby (For A Black Mother)*
- Hughes, L. (2012). *I, Too, Sing America*
- Jordan, D. (2010) *Baby Blessings: A Prayer for the Day You Were Born*
- Nelson, K. (2005). *He Got The Whole World In His Hands*
- Nelson, V. N. (2015). *The Book Itch: Freedom, Truth & Harlem's Greatest Bookstore*
- Perkins, U.E. (2003). *Hey Black Child*
- Reynold, V. (2017). The Joys of Being a
- Shabazz, I. (2014). *Malcolm Little: The Boy Who Grew Up to Become Malcolm X*
- Smith, C. R. (2007). *12 Rounds to Glory: The Story of Muhammad Ali*
- Steptoe, J. (2016). *Radiant Child: The Story of Young Artist Jean Michel Basquiat*
- Weatherford, C.B. (2008). *Before John Was A Jazz Giant: A Song of John Coltrane*

one-dimensional view of Black masculinity and does not always have a positive impact on the academic outcomes of Black boys in early childhood education. By contesting the one-dimensional view of Black masculinity, Stevenson and Ross found alternative forms of Black masculinity in their work, and the ways in which the celebration of that masculinity can aid in literacy education. As previously mentioned in Chapter 2, Black boys and men are often not afforded the rights to express alternative forms of Black masculinities or varying ways to express boyhood (and manhood; Curry, 2017). Yet, diverse and multiple expressions of Black masculinity can inform not only Black Masculine Literacies, but also sports and hip-hop that inform the identities of Black boys in and beyond early childhood education. To that end, early childhood educators should find ways to integrate Black Masculine Literacies beyond the notion of hegemonic masculinity into teaching and learning processes that support Black boys' academic outcomes in reading, hence, the purpose of BlackBoyCrit Pedagogy. Furthermore, Black Masculine Literacies are inclusive of books and other texts that honor and celebrate Black boys as a way to contest not only literacy normativity, but also anti-Black misandry in classrooms. Although it is not exhaustive, Table 5.2 provides a list of books that positively represent Black boys and boyhood.

Black Male Teachers as Black Masculine Literacies

It is also important to note that, given that the body is text as described in Chapter 4 (Yancy, 2017), the presence of Black male teachers can serve as a kind of Black Masculine Literacies that Black boys can read and emulate in early childhood classrooms, especially when these teachers embody a range of Black masculine identities and position themselves as those who are committed to challenging anti-Black misandry in classrooms. For this reason, Roland, introduced in Chapter 4, was motivated to attend school because he had a "Brown" teacher, Mr. Henry. As such, there is a need to recruit and retain Black male teachers, or better yet, BlackBoyCrit Pedagogues, who are courageous and are intentional about dismantling not only literacy normativity but also anti-Black misandry in early childhood classrooms.

Conclusion

All in all, there is a need to protest literacy normativity in early childhood classrooms, which takes me back to my personal accounts relating to literacy experiences in school and insights into how literacy normativity negatively impacted my early years and schooling experiences, as well as my relationship to reading. I am indebted to the pedagogical practices of teachers, including my former kindergarten teacher, Mr. C., who challenged literacy normativity in early childhood classrooms to ensure that Black boys like me saw themselves positively reflected in Black Masculine Literacies as a praxis of BlackBoyCrit Pedagogy.

References

Alim, H. S., & Smitherman, G. (2012). *Articulate while black: Barack Obama, language, and race in the U.S.* Oxford University Press.

Aratani, Y., Wight, V. R., & Cooper, J. L. (2011, May). *Racial gaps in early childhood: Socio-emotional health, developmental, and educational outcomes among African-American boys.* National Center for Children in Poverty. http://www.nccp.org/publications/../text_1014

Baines, J., Tisdale, C., & Long, S. (2018). "We've been doing it your way long enough": Choosing the culturally relevant classroom. Teachers College Press.

Baker-Bell, A. (2020a). *Linguistic justice: Black language, literacy, identity, and pedagogy.* Routledge.

Baker-Bell, A. (2020b). Dismantling anti-black linguistic racism in English language arts classrooms: Toward an anti-racist black language pedagogy. *Theory into Practice,* 59(1), 8–21.

Baker-Bell, A. (2017). I can switch my language, but I can't switch my skin: What teachers must understand about linguistic racism. In E. Moore, Jr., A.Michael, & M. W. Penick-Parks (Eds.), *The guide for white women who teach black boys* (pp. 97–107). Corwin Press.

Baldwin, J. (1979, July 29). If black English isn't a language, then tell me, what is? *The New York Times.* https://www.nytimes.com/1979/07/29/archives/if-black-english-isnt-a-language-then-tell-me-what-is.html.

Boutte, G. (2016). *Educating African-American students: And how are the children?*Routledge.

Connell, R. W. (2005). *Masculinities.* University of California Press.

Curry, T. (2017). *Man-not: Race, class, genre and the dilemmas of black manhood.* Temple University Press.

Dunham, Y., Baron, A. S., & Banaji, M. R. (2008). The development of implicit intergroup cognition. *Trends in Cognitive Science,* 12(7), 248–252.

Freire, P. (1970). *Pedagogy of the oppressed*. Continuum.

Gay, G. (2010). *Culturally responsive teaching: theory, research, and practice*. Teacher College Press.

Husband, T. (2012). Why can't Jamal read? There's no simple answer why black males struggle with reading, but part of the problem stems from correctable factors that tend to lead to an early disconnect. *Phi Delta Kappan*, 93(5), 23.

Kelly, D., Quinn, P. C., Slater, A. M., Gibson, A., Smith, M., Liezhing, G., & Pascalis, O. (2005). Three-months-olds, but not newborns, prefer own-race faces. *Developmental Science*, 8(6), F31–F36.

King, J. (1991). Dyconscious racism: Ideology, identity, and the miseducation of teachers. *The Journal of Negro Education*, 60(2), 133–146.

Kinloch, V. (2010). *Harlem on our minds: Place, race, and the literacies of urban youth*. Teachers College Press.

Kirkland, D., & Jackson, A. (2019). Toward a theory of black masculine literacies. In T. Ransaw, C. P. Gause, & R. Majors (Eds), *The handbook of research on black males: Quantitative, qualitative, and multidisciplinary* (pp. 367–396). Michigan State Press.

McCready, L. (2010). *Making space for diverse masculinities: Difference, intersectionality, and engagement in an urban high school* (Adolescent Cultures, School and Society). Peter Lang.

Miller, E. (2015). Race as the Benu: A reborn consciousness for teachers of our youngest children. *Journal of Curriculum Theorizing*, 30(30), 28–244.

MrLilmar. (2015, December 31). Two little white girls react to receiving black dolls for Christmas. YouTube. https://www.youtube.com/watch?v=Hv1K9roa4cc

Olsen, K. (2009). *Wounded by school: Recapturing the joy of learning and standing up to old school culture*. Teachers College Press.

Perry, T., & Delpit, L. (Eds.). (1998). *The real Ebonics debate: Power, language, and the education of African-American children*. Beacon.

Pritchard, D. E. (2017). *Fashioning lives: Black queers and the politics of literacy*. Southern Illinois Press.

Richardson, E., & Ragland, A. (2018). #Staywoke: The language and literacies of the #BlackLivesMatter movement. *Community Literacy Journal*, 12, 27–56.

Rickford, J. R., & Rickford, R. J. (2000). *Spoken soul: The story of black English*. Wiley.

Sims-Bishop, R. (1990). Mirrors, windows, and sliding glass doors. *Perspectives: Choosing and Using Books for the Classroom*, 6(3), ix–xi.

Smitherman, G. (1999). *Talkin that talk: Language, culture, and education in African America*. Routledge.

Stevenson, A., & Ross, S. (2015). Starting young: Emergent black masculinity and early literacy. *Journal of African American Males in Education*, 6(1), 75–90.

Watson, D., Hagopian, J., & Au, W. (2018). *Teaching for black lives*. Rethinking Schools.

Wheeler, R., & Swords, R. (2010). *Code-switching lessons: Grammar strategies for linguistically diverse writers*. Firsthand Heinemann.

Wright, B. (2017). Five wise men: African-American males using urban critical literacy to negotiate and navigate home and school in an urban setting. *Urban Education*.

Yancy, G. (2017). *Black bodies, white gazes: The continuing significance of race* (2nd ed.) Rowman & Littlefield.

Young, V., Barrett, R., Young-Rivera, Y., & Lovejoy, K. (2014). *Other people's English: Code-meshing, code-switching, and African American Literacy*. Teachers College Press.

6

CULTIVATING BLACK MASCULINE LITERACIES AS A PRAXIS OF BLACKBOYCRIT PEDAGOGY

Black Boys' Portraits of Mr. Tal, Mr. Henry, and Mr. Javien

Considering my own struggle with literacy in early childhood education, I wonder if my experiences would have been different had my teachers (much like my kindergarten teacher, Mr. C.) centered my interests and cultural ways of knowing and being in the books they selected and the literacy practices they embraced. How do we imagine and reimagine early childhood classrooms as spaces that acknowledge, value, and embrace Black Masculine Literacies as a praxis of BlackBoyCrit Pedagogy? How could this shift the so-called underperformance and lacking motivation of Black boys in reading? To answer these questions, I highlight the perceptions of Braden, a 6-year-old Black boy, on the pedagogies, literacy, and schooling practices of Mr. Tal; Joshua, 6-year-old kindergartener, on Mr. Henry's; and Ameer, another 6-year-old boy, on Mr. Javien's. These boys describe how their Black male teachers used Black Masculine Literacies as a praxis of BlackBoyCrit Pedagogy to engage them in literacy teaching and learning. Much like my own personal experiences with my kindergarten teacher, Mr. C., I chose to highlight Braden, Joshua, and Ameer in this chapter because they were passionate about the books their teachers gave and shared with them.

In Chapter 5, I explained the importance of protesting literacy normativity and using Black Masculine Literacies in early childhood classrooms. Using the portraits of Black boys and male teachers, this chapter serves to position Black boys as those who are interested in reading books and other texts, and Black male teachers as those who are able to infuse Black Masculine Literacies as a praxis of Black BoyCrit Pedagogy in early childhood education to support the interests of Black boys. Early childhood educators must be reminded that Black boys drive how BlackBoyCrit Pedagogy and subsequently Black Masculine Literacies are enacted in classrooms and Black male teachers support them by providing a humanizing and healing environment where books and other texts that honor and celebrate diverse and multiple expressions of

DOI: 10.4324/9780429287619-7

TABLE 6.1 Characteristic of Classrooms Embracing Black Masculine Literacies as a Praxis of BlackBoyCrit Pedagogy

---

- Developing a broad understanding of Black boy interests and male masculinity when selecting books
- Going beyond just offering books to interest Black boys
- Connecting Black boys' interest across the curriculum
- Providing a model of Black men as readers
- Using Black boys' engagement with motivating texts to assess them as readers
- Seeing Black boys as readers instead of nonreaders
- Embracing oral narratives as a Black masculine literacy practice
- Abandoning literacy normativity practices
- Using Black Masculine Literacies to support math and reading growth
- Getting to know Black boys' community cultural wealth
- Choosing books to uphold the joys of Black boyhood
- Drawing on the resources of the Black community
- Valuing Black language

Black masculinities are readily available. Against this backdrop, I want to be clear. The implementation of Black Masculine Literacies as a praxis of BlackBoyCrit Pedagogy will look differently across early childhood classrooms and Black male teachers will support such expressions in their own way. Table 6.1 describes how Black Masculine Literacies is operationalized in this chapter as a praxis of BlackBoyCrit Pedagogy. Readers should note that much like what I have done in Chapter 4, I have used the "Zoom Out" sections of the chapter to include italicized sub-headings that identify the characteristics of classrooms that embrace Black Masculine Literacies as a praxis of BlackBoyCrit Pedagogy.

Similar to what I have done in previous chapters, I first introduce the Black boys, their family members, and male teachers I am highlighting here. Then, I share the portraits of each teacher as informed by the insights and perceptions of the young boys.

Introduction of Key Players

In this section, I briefly introduce new key players in my stories about children, families, and teachers who uphold and benefit from BlackBoyCrit Pedagogy: Braden and his father, Mr. Raton, as well as Joshua and his mother, Mrs. Felice and I briefly reintroduce Ameer and his grandmother, Mrs. Martha. Table 6.2 provides a brief overview of the Black boys, their male teachers, and their biological parents and caregivers. Similar to Chapter 4, I provide more intimate details about each participant in the portraits to follow. Because I have introduced Mr. Tal, Mr. Henry, and Mr. Javien in Chapter 4, I will not further introduce them here.

TABLE 6.2 Black Boy Kindergartners and Caregivers

Black Boys	Ages	Teachers	Family Member	Familial Relationship
Braden	6	Mr. Tal	Mr. Raton	Father
Joshua	6	Mr. Henry	Mrs. Felice	Mother
Ameer	6	Mr. Javien	Mrs. Martha	Grandmother

Braden and His Father, Mr. Raton

Braden, a six-year-old Black boy, was a student at Tillers Plain Elementary School, located in the Lowcountry of South Carolina. He was enrolled in Mr. Tal's kindergarten class. Braden demonstrated his brilliance in quiet yet academically-focused ways: though he was oftentimes quiet, he was always academically engaged. He excelled in all academic areas, was extremely interested in sports, and very fond of books that addressed sports-related themes. He said that he liked school because there, he could play with his friends. Mr. Raton, Braden's father, is a single parent who is actively involved in his son's life and education. He found opportunities to be involved in every aspect of Braden's schooling experiences including those aspects that are unfortunately far too often expected and highly regarded by teachers and school administrators as being the only way to be "involved" in children's educational experiences (i.e, attending parent-teacher conferences, and communicating regularly with Mr. Tal over the phone). The purpose of his communication was to become informed of Braden's progress in Mr. Tal's class. Such interactions between Black fathers and teachers are, more often than not, constructed as anomalies. Oftentimes, the research literature constructs Black fathers (and mothers) as uninvolved in the lives and the schooling experiences of their children (Baker, 2017; Boutte & Johnson, 2014). Typically, that is because "involvement" is often only seen as coming to school conferences and participating in school events when there is a wide range of ways that Black families support their children often unrecognized by teachers (Myers, 2013). Mr. Raton said that he appreciated Mr. Tal because Mr. Tal "understands [Black] culture." He further stated that, because "[Mr. Tal] understood the culture, he would not easily write [Braden] up," or send him out of the classroom for minor behavioral infractions including talking too much or talking out of turn. Reflecting on his own schooling experiences, Mr. Raton stated that he noticed that White teachers did not seek to understand Black boys' behaviors, exhibited bias toward White boys displaying the same behaviors, and often struggled to support him and his classmates when he attended school.

Joshua and His Mother, Mrs. Felice

Joshua is a 6-year-old who attended Ponce De Leon Elementary School (Lower Campus). He was one of three Black boys in Mr. Henry's class. Joshua loved math and, according to Mr. Henry, math was naturally easy for him. However, Joshua was not as fond of reading, his mother, Mrs. Felice, stated that she noticed he struggled to read; however, she was pleased with how Mr. Henry encouraged him in spite of his difficulties. According to Mrs. Felice, Mr. Henry did "little things," like giving Joshua books to take home to read to her, and Mr. Henry would promise Joshua he would test him on them the next day. Joshua also enjoyed sports; he played football for a community-league team, and frequently engaged in conversations with Mr. Henry about sports during class, lunch, and recess. Joshua enjoyed talking about sports so much that, instead of playing with classmates during recess, he often spent time with Mr. Henry discussing athletes and their statistics. Mrs. Felice is also a teacher at Ponce De Leon. She appreciated the deep care and concern Mr. Henry had for Joshua and the other children under his tutelage. She had previously witnessed White teachers at the school discriminate against Black boys before they even entered their classrooms. She once witnessed some of the teachers in her building compare attendance lists to see which of them had most of the "bad" Black boys. Mrs. Felice stated that schools needed to recruit and retain more Black male teachers like Mr. Henry because they served as Role Models for Black boys like Joshua. Like Mrs. Boins, Mrs. Felice suggested that, even though her husband is a professional who is actively involved in Joshua's life, Joshua needed to see other positive Black male Role Models like Mr. Henry in professional positions like teaching.

Portraits by Black Boys About Black Male Teachers

Zoom In

"He gave me fifteen race car books to take home."

—*Braden*

Braden was especially interested in Mr. Tal's children's books. Mr. Tal's classroom library was full of books from which Braden could choose. Braden suggested that the most interesting books were those that sparked his interest in race cars. Braden was an active young child and needed a teacher like Mr. Tal who understood that teaching in energetic and active ways were keys to keeping him engaged in the teaching and learning process. Mr. Raton, Braden's father, noted that Braden "is a bright kid, but the energy is intensively spoken at times, so whatever [Mr. Tal] needs to do to reel him back in, he has my blessings.". The most effective way Mr. Tal "reeled" Braden in was through books that piqued his interest: books about race cars. As such, Mr. Tal adhered to the important insights of Mr. Raton (e.g. "reel him back in") to support him in the classroom.

Understanding Braden's fascination with the sport, Mr. Tal filled his classroom library with race car books. He sought out and purchased race car books from educational supply stores with his personal funds so Braden could have access to them in the classroom and take them home. As Braden related during an interview, "He [Mr. Tal] gave me fifteen race car books to take home." Braden knew that, when he was on task, Mr. Tal often told him he could "get a race car book" as a reward. Mr. Tal explained that he used race car books as a motivational tool to encourage Braden and other Black boys who did not like reading and writing to experience the joys thereof and preparing them to seek motivating texts in and beyond the early childhood classroom. According to Mr. Tal, after he supplied the books, Braden became more engaged in the reading and writing process, and could frequently be found tucked away in the classroom corner reading his race car books. During Morning Meeting, Mr. Tal also held space for Braden to give book talks, during which he shared information about the book he read with his classmates. He also noted that, consequently, Braden's academic achievement in reading improved significantly on quarterly reading assessments. As a classroom visitor, even I noticed Braden's engagement and academic improvement. Mr. Tal also found opportunities to use race car books in his math and science lessons. He allowed Braden to draw race cars to aid in visualizing addition and subtraction problems, and also enabled him to build ramps to use in racing toy cars, which became both early childhood math and science lessons for Braden.

Zoom Out

National reading data perpetuate the myth that Black boys cannot and do not read (Tatum, 2005; Wright, 2017). Braden's interest in race car books and his desire to read about them serves as counternarratives to dominant anti-Black misandric myths that suggest Black boys are neither interested in books nor actively reading them. Given that, in most early childhood literacy programs and in most classroom book collections, texts are dominated by Whiteness (Baines et al., 2018; Henderson et al., 2020), and most prescribed instructional programs do not provide many opportunities for children to choose books that interest them (Henderson et al., 2020; Souto-Manning & Martell, 2016), Mr. Tal's approach and his successes with Black boys as readers provide critical evidence for incorporating into classrooms and lessons books and other texts that both interest and encourage Black boys to read and write more. As previously mentioned, early childhood teachers like Mr. Tal, who find the utility in BlackBoyCrit Pedagogy, must understand the academic needs, Black masculine identities, and interests of their students, and work to ensure those interests are an integral part of the teaching and learning process. While many teachers will recognize that this is not a new concept – the importance of connecting literacy to the individual realities of Black children (Ladson-Billings, 2009; Lee, 2007) – the fact that it is not widely adopted as foundational in early childhood classrooms means that we continue to inflict anti-Black misandric violence on Black boys and impede the progress they might make.

Developing a Broad Understanding of Black Boy Interests and Male Masculinity when Selecting Books

Although such might not have been the case for Braden, sports-related books such as race car books are more readily available in early childhood classrooms than books that address other aspects of Black boys' masculine identities. Indeed, not all boys are interested in sports-related books about subjects like race car driving (Bryan, 2019). According to Black masculinity scholars (Davis, 2003; Howard, 2014; Lynn, 2006a/b), to suggest otherwise is to essentialize the experiences of Black boys, which minimizes the diversity that exists among them (Howard, 2014). Teachers should not assume that all Black boys enjoy and are interested in sports, but they should enable Black boys to express their own individual identities and interests in classroom books so that they, as teachers, can make accessible books and other texts that best interest their students (Kirkland & Jackson, 2009; 2019).

This look at a broad range of Black boy interests extends also to the breadth of ways to be Black and boy discussed in Chapter 2. That is the case again here as we consider the importance for Mr. Tal to include not only books that portray Black boys who engage in cheerleading and other non-hegemonic sports-related activities, but also books focusing on families with two dads, single Black fathers, transgender men, and Black men in a range of professions which are not often found in early childhood classrooms. Thus, while it is a positive characteristic that most of Mr. Tal's book collections were grounded in Black masculine identities, he could have done more to expose his Black boys to books that demonstrated a range of ways of being a Black male and diverse activities and professions in which Black boys and men engage. Of course, this is not intended to indict Mr. Tal, however, it is an attempt to point out a blindspot that exists in many classrooms which otherwise challenge anti-Black misandry through BlackBoyCrit Pedagogy. Thus, it is important that teachers not view sports-related texts books as the only kinds of books that can achieve this; rather, they should view them as one possible form of Black Masculine Literacies that motivates Black boys to engage in literacy processes. This requires that teachers make every effort to listen, hear, and understand Black boys, like Mr. Tal, who spent time speaking with and learning about the lives of his Black boys, became aware of their interests, and infused those interests into the teaching and learning process. All these practices are consistent with BlackBoyCrit Pedagogy.

Going Beyond Just Offering Books to Interest Black Boys

Nevertheless, it is important to note that the use of Black Masculine Literacies as a praxis of BlackBoyCrit Pedagogy is not as easy as simply making accessible the books that interest Black boys. Although Mr. Tal used those books to motivate and encourage Braden as well as other Black boys to engage in reading and writing, he also used books to build on their prior knowledge, and to help them see not only the mirrors and windows, but sliding doors and opportunities; in this case, he encouraged them to see themselves as more than athletes. He wanted them to embrace their scholarly identities, and envision their academic and social potential. As he spoke daily about and highlighted images of Black historical male sport figures, Mr. Tal also encouraged Braden and other Black boys to see themselves as teachers, lawyers, and other professionals who could positively contribute to society.

Mr. Tal often shared with his students what it means to be a Black male teacher, and he was concerned by the lack of children's books available to them—especially books that highlighted Black males working as teachers. He suggested that, as a result, Black boys might not be able to see themselves as or respect Black male teachers. Early childhood teachers like Mr. Tal, who employ Black-BoyCrit Pedagogy, are proficient at centering their own lived realities, centering positive views of Black men, contesting anti-Black misandric images of Black men that may not position them positively in the world, and encouraging Black boys to see themselves and people who look like them positively in school curricula traditionally built on anti-Black misandry.

Connecting Black Boys' Interests across the Curriculum

Mr. Tal not only saw intimate connections between the interest of his Black boys and literacy, but also math and science. Early childhood teachers like Mr. Tal understand the inter-curricular nature of anti-Black misandry in early childhood education. As such, he understood that countering anti-Black misandry in math and science through Black Masculine Literacies and subsequently BlackBoyCrit Pedagogy was just as important as doing so in reading.

Providing a Model of Black Men as Readers

The fact that Mr. Tal often used his own personal funds to purchase race cars books to motivate Braden to read and write was a type of Black masculine literacy that Black boys can "read" as not only an instance of an adult promoting the importance of reading and writing, but also as an opportunity to view Black men as both readers and writers who, in turn, care deeply about Black boys' reading and writing abilities. Black men have always inspired other Black men and boys to develop a love and passion for reading and writing; this can be traced back to the era of the enslavement of African people, when anti-literacy laws prohibited Black men and women from legally learning to read and write (Perry et al., 2003; Williams, 2005). However, some enslaved Africans defied the laws and taught themselves and other enslaved Africans these necessary skills (Williams, 2005). For example, Elijah Marrs, an enslaved man, taught and gave books to enslaved men who wanted to learn to read and write (William, 2005). Indeed, even during an era where teaching themselves and other enslaved Africans was forbidden, literate enslaved African men became teachers, or better yet BlackBoyCrit Pedagogues, who motivated and encouraged other Black men and boys to educate themselves.

Using Black Boys' Engagement with Motivating Texts to Assess Them as Readers

After Mr. Tal introduced Braden to books that interested him, Braden's motivation and engagement significantly improved. When teachers like Mr. Tal, who infuse BlackBoyCrit Pedagogy, center the interests of Black boys in the teaching and learning of reading (Husband, 2012, Meier, 2015; Tatum, 2005, 2015), such is typically the outcome. Nevertheless, national and state-level reading assessments do not take these outcomes into consideration, nor note when teachers use books and other texts (other than those required in the assessments) that are applicable to the lives of Black boys (Henderson et al., 2020; Husband, 2012; Meier, 2015; Kirkland & Jackson, 2009). Rather, these formal assessments paint bleak pictures about Black boys' performance in reading as early as early childhood education, and teachers use the assessments to essentialize Black boys' reading performances.

Early childhood educators should be careful about the use and application of such data to define Black boys' abilities or to inform how and what they teach. These data do not indicate how the anti-Black misandric nature of books, texts, and reading assessments may cause Black boys to become disinterested in and disenfranchised from reading. Similar to Mr. Tal, they should instead assess students as readers while they are engaged and motivated to read and write beyond literacy normative practices. This gives a truer sense of what children can do as readers, the strategies they use, the words they know, the letter-sound correspondences they are able to make, and their ability to comprehend texts.

Seeing Black Boys as Readers Instead of Nonreaders

Consistent with BlackBoyCrit Pedagogy, Mr. Tal saw Braden as a reader instead of a nonreader. I believe the first solution to confronting anti-Black misandry in early literacy is to confront teachers' mindsets about who can and cannot read. By that, I mean that much like Mr. Tal, early childhood educators must begin to see Black boys like Braden as readers and to understand that Black boys are engaged in literacy practices in their homes and communities that go unnoticed in early childhood classrooms (Tatum, 2005; Kirkland & Jackson, 2009; Wright, 2017). Alfred Tatum (2005, 2015) has long sought to help teachers shift their mindsets about the literacy abilities of Black boys in and beyond early childhood education. Reflecting on my own early literacy experiences, I believe most of my early childhood teachers, with the exception of Mr. C., thought I was unable to read, and presently, most early childhood teachers continue to perceive Black boys as nonreaders. Indeed, we have much more work to do to confront teachers' mindsets about Black boys' reading abilities.

Embracing Oral Narratives as a Black Masculine Literacy Practice for Black Boys

When he held space for Braden to orally share the books he read during Morning Meeting, Mr. Tal understood the importance of engaging Braden in oral narrative as a Black masculine literacy practice. Oral narrative centers the voices and insights of Black ways of knowing and being among Black boys (Gardner-Neblett & Sideris, 2017). Because Black boys are often silenced in early childhood classrooms, engaging Braden in oral narratives is a solution that is not only grounded in the lived realities and experiences of Black boys, but also humanizes, heals, and uplifts them from hegemonic schooling practices that silence their voices in classrooms. Given Braden's significant gains on quarterly reading assessments, it is important to note that Mr. Tal's infusion of oral narratives was instrumental in supporting Braden's literacy outcomes. We should be further encouraged by the scholarship of Gardner-Neblett and Sideris (2017), who found that promoting the use of oral narrative skills in early childhood education has the potential to improve Black children's reading skills, and especially among Black boys in the study who demonstrated success in reading throughout the school years. In other words, one can surmise that BlackBoyCrit Pedagogues like Mr. Tal, who embrace oral narrative as a Black masculine literacy practice, can potentially lead to building strong early literacy skills among Black boys like Braden for years to come.

Abandoning Literacy Normative Practices

As he drew on his own lived realities as a Black man and, subsequently a Black male teacher, Mr. Tal's Role Modeling served as a way of incorporating BlackBoyCrit Pedagogy and, by extension, Black Masculine Literacies into the teaching and learning process (Kirkland, 2011; Kirkland & Jackson, 2019). Collectively, through books, texts, and his position as a Black male teacher, Mr. Tal encouraged Braden and other boys to make connections to texts through Black Masculine Literacies (which is rare when early childhood books do not draw on the individual identities of Black boys; Tatum, 2005)), draw comparisons and contrast across texts, use abilities to read one text to support abilities to read others, and use texts as windows to being able to read the world.

Zoom In

"Mr. Henry, You're really good at drawing basketballs."

—Joshua

Joshua was always excited during math time, and it was clear he was a gifted math learner in the way that he readily engaged in math literacies, using numbers as a way to read the word as well as the world. Although his parents and Mr. Henry felt that Joshua did not enjoy reading, math was Joshua's preferred literacy practice. Because of his excitement and interest in math, Joshua often dominated math lessons, yelling out responses before other students had a chance to answer. On one occasion during one of my observations, Mr. Henry had to remind Joshua about the need to allow other students to participate. Responding to Joshua's excitement about knowing all the answers, Mr. Henry told him, "Yes, I know you know the answer, but you have to give other people a chance to answer, just like you. I need to see that they know too. So, raise your hand next time, so I can call on you."

Joshua also loved sports, and was an avid football player who played for a local community football team. After learning about Joshua's interest in athletics, Mr. Henry found ways to infuse them into his math lessons. He used sports-related semiotic systems (e.g., signs and symbols) to help Joshua and other students solve complex problems and make the lesson relevant. By drawing basketballs on the Smartboard, Mr. Henry taught his students to add double-digit numbers. During this lesson, Joshua stated, "Mr. Henry, you're really good at drawing basketballs."

Through sports, Joshua and Mr. Henry had built a strong bond inside and outside the classroom; they often spent time during lunch and recess discussing sports and statistics. Joshua was fascinated with Mr. Henry's Apple watch which gave sports updates regarding the latest trades and games scores. Each time Joshua heard the chime from Mr. Henry's watch, he knew there were sports developments of which he needed to be aware. Mr. Henry explained how, during one of his class sessions, his watched sounded and, learning that Darryl Williams, a football player, had been traded to another team, he relayed the information to Joshua. Later that day, he spoke with Joshua's mother, Mrs. Felice, who mentioned that she too had learned the news and could not wait to share what she had learned with Joshua. When she eagerly told him as he was entering the family car to go home after a long school day, Joshua looked at her and said, "Oh, I already know. Mr. Henry told me."

To further build a relationship beyond the classroom, Mr. Henry also attended Joshua's community sports events. Like Mrs. Boins (Roland's mother), Mrs. Felice was appreciative of the fact that Mr. Henry made himself not only a part of Joshua's school life, but also his personal and familial lives. According to her, Joshua was excited to see Mr. Henry at his game because he knew they would have an opportunity to discuss it the next school day.

The sport-related conversations in which Joshua and Mr. Henry engaged were also centered on Mr. Henry's lived experiences as a former high school and college football player, and as a current football coach. Mr. Henry shared stories about how his parents required him to do well in school and that, if he did not do well, he was not allowed to play. This was Mr. Henry's way of encouraging Joshua to also excel in school and spend more time reading at home.

Mr. Henry not only integrated sports into his math lessons as a way to teach Joshua and his classmates, but he also introduced a math approach he learned at a professional development conference. Joshua was extremely fond of the *NOWA* graphic organizer, which helped him to quickly and easily solve math problems. During a classroom visit, Joshua introduced NOWA to me, and demonstrated its use and applicability as he easily solved several math problems. Even when math lessons did not require it, Joshua constantly asked, "Mr. Henry, can we do *NOWA*?"

Zoom Out

Similar to the ways in which research studies negatively describe the academic performance outcomes of Black boys in reading, they also describe Black boys as underperforming in math. These studies rarely highlight the academic potential of Black boys like Joshua, who excel in math, and the teachers who are able to teach math in ways that meet their needs. In fact, Joshua's and Mr. Henry's examples serve as counternarratives to dominant anti-Black misandric research narratives, which suggest that Black boys are underperforming in math, and that Black male teachers cannot effectively teach it (Hunter & Stinson, 2019; Jett, 2013; Jett et al., 2015).

Particularly important are the ways Mr. Henry fosters Joshua's love for math and his skills as a gifted math learner, and the ways he illustrates that teachers who teach against anti-Black misandry recognize the possibilities of Black boys, and find ways to develop their innate gifts, talents, and abilities in and beyond the classroom. In other words, Black male teachers affirm Black boys' potential as well as their Black masculine identities.

Unfortunately, however, because many teachers view Black boys from deficit perspectives and in anti-Black misandric ways, by the third grade, most students like Joshua become discouraged and afraid to embrace their scholarly identities in math and other content areas (Ford, 2013; Jett, 2013; Whiting, 2009). Consequently, they are positioned for every teacher that follows to see them as perils instead of promises (Howard, 2014). For this reason, Mrs. Felice revealed that she was concerned for Joshua and other Black boys in schools, and saw the necessity of Black male teachers like Mr. Henry to counter anti-Black misandry. As she stated,

> I think what concerns me most as he gets older ... you know what ... not even as he gets older. As he is going through school, people will look at the fact that he is an African American male. And not necessarily him ... it could be boys that look like him and [they] perceive them to be a problem without giving him a chance to show them what kinda person he really is. A lot of it has to do with us as educators and how open are we to accepting and embracing every child. Some of us are more open to embracing other races more than others. That is why we need more Black male educators.

I, too, have similar concerns. In my current professional capacity as a preservice teacher educator, I see White preservice teachers who enter early childhood classrooms with anti-Black misandric assumptions about the intellectual capabilities of Black boys. On a course evaluation, one White female preservice teacher wrote that she thought my expectations for the future children she would teach were too high because the children, mostly Black boys, whom she encountered in her field/practicum experiences "were not gifted children."

Using Black Masculine Literacies to Support Math and Reading Growth

Consistent with BlackBoyCrit Pedagogy, Mr. Henry not only humanized, healed, and inspired Joshua, but he also used Black Masculine Literacies to support Joshua's academic potential in math and reading. He infused Joshua's identity as both athlete and scholar into his pedagogies and schooling practices. When Joshua mentioned that Mr. Henry was good at drawing basketballs, he basically suggested that Mr. Henry was also effective at engaging him in the math lesson by using Black masculine referents with which he was familiar. These referents were a part of their daily conversations outside the classroom, and easily facilitated the teaching and learning of math in it. Additionally, Joshua was proud that Mr. Henry gave him a math technique (NOWA) that increased his proficiency in solving math problems. For Joshua, it seemed like NOWA was akin to a sports play book that coaches provide to athletes to help them strategize and win games. NOWA helped Joshua continue to win the game of math, and this became another way that Mr. Henry fostered Joshua's identity as both a gifted math learner and athlete.

Although he knew Joshua was not motivated to read, Mr. Henry did not foster negative and anti-Black misandric perceptions of Joshua's reading ability. Instead, he assigned him books he could take home to read to his mother, Mrs. Felice, as motivation. He refused to perceive Joshua as having academic deficiencies or assign him to special education and/or pullout programs just as I was sent to the computer lab to receive supposed remediation in reading. On the contrary, once Mr. Henry understood Joshua's excitement for math, he did not remove him from the classroom for his reading deficiencies, nor for misbehavior when he yelled out answers during math lessons before other students could answer. Instead, he reminded Joshua of his need to allow other students to participate. This is undoubtedly because Mr. Henry understood the reasons behind Joshua's behavior and, like Mrs. Felice, he worried about how Black boys were (mis)treated in schools. As Mr. Henry stated,

> Yes, I worry about the fact [of] how they fit in the school entity first. There aren't many chances for them to be Black boys. For example, we ask five-, six-, and seven-year-old boys to come to school for 7.5 hours and sit in a desk or on a small square on the carpet still, and not bother anyone. We ask them to walk in straight lines downs long hallways, sit quiet at lunch and during dismissal. It's most of the things we do that make school not a good place for Black boys. Then people discipline them for not following the rules that they think keep them in line … Crazy! We should do more to meet the need of our Black boys.

What Mr. Henry described was the preschool-to-prison nexus, wherein every aspect of the schooling process is representative of and is preparing Black boys for what Alexander (2010) referred to as the prison industrial complex. Knocked down again and again and again, Black boys have little recourse except to believe the anti-Black misandric identities being thrust upon them. Black male teachers like Mr. Henry, who employ BlackBoyCrit Pedagogy, are consciously aware of the anti-Black violence inflicted upon Black boys, and are deliberate in teaching to counter anti-Black misandry. They work daily to interrupt and, if possible, dismantle anti-Black misandric structures put in place to annihilate Black boys early on in schools (Essien, 2017; Kunjufu, 2005).

When Mr. Henry asked Joshua to allow other students the opportunity to answer his questions during the math lesson, Joshua responded to Mr. Henry's request immediately. Joshua's immediate response demonstrated the mutual respect and symbiotic relationship between him and Mr. Henry. In other words, there was no cultural mismatch between the two, as is often the case with White early childhood teachers, who engage in cultural tugs-o-war with Black boys, all because of the cultural mismatch between both groups (Wood et al., 2017; Wright & Counsell, 2018). Stated more pointedly, White teachers do not—and, in most cases, refuse—to understand Black boys, and Black boys do not understand White female teachers (Moore et al., 2018). Let me be clear! This idea does not mean that White teachers cannot successfully teach Black boys. When White teachers respect and see the brilliance of Black boys like Joshua, they become successful teachers of Black boys. As such, Black boys demonstrate mutual respect between them and their White teachers.

Getting to Know Black Boys' Community Cultural Wealth

Joshua was not only excited about the opportunity to build a positive relationship with Mr. Henry in the classroom; he was also excited to build one with him outside it. Joshua appreciated that Mr. Henry attended his football games, which is a rarity among most early childhood educators, who rarely spend time in young Black children's communities. The reality is that most White teachers are afraid to visit the homes and communities of Black boys. They often possess deficit views not only of the children, but of the communities in which the children live (Carey, 2019). Preservice and inservice teachers with whom I have worked often speak negatively about their students' communities. Most admit they are afraid to go into spaces where children live. However, in my language and literacy course for early childhood teachers, I assign a culminating project titled The Community Mapping Project (Jackson & Bryson, 2018; Lopez-Robertson et al., 2010). It enables preservice teachers to visit communities of Color to highlight the cultural wealth and capital of those communities as a way to center heritage knowledge in the teaching and learning process. And yet, even after several course lectures on community cultural wealth (Yosso, 2005), in which I purport to shift deficit views about communities of Color, White preservice teachers still hold deficit views of these communities. As such, teachers like Mr. Henry remain an anomaly in schools, but are desperately needed to embrace not only the brilliance of Black boys, but the cultural wealth and capital of the communities in which they live.

While previous research studies on Black Masculine Literacies (Kirkland & Jackson, 2009, 2019; Stevenson & Ross, 2015) have delineated the ways in which Black boys perform literacies based on their identities as informed by hegemonic masculinity, sports, and hip-hop culture, Black Masculine Literacies can be defined as the literacies Black male teachers perform in *collaboration* with Black boys, their parents, and their communities to support their academic and social success in classrooms, and to contest the anti-Black misandric conspiracy to destroy them in schools. Black male teachers, who employ BlackBoyCrit Pedagogy, can embody literacies and/or literacy practices in the form of pedagogies and in-/out-of-school practices that effectively and appropriately influence Black boys in both the classroom and the community. This idea contests anti-Black misandric and hegemonic masculine constructions of Black male teachers, who are solely constructed as disciplinarians and father-figures whose tasks are to keep Black boys under control due to their so-called "deviant" behaviors (Brockenbrough, 2012).

Reconstructing an image of the Black male teacher beyond hegemonic masculine expectations constructs them as empathetic instructors who are active and collaborative participants in the uplift of Black boys in early childhood classrooms and schools. Because Black male teachers can employ Black Masculine Literacies that are also informed by *empathetic masculinities* or masculinities grounded in empathy, they can engage in similarly informed Black Masculine Literacies, even as their identities are informed by hip-hop and sports culture.

Zoom In

"He always be reading the good books ... you can listen to kinda like a rap"
—*Ameer*

Ameer's grandmother, Mrs. Martha, shared with me that Ameer has autism. She felt that this was one reason why he was a quiet student. Sometimes he did not speak unless he was spoken to. Mrs. Martha acknowledged that, prior to being a student in Mr. Javien's class, Ameer went days without talking to anyone but that, under Mr. Javien's tutelage, Ameer found his voice. Laughing, Mrs. Martha stated that Mr. Javien did too good of a job with Ameer because as she said, "Now he now talks too much." Over time, I, too, noticed that Ameer had found his voice and started to communicate more with me and his classmates. During a brief classroom conversation, I asked him about what he liked about school as a way to encourage him to share his insights about his teacher, Mr. Javien. When asked about what he liked most about Mr. Javien, Ameer stated, "He always be reading the *good books* ... you can listen to kinda like a rap." Based on my observations, Mr. Javien often used books that were accompanied by hip-hop music to engage his students and he used hip-hop examples in his teaching. Understanding his students' interest in hip-hop culture and artists such as Jay-Z and Beyonce, Mr. Javien activated his students' prior knowledge to help them understand words and concepts that were new to them. For example, Mr. Javien used the term "headliner" in a sentence to help his students understand the importance of community rather than individualism. He explained to the children, "There ain't no headliners in this classroom." Immediately, one of his Black boys, Keith (pseudonym), who was sitting at the front of the classroom asked, "What is that?" Mr. Javien then explained to his students, "Let me help you understand what a headliner is. You know when you go to Jay-Z's or Beyonce's concert, they are the headliners because they are in-charge on the stage. There ain't no headliners in this class."

Mr. Javien also invited Black men and women including his students' mothers and fathers from the local community to read to his students through his *Mystery Reader* initiative. Mystery Reader took place once a month and readers were provided opportunities to read books that mirrored the experiences of the students. To ensure this, Mr. Javien selected the book the mystery readers would share. Much like most of his classmates, Ameer always enjoyed the guests and was engaged, raising his hands and answering questions. On one occasion, the school district's superintendent, a Black male, served as guest reader. Ameer stated that he enjoyed the book that the superintendent read and wanted to take it home to read.

Zoom Out

Given the Eurocentric nature of books and other texts in most early childhood classrooms (Boutte et al., 2008), what Ameer refers to as the "good books" are not readily available in classrooms. Per Ameer's perspective, good books are those that reflect his cultural ways of knowing and being, and are grounded in his experiences. As Ameer's stories demonstrated, these books promoted the strength and possibilities of his culture; humanized, healed, restored, and uplifted Ameer and his classmates; and accounted for the collective and individual identities of Ameer and his classmates in their rural elementary school. Finally, but perhaps most important, Mr. Javien's good books upheld the richness and joy of Black boyhood. These are attributes of BlackBoyCrit Pedagogy and Black Masculine Literacies described along with others from Ameer's stories in the following sections.

Choosing Books to Uphold the Joys of Black Boyhood

Ameer's announcement that Mr. Javien used "good books" in his classroom likely indicates that Ameer may have had previous experiences with bad books, books that fall under the category of literacy normativity described in Chapter 2 and 5 as that which centers White ways of knowing and being thereby negatively impacting literacy outcomes of Black boys in early childhood education (Husband, 2012; Meier, 2015; Pritchard, 2017; Rashid, 2009; Tatum, 2005, 2015; Wright, 2017). When Ameer suggested that Mr. Javien used *good books*, he implicitly suggested that he must have had teachers previously who used books to which he could not relate and that did not uphold the richness and joy of Black boyhood. Research studies focused on children's literature repeatedly report an overwhelming number of Eurocentric books – meaning focused on primarily

White characters and written by White authors – in early childhood classrooms (Boutte et al., 2008; Cooperative Children's Book Center, 2019; Henderson et al., 2020). While many of these are not "bad" books in terms of quality, style, story, etc., they *are* bad when we consider classrooms filled with them rather than dominated by "good books" that reflect the lives, communities, heritage, and masculine identities of Black boys like Ameer. With Ameer in mind, we can then think of bad books as those omitting the Black cultural ways of knowing and being that are familiar to Ameer and other Black boys. They are "bad" in that, by disregarding the strength and possibilities of Black culture, they harm, oppress, and dehumanize Black children like Ameer. Thus, classroom book collections can be decidedly dehumanizing and anti-Black misandric in nature. Even books that have Black characters can be labeled as "bad" and anti-Black misandric (Curry, 2017) in nature, when they uphold specific stereotypes and biases about Black boys, for example, when they portray Black boys solely as antagonists or when they disregard the individual and collective differences among Black children by promoting stereotypes and biases about them.

Drawing on the Resources of the Black Community

An important feature of Mr. Javien's infusion of BlackBoyCrit Pedagogy is his ability to draw on the wealth of the local community to support the literacy experiences and outcomes of students. His Mystery Reader initiative was an important practice that enabled Ameer and other Black boys to see Black men (and women) as readers, as Mr. Javien invited them to read to his students. This was another way for Black men and women to become informants and partners in the academic enterprise. As previously mentioned, BlackBoyCrit Pedagogy requires teachers to provide windows and mirrors for Black boys, and to incorporate Black families and communities as integral parts of the teaching and learning process.

Valuing Black Language

Although not a large part of Ameer's portrait of Mr. Javien, the boys' and teachers' use of Black Language in all of my observations was an important element in their enactment of BlackBoyCrit Pedagogy. In response to one of my questions, Ameer responded, "He always be reading good books." Many early childhood educators might suggest that Ameer used "broken English" and/or "incorrect English" in this response. However, such was not the case; he was speaking a rule-governed, historically-based language accepted by the Linguistic Society of America as, not bad English or even a dialect, but a language (Baker-Bell, 2020). Thus, Black Language is neither broken nor incorrect, and children like Ameer who speak it reveal expertise and fluency. Ameer invoking his right to use Black Language as he described his teacher's literacy practice: "Mr. Javien always be reading good books." Here he demonstrated Black Language proficiency by using the habitual "be," a strong linguistic feature of Black Language that suggests an event is ongoing. Thus, Ameer used it to explain Mr. Javien's use of what Ameer termed as good books as an ongoing process in his early classroom.

Much like Mr. Javien, teachers who use BlackBoyCrit Pedagogy value all the experiences Black boys bring to classrooms, which includes the linguistic ones. Mr. Javien is also an avid Black Language speaker and uses the language in his classroom. Mr. Javien's response to his student—"There ain't no headliner in this class"—is one example of his use of Black Language in his early childhood classroom. Given the humanizing and healing environment Mr. Javien provided as he modeled for Ameer the right to use his own language, Ameer felt comfortable speaking Black Language. Teachers who prohibit Black boys like Ameer from using Black Language also engage in anti-Black misandry, but such was not the case for Mr. Javien.

Practical Recommendations for Early Childhood Educators

Considering the pedagogical, literacy, and schooling practices of Black male teachers highlighted in this chapter, the following sections suggest how characteristics of Black Masculine Literacies as a praxis of BlackBoyCrit Pedagogy can inform teaching in other early childhood classrooms. Thus, given the context of teaching that goes beyond just offering books to interest Black boys, connects Black boys' interests across the curriculum, provides a model of Black men as readers, using students' engagement with texts to assess them as readers, appreciates students' community cultural wealth, chooses books to uphold the joys of Black boyhood, draws on the resources of the Black community, and values Black Language, consider the following practical recommendations provided in Table 6.3.

Use and Integrate Black Boy-centric Books and Other Texts

We should all refuse to believe the hype that Black boys do not love to read; they, in fact, are avid readers, and images of Black boys as readers are reflected throughout this book, and particularly this chapter. Even so, early childhood teachers should work to infuse into their curricula what Ameer called the *good books*, those books that are humanizing to Black boys. We should work toward building classrooms and home libraries that are supporting in critical ways the academic, literacy, and

TABLE 6.3 Practical Recommendations for Early Childhood Educators

- Use and integrate Black boy-centric books and other texts
- Infuse oral narratives as a Black Masculine Literacy Practice into early literacy
- Foster Black boys' math identities
- Acknowledge, value, and appreciate Black language

schooling outcomes of Black boys in and beyond early childhood classrooms. As such, teachers can purchase and incorporate into early childhood curricula books that celebrate Black boys and boyhood. In Chapter 5, I provided the names of a few such books. However, several websites, including Sidney Keys III's www.booksandbros. com, and the Conscious Kid's *Black Books Matter: Children's Books Celebrating Black Boys* (www.Theconsciouskid.org) can also provide useful support to early childhood classrooms. Additionally, early childhood educators can begin (or empower Black boys to begin) their own book clubs. For example, Mrs. Janelle W. Henderson, an early childhood teacher in Louisville, Kentucky, realized that she was not meeting the needs of Black boys, so she started a book club to support their literacy needs and desires. Early childhood teachers who are interested in Janelle's work can check out her blog titled *How Curious George Showed Me I Wasn't Meeting the Needs of My Black boys* (https://blog.heinemann.com/curious-george-showed-me-i-I-meeting-needs). Teachers can also follow Mr. Javien's lead, and integrate a *Mystery Reader* initiative, where they invite Black men (and women) from the community to serve as readers of Black Masculine Literacies

Teachers can also create a Black boy virtual space. Mr. Johnny Jackson, a doctoral student at Miami University and a diversity and equity officer, created a Black boy virtual space called Harambe at a local elementary school in his community. Harambe is an Afrocentric and boy-centric mentoring program that meets weekly online to support the educational experiences of Black boys in Marion, Ohio. Harambe is a humanizing and healing space for Black boys. It is also guided by four important Afrocentric principles: *ubuntu*, Black boy joy, mindfulness, and cultural literacy and memory (Jackson, personal communication, 2020). The guiding principle—*ubuntu* (i.e., I am because we are)—purports to help Black boys understand the importance of community. Black boy joy is important because it helps Black boys understand the importance of experiencing the best of oneself and other Black boys. Mindfulness, or deep-breathing, aims to help Black boys look inside themselves for individual and collective healing. Last, and certainly not least, cultural literacy and memory purports to help Black boys to come to know themselves through boy-centric books and other texts. All of the Afrocentric principles of Harambe are consistent with Black Masculine Literacies as a praxis of BlackBoyCrit Pedagogy.

Infuse Oral Narratives as a Black Masculine Literacy Practice into Early Literacy

Mr. Tal's use of oral narrative as a Black masculine literacy practice yielded powerful literacy outcomes among Braden. As such, oral narrative as a Black masculine literacy practice should not only challenge early childhood teachers to rethink the teaching of early literacy skills in classrooms, but should prompt them to consider the importance of replacing those skills with Black masculine literacy practices, which lead to higher performance outcomes for Black boys. To that end, to improve Black boys' literacy outcomes, early childhood educators should capitalize on oral narrative as a Black masculine literacy practice across early childhood curricula, incorporating it into all disciplines, from literacy to math. Much like Mr. Tal, teachers can infuse oral narrative as a Black masculine literacy practice into Morning Meetings (Kriete & Davis, 2014) and culture circles (see Souto-Manning [2013] for more information). Doing so allows Black boys like Braden to share their personal lived experiences, and bolsters their academic, literacy, and schooling outcomes.

Foster Black Boys' Math Identities

Joshua loved math. Mr. Henry knew it and supported his academic prowess in math. Early childhood educators like Mr. Henry can foster Black boys' math identities by centering their lived realities and experiences in math. By that, I mean early childhood educators can draw on the rich everyday cultural, individual, and collective experiences to support the teaching and learning of early mathematics (Martin, 2012; Shonkoff & Phillips, 2000; Wright et al., 2016). Much like building Black boys' STEM identities, early childhood educators can partner with community agencies such as children's museums and programs that draw on out-of-school experiences to teach math (Wright et al., 2016).

Acknowledge, Value, and Appreciate Black Language

Black children, like Ameer, are oftentimes bilingual and/or multilingual; yet, most early childhood educators ignore the linguistic practices in which Black boys (and girls) engage while they are in classrooms. This is beyond tragic. It means that early childhood educators sacrifice the diverse linguistic practices in which Black boys engage for other linguistic and normative literacy practices. However, throughout this chapter, I have encouraged teachers to interrupt such practices by highlighting Black male teachers in early childhood education who were courageous enough to "teach against the grain" and infuse Black Masculine Literacies as a praxis of BlackBoyCrit Pedagogy in their classrooms. In so doing, they acknowledged Black boys' rights to their own languages, and refused to promote a classroom environment steeped in code-switching methodologies and practices. Instead, they "loved on" Black linguistic practices (Baker-Bell, 2020), as most of them were also Black Language speakers. Teachers who love on Black Language replace code-switching practices with code-meshing methodologies, a pedagogical approach that enables students to naturally blend linguistic varieties such as Black Language with White Mainstream American English (Baker-Bell, 2020).

Conclusion

Early childhood teachers who teach against anti-Black misandry and apply Black Masculine Literacies as a praxis of BlackBoyCrit Pedagogy see opportunities through teaching and learning to simultaneously foster Black masculine identities as well as academic and social interests. The pedagogies, literacies, and schooling practices of the Black male teachers presented in this chapter were vitally important to the experiences of Braden, Joshua, and Ameer. I am sure they can be equally vital to other Black boys. As such, early childhood educators can strive to model these practices, while simultaneously finding their own practices to support the experiences of Black boys beyond anti-Black misandry in early childhood education. Most Black male teachers are more willing to do this critical work in classrooms. Yet, this is not just about hiring more Black male teachers. We should search specifically for teachers like Mr. Tal, Mr. Henry, and Mr. Javien who simultaneously teach against anti-Black misandry, and are able to support the academic and social successes of Black boys like Joshua, Braden, and Ameer in early childhood education. Given that some Black male teachers are prepared to uphold deficit and even anti-Black misandric assumptions about themselves and Black boys, those who are not prepared to teach against anti-Black misandry can and will do more harm than good. W. E. B. DuBois (1935) contended that

> We shall get a finer, better balance of spirit; and infinitely more capable and rounded personality, by putting [Black] children in schools where they are wanted, and where they are happy and inspired, than in thrusting them into halls where they are ridiculed and hated. (p. 331)

In other words, we need teachers who will humanize, heal, and inspire rather than discourage Black boys in early childhood classrooms and schools. While race and gender might be crucial in this search, so too is countering anti-Black misandry. Furthermore, White teachers should also be inspired to teach against the grain and anti-Black misandry as to reassure Black boys they are wanted in schools and classrooms and can be happy and inspired therein.

References

Alexander, M. (2010). *The new jim crow: Mass incarceration in the age of colorblindness.* The New Press.

Baines, J., Tisdale, C., & Long, S. (2018). *"We've been doing it your way long enough": Choosing the culturally relevant classroom.* Teachers College Press.

Baker-Bell, A. (2020). *Linguistic Justice: Black language, literacy, identity, and pedagogy.* Routledge.

Baker, C. (2017). Father involvement and early childhood development in African American families: Implications for research, practice, and policy. In I. Iruka, S. M. Curenton, and T. Durden (Eds.), *African American children in early childhood education: Making the case for policy investments in families, schools, and communities* (pp. 201–219).

Boutte, G., & Johnson, G. (2014). Community and family involvement in urban schools. In H. R. Milner and K. Lomotey (Eds.), *Handbook on urban education* (pp. 167–182). Routledge.

Boutte, G., Hopkins, R., & Watlaski, T. (2008). Perspectives, voices, and worldviews in frequently read children's book. *Early Education and Development*, 19(6), 1–22.

Boykin, A. W. (1994). Afro cultural expression and its implications for schooling. In E. Hollins, J. King, & W. Hayman (Eds.), *Teaching diverse populations: Formulating a knowledge base* (pp. 243–273). State University of New York Press.

Brockenbrough, E. (2012). "You ain't my daddy": Black male teachers and the politics of surrogate father. *Teacher College Records*, 114(5), 1–43.

Bryan, N. (2019). Playing with or like the girls: Advancing the performance of 'multiple masculinities in black boys' childhood play in US early childhood classrooms. *Gender and Education*, 31(3), 309–326.

Carey, R. (2019). Imagining the comprehensive mattering of black boys and young men in society and schools: Toward a new approach. *Harvard Educational Review*, 89(3), 370–396.

Cooperative Children's Book Center. (2019). *Publishing statistics on children's/YA books about people of color and First/Native Nations and by people of color and First/Native Nations authors and illustrators*. https://ccbc.educstion.wisc.edu/books/pcstats.asp

Curry, T. (2017). *Man-not: Race, class, genre and the dilemmas of black manhood*. Temple University Press.

Davis, J. E. (2003). Early schooling and academic achievement of African American males. *Urban Education*, 38(5), 515–537.

DuBois, W. E. B. (1935). Does the negro need separate schools? *The Journal of Negro Education*, 4(3), 328–335.

Essien, I. (2017). Teaching black boys in early childhood education: Promising practices from exemplar teachers. *Journal of African American Males in Education*, 8(2). http://journa lofafricanamericanmales.com/wp-content/uploads/2017/12/2-Essien- 2017- Teaching-Black-Boys-in-Early-Childhood-Education.pdf

Ford, D. (2013). *Recruiting and retaining culturally different students in gifted education*. Prufock Press.

Gardner-Neblett, & Sideris, J. (2017). Different tales: The role of gender in the oral-narrative reading link among African American children. *Child Development*, 89(4), 1328–1342.

Henderson, J., Warren, K., Whitmore. K. F., Flint, A. S., Laman, T. T., & Jaggers, W. (2020). Take a close look: Inventorying your classroom library for diverse books. *The Reading Teacher*, 73(6), 747–755.

Howard, T. (2014). *Black maled: Perils and promises in the education of African American males*. Teacher College Press.

Hunter, J. G., & Stinson, D. W. (2019). A mathematics classroom of caring among a black male teacher and black male students. *Curriculum & Teaching Dialogue*, 21(1/2), 21–34.

Husband, T. (2012). Why can't Jamal read? There's no simple answer why black males struggle with reading, but part of the problem stems from correctable factors that tend to lead to an early disconnect. *Phi Delta Kappan*, 93(5), 23.

Jackson, J. (personal communication, 2020). Black boy virtual space.

Jackson, T., & Bryson, B. (2018). Community mapping as a tool for developing culturally relevant pedagogy. *New Educator*, 14(2), 109–128.

Jett, C. C., Stinson, D. W., & Williams, B. A. (2015). Communities for and with black male students. *The Mathematics Teacher*, 109(4), 284–289.

Jett, C. C. (2013). HBCUS propel African American male mathematics majors. *Journal of African American Studies*, 17(2), 189–205.

Kirkland, D. (2011). Books like clothes: Engaging young black men with reading. *Journal of Adolescent and Adult Literacy*, 55(3), 199–208.

Kirkland, D., & Jackson, A. (2019). Toward a theory of black masculine literacies. In T. Ransaw, C. P. Gause, & R. Majors (Eds.), *The handbook of research on black males: Quantitative, qualitative, and multidisciplinary* (pp. 367–396). Michigan State Press.

Kirkland, D., & Jackson, A. (2009). Beyond the silence: Instructional approaches and students' attitudes. In J. C.Scott, D. Y.Straker, & L. Katz (Eds.). *Affirming students' right to their own language: Bridging language policies and pedagogical practices* (pp. 132–150). Routledge.

Kriete, R., & Davis. (2014). *The morning meeting book: K-8* (3rd ed.). Center for Responsive Teaching.

Kunjufu, J. (2005). *Keeping black boys out of special education*. African American Images.

Ladson-Billings, G. (2009). *The dreamkeepers: Successful teachers of African American children* (2nd ed.). Jossey-Bass.

Lee, C. (2007). *Culture, literacy, and learning: Taking blooming in the midst of thewhirlwind*. Teacher College Press.

Lopez-Robertson, J., Long, S., & Turner-Nash, K. (2010). First steps in constructing counter narratives of young children and their families. *Language Arts*, 88(2), 93–103.

Lynn, M. (2006a). Dancing between two worlds: A portrait of the life of a black male teacher in South Central L.A. *International Journal of Qualitative Studies in Education*, 19 (2), 221–242.

Lynn, M. (2006b). Education for the community: Exploring the culturally relevant practice of black male teachers. *Teachers College Record*, 108(12), 2497–2522.

Martin, D. (2012). Learning mathematics while black. *Educational Foundations*, 26(1), 47–66.

Meier, T. (2015). "The brown face of hope": Reading engagement and African American boys. *The Reading Teacher*, 68(5), 335.

Moore, E., Michael, A., & Penick-Parks, M. (2018). *A guide for white women who teach black boys*. Corwin.

Myers, M. (2013). *A study of the intersections of race, schooling, and family life in a rural black community* [Doctoral dissertation, University of South Carolina]. Unpublished dissertation. https://scholarcommons.sc.edu/cgi/viewcontent.cgi?article=3542& context=etd.

Perry. T., Steele, C., & Hilliard, A. III. (2003). *Young, gifted, and black: Promoting high achievement outcome among African-American students*. Beacon Press

Pritchard, D. E. (2017). *Fashioning Lives: Black queers and the politics of literacy*. Southern Illinois Press.

Rashid, H. (2009). From brilliant baby to child placed at risk. The perilous path of African American boys in early childhood education. *Journal of Negro Education*, 78(3), 347–358.

Shonkoff, J. P., & Phillips, D. A. (Eds.). (2000). *From neurons to neighborhoods: The science of early childhood development*. National Academies Press.

Souto-Manning, M. (2013). *Multicultural teaching in the early childhood classroom*. Teacher College Press.

Souto-Manning, M., & Martell, J. (2016). *Reading, writing, and talk inclusive teaching strategies for diverse learners, K-2*. Teachers College Press.

Stevenson, A., & Ross, S. (2015). Starting young: Emergent black masculinity and early literacy. *Journal of African American Males in Education*, 6(1), 75–90.

Tatum, A. (2015). Engaging African American males in reading (reprint). *Journal of Education*, 195(2), 1–4.

Tatum, A. (2005). *Teaching reading to black adolescent males: Closing the achievement gap*. Stenhouse Publishers.

Whiting, G. W. (2009). The Scholar Identity Institute: Guiding Darnel and other black males. *Gifted Child Today*, 32(4), 53–56.

Williams, H. (2005). *Self-taught: African American education in slavery and freedom.* University of North Carolina Press.

Wood, J. L., Essien, I., Blevins, D. (2017). Black males in kindergarten: The effects of social skills on close and conflictual relationships with teachers. *Journal of African American Males in Education,* 8(2), 30–50.

Wright, B. (2017). Five wise men: African-American males using urban critical literacy to negotiate and navigate home and school in an urban setting. *Urban Education* .

Wright, B., & Counsell, S. (2018). *The brilliance of black boys: Cultivating success in the early grades.* Teacher College Press.

Wright, B. L., Counsell, S. L., Goings, R. B., Freeman, H., & Peat, F. (2016). Creating access and opportunity: Preparing African American male students for STEM trajectories preK- 12. *Journal of Multicultural Education,* 10(3), 384–404.

Yosso, T. J. (2005). Whose culture has capital? *Race, Ethnicity and Education,* 8(1), 69–91.

7
UNDERSTANDING BLACK BOYHOOD PLAY EXPERIENCES IN EARLY CHILDHOOD EDUCATION

BlackBoyCrit Pedagogy centralizes play as an important part of boyhood experiences and requires teachers to understand, acknowledge, and confront the anti-Black misandric violence Black boys face during play in and beyond schools. My own boyhood play experiences were subjected to such anti-Black violence. When I was 9 years old, I was dribbling a basketball in the streets of my community, near Mall Park (Figures 7.1 and 7.2) on Charleston's eastside where I often played, when I suddenly heard the sound *Click! Click!* As I raised my head, I saw an older White woman staring at me as she locked her car door. Apparently, she was afraid of me, and negatively perceived me as a threat to her in *my* community. In that moment, I wished I had possessed the language to retaliate when she murdered me with her eyes. As I reflect on that incident, it reminds me of the same kind of fear and negative perceptions that were the catalysts for Tamir Rice's death in a playground in Cleveland, Ohio. Fearful of Tamir, a White male citizen called the local police department to complain about a 21-year-old man (when it was, in fact, a 12-year-old boy) brandishing a toy gun and threatening nearby citizens (Dumas & Nelson, 2016; Lewis-Ellison et al., 2018). Tamir was shot immediately on officers' arrival at the park, and his death is indicative of what it means to live and play in what Hartman (2007) has called the *afterlife of slavery*: the ongoing dehumanization of Black life "by a racial calculus and a political arithmetic that were entrenched centuries ago" (p. 6).

Returning to my own victimization during play, this harrowing event was the beginning of my awareness of the White gaze: how White people negatively perceived the bodies of Black boys (Yancy, 2017). It is this gaze that leads to White people's fearful responses to the mere sight of the Black body (Yancy, 2017). While reflecting on her Black girlhood experiences, the Black feminist scholar and activist Audre Lorde (1984) described an experience during which she sat next to a White woman on a train and inadvertently brushed against her. The White woman gave

DOI: 10.4324/9780429287619-8

FIGURE 7.1 Mall Park

FIGURE 7.2 Playground Area of Mall Park

Lorde a disgusting look. Analyzing Lorde's Black girlhood experience, Yancy (2017) asserted what Lorde experienced was the White gaze, "its penetrating hatred, its impact on her body" (p. 67). During the moment when I was victimized during play, I, too, learned of the impact of the White gaze.

Black children of every gender should not have to live in a world where playing in their own schools and communities puts them at risk of White people's stereotypes and biases. In the same manner that Black children and other children of Color have the rights to their own languages, they should also have the right to play. However, many children are victims of racialized and gendered violence during play. For example, on October 16, 2018, two Black boys (whose names were not mentioned) were accosted for playing with a BB gun in their community in Columbus, Ohio. Officer Peter Casuccio stopped and berated the two, telling them that, "This is getting kids killed all over the country" (Fiedstadt, 2018, n.p.). He also told the boys, "Your life hasn't even gotten started, and yet [it] could have ended. Cause I wouldn't have missed"—a thinly veiled reference to the probability that he would have fired his gun at the two boys (n. p.). The boys were briefly detained before being released to their parents, and the Columbus Police Department chalked up their interaction with Officer Casuccio as a "lesson learned" (Hauser, 2018, n. p.).

We now know that playing with toy guns is getting Black children—and Black boys in particular—killed. We know that, when Black boys are engaged in innocent childhood play activities, they are stereotyped and racially profiled, unlike their White boy counterparts. Black boys are also those who must be painstakingly taught life lessons to avoid becoming victims of anti-Black misandric violence in schools and communities. Reflecting on his early childhood play experiences, Clint Smith, a Black male author and poet, shared a similar story about his experience playing with a toy gun with his White friends in a hotel parking lot during a school field trip (J. Howard, 2019). Smith's father rebuked him for playing with the toy in a public space, and helped him to understand the potential cost for living and playing while Black. His father also informed him about the privileges and advantages of being White, which were not afforded to him but *were* afforded to his White friends, and the possibility of Black death for simply engaging in innocent play.

Play is both a language and literacy practice (Hale & Bocknek, 2016; Lewis-Ellison et al., 2018; Souto-Manning & Martell, 2016). However, Black boys' play is a language and literacy practice that is far too often misread, misunderstood, devalued, and unacknowledged in and beyond early childhood classrooms. Given that Black boys are socially constructed as monstrous and their bodies misread as dangerous, the ways in which they play are often described in the same manner (Bryan, 2020; J. Howard, 2019; Howard, 2014; Ulen, 2016). And yet, play is seen in many cultures in the United States, as an important element in children's positive academic, emotional, and social development (Trawick-Smith, 2020) which means that play is a right that is often denied to children of Color and especially Black boys (Bryan, 2020; Souto-Manning & Martell, 2016).

In this chapter, I confront the anti-Black misandric violence Black boys face during play in early childhood education. In so doing, I briefly discuss play, the types of play in which children engage, and the mischaracterization of Black boys' play in early childhood education and communities. Understanding its vital importance to the development of Black boys, my hope is that early childhood educators will learn to value, acknowledge, and appreciate the varying ways in which Black boys play. Such valuation, acknowledgement, and appreciation will require a paradigm shift in the ways many teachers view Black boys which requires reflection on their own stereotypes and the biases that inform the ways they view Black boys and boyhood play.

Understanding Play

Developmentalists such as Piaget, Vygotsky, and Erickson defined play as one of the most important elements of children's lives (Hale & Bocknek, 2016). Play is a child-selected event (Lewis-Ellison et al., 2018), and "a child's play is believed to reflect the degree to which they can impose their own sense of structure and sequence on the external environment" (Hale & Bocknek, 2016, p. 77). Nevertheless, there is no standard definition of play (Bergen & Fromberg, 2009). It is a diverse and multi-dimensional phenomenon, and "[in order] for an activity to count as play, it must be voluntary and self-organized" (p. 427). This particular definition is consistent with those of other definitions of play (Souto-Manning, 2017).

Play is an event through which children from diverse cultural backgrounds and with varying abilities experience joy and pleasure alone or with each other, and without the interference of adults (Trawick-Smith, 2020). It is a type of language and literacy practice wherein children engage in "scaffolding, but also … explore [their] multiple worlds" (Souto-Manning & Martell, 2016, p. 57) and is grounded in the cultural identities, experiences, and practices of those who are engaged in it (Dumas & Nelson, 2016); according to Dumas and Nelson (2016), play is not limited by age nor is it a restricted event, as it can be planned or unplanned. In the same way that Black boyhood can be understood as diverse, so too are the ways in which Black boys play (Dumas & Nelson, 2016). The diverse ways Black boys play, including defying hegemonic masculine and heteronormative expectations of boyhood play; e. g., the established societal norms and rules to which all men and boys are expected to adhere as defined by birth-assigned gender have been documented (Connell, 2005; Howard, 2019; Lewis-Ellison et al., 2018; McCready, 2004; Sumison, 1999).

Types of Play

Despite the varying definitions of play, several types of play in which young children engage have informed our thinking about play, at least in the United States. While an exhaustive list of the types of play is not presented in this section, several types of play are widely recognized in the field of early childhood education in this country. Here I focus on six of them: *motor play, pretend play, construction play, games, exploration*, and *digital play* (Trawick-Smith, 2020).

Motor play is a type of play experience during which "children perform spontaneous physical actions using different parts of their bodies" (p. 29). Examples of motor play include (but are not limited to) arts and crafts, board games, and geoboards, which enhance motor skills. Motor play is the most prevalent type of play among young children (Trawick-Smith, 2020). *Pretend play* or imaginative/fantasy play occurs when young children create make-believe events and scenarios (Bergen, 2013; Trawick-Smith, 2020). For example, Black boys who "play school," or imitate pedagogical and schooling practices are engaging in pretend play (Bryan & Jett, 2018). *Construction play* is defined as a type of play experience wherein young children use material items to build multidimensional structures, and young children may use cardboard boxes to build a fort (Trawick-Smith, 2020). *Game play* is a competitive event during which young children compete for rewards; it is also rule-based (Trawick-Smith, 2020). For some Black boys, playing basketball, football, or any sport-related activity constitutes game play. Game play is also inclusive of videogaming (Lewis-Ellison et al., 2018). Finally, Trawick-Smith (2020) contended that *exploration/problem-solving play* is a type of play during which children explore phenomena and/or work to solve problems. *Digital play*, which includes children's use of digit technology, including I-Pads (Lewis-Ellison et al., 2018). Each of these types of play can occur either solitarily or socially (Lillard et al., 2013).

Given the oral traditions of Black culture (Boykin, 1994), play is not only a habit of physical activity, but also one of linguistic expression (Dumas & Nelson, 2016). In Black communities, children engage in activities like *playing the dozens* (Smitherman, 1999), a game of playful linguistic expression used to jokingly embarrass someone and/or a member of someone's family, especially the mother. Such expression is often called *your momma's jokes* (Alim & Smitherman, 2012; Smitherman, 1999). Grounded in Black cultural ways of knowing and being, hip-hop play, coined by Broughton (2017) is a type of play experience that is informed by the elements of hip-hop including breakdancing, rapping, emceeing, and graffiti art. Although her scholarship does not focus on Black boys, Gaunt (2006) has identified the "games Black girls play" including *double dutch* and *hand games* that are informed by Black musical traditions including hip-hop. Perhaps collectively, the works of Broughton (2017) and Gaunt (2006) align with BlackBoyCrit Pedagogy, and can serve as a blueprint for providing possibilities for seeing and imagining Black boyhood play beyond the language of hypermasculinity that typically defines it.

The Academic and Social Benefits of Play

Regardless of the type of play in which young children engage, we know that play can lead to rich academic, social, emotional, cognitive, and physical benefits of play (Bergen, 2002, 2013; Broughton, 2017; Bruce et al., 2017; Hale & Bocknek, 2016; Lillard et al., 2013; Paley, 1992). As such, play is important in the lives of all children. However, because of its importance to the educational experiences of young children, I will focus (albeit briefly) on the academic and social benefits of play. In terms of academic benefits, young children who engage in play on a regular basis are far more likely to perform better in academic areas, including math and reading (Bulotsky-Shearer et al., 2011). Precisely, children who engage in frequent play can increase language proficiency by increasing the number of words they learn and by using more complex language structures, including verb tenses (Cohen & Uhry, 2007). Similarly, in math, young children who play can bolster mathematical reasoning and logical skillsets (Worthington & van Oers, 2016).

Children also benefit socially as they engage in frequent play experiences. One important social benefit of play is that young children learn to build positive relationships with other children and adults (Lewis-Ellison et al., 2018). They learn to be resilient (Hale & Bocknek, 2016). Children also learn appropriate social skills, including the ability to interact and collaborate with others. As such, play becomes an important part of young children's socioemotional development (Broughton, 2017; Hale & Bocknek, 2016). And yet, there is a growing movement to remove play from the early childhood curricula in order to allocate more time for the teaching of rigorous subject areas like math and reading, which are important for testing (Souto-Manning, 2017). Play and playtime are frequently being replaced by preparation for standardized testing (Lewis-Ellison et al. 2018).

Despite decades of research into children's play and the concomitant academic and social benefits, we know that most studies on play have remained color evasive, ignoring race and the racialized histories of children's play, and focusing largely on the play styles, behaviors, and experiences of White middle-class children (Adair & Doucet, 2014; Broughton, 2017; Bryan & Jett, 2018; Dumas & Nelson, 2016; Earick, 2010; Lewis-Ellison et al., 2018; Van Ausdale & Feagin, 2001). Most of those color evasive studies have also conflated race and socioeconomic status (Hale & Bocknek, 2016). Despite the fact that developmental processes are different across cultures (Bronfenbrenner & Morris, 1998; Cannella, 1997), there is a tendency in early childhood education to apply "data from non-diverse samples of children to Black American children ... in regard to play research" (Hale & Bocknek, 2016, p. 78). For example, scholars (Paley, 1992; Tobin, 1997) have promoted the importance of cross-cultural play (or the idea that play looks differently across cultural groups). However, in the cross-cultural play scholarship, the play behaviors, styles, and, experiences of White middle-class children are still centered as the norm against which other cultural groups are judged and measured (Rogoff, 2003). Therefore, cross-cultural play has ignored specific focus on the play experiences of Black children and boys in this case. Gregory et al. (2013) have emphasized the importance of moving beyond cross-cultural play to focus specifically on young children's engagement in syncretism: literacy processes that enable them to draw expertly on their own cultural backgrounds to create new spaces for play, teaching, and learning. Further contesting the literature on cross-cultural play, Hale and Bocknek (2016) have called for a framework that moves beyond the White gaze to honor the cultural backgrounds and play experiences of Black children. If we are to employ Black-BoyCrit Pedagogy in early childhood education, we must move beyond the White gaze and must learn more about the typology of Black children's play in general and boys' in particular, and perhaps such knowledge could possibly minimize the mischaracterization of Black boyhood play (Hale & Bocknek, 2016).

Exploring the Mischaracterization of Black Boys' Play

There are a few educational research studies that have been consistent with the developing ideas of BlackBoyCrit Pedagogy and have brought attention to the anti-Black misandric violence Black boys experience during play. For example, Rosen's (2017) 18-month ethnographic study on imaginative play examining "the responses of both children and educators to children's playful enactments of monster and the monstrous" (p. 179) in a London-based preschool/nursery found that the inscription of monsters were repeatedly placed on the bodies of Black boys (and other children of Color). In short, the roles of antagonists or "bad guys" that children enacted during imaginative play experiences were predominantly affixed to Black children. When Black boys and other children of Color engaged in imaginative play roles as monsters, early childhood educators attached socially constructed ideas of "monster" onto their bodies—ideas that became difficult to interrupt after those play experiences. In contrast, when White children played similar monstrous roles, they were not attached to such monstrosity after play.

A recent, groundbreaking study on play not only reaffirms early childhood teachers' biases, fears, and stereotypes about Black boys, but also confirms their suspicions regarding their play experiences in preschool classrooms. Employing eye-tracking technological devices, Gilliam et al. (2016) followed the eye movements of 135 Black and White early childhood educators as they watched videos of four children (a Black boy and girl and a White boy and girl) playing in preschool settings. Although there were no incidents of misbehavior reflected in the videos, the teachers were asked to pay particular attention to misbehavior among the children. It was discovered that both Black and White early childhood teachers disproportionately identified misbehavior in Black boys' (and girls') play. Similarly, reflecting on a personal narrative about his experiences searching for a preschool he thought suitable for his Black daughters, Rich Milner (2020) recalled witnessing a teacher's hyperfocus on the perceived misbehavior of a Black boy. As he related,

> During one visit, I witnessed a group of five students (one Black and four White students) playing together in a classroom. As I watched, the preschool teacher told "Jamal," the Black student, "You're too loud. Let's use our indoor voice, please." The teacher turned back to me and continued answering my questions. Soon, she turned again to the five youngsters, but

again focused her words only on one: "Jamal, you are too loud. I'm going to have to ask you to take a seat if you keep it up." (p. 152)

Milner (2020) was stunned by the teacher's actions because he had witnessed a group of five students—not just Jamal—yelling and not using their "indoor voice [s]" (p. 152). The teacher's reaction to Jamal's play style is an example of anti-Black misandric violence and is clearly inconsistent with the developing ideas of BlackBoyCrit Pedagogy, which were discussed in Chapter 2.

Given teachers' stereotypes and biases relating to Black boys' play styles (Gilliam et al., 2016), Black boys far too often experience exclusionary discipline during play. They are removed from play and recess time, and the overall recess time they receive in school decreases as the school year progresses (Bryan, in progress). As a former teacher and a current teacher educator, I have personally witnessed Black boys' exclusion from play. During these moments, Black boys are summoned to "stand against the wall" or to remain in the classroom to complete academic work during playtime. In other play-exclusionary measures, Black boys (and girls) are often removed from creative play to engage in more teacher-led academic activities (Earick, 2010; Lewis-Ellison et al., 2018). Considering the academic and social benefits of play, and teachers' biases against Black boyhood play, early childhood educators should consider the negative impact of exclusionary discipline on the reading and disciplinary outcomes of Black boys in early childhood education (Bryan, in progress).

Racial complexities can further complicate the play experiences of Black boys. While investigating the play styles and experiences of Black mixed-race boys in their schools, homes, and communities, Howard (2019) found that Black mixed-race boys are often subjected to anti-Black misandric violence during play. They often face difficulties navigating the Black-White binary, or the complexities of being both Black and White during play. In other words, these boys can't "just play," and be boys without being subjected to racial scrutiny (Howard, 2019). Particularly important to point out in the study are White mothers' denial of the racialized and gendered experiences of Black people in general and their Black mixed-race sons in particular. As such, White mothers who have Black mixed-race sons can inadvertently contribute to the types of anti-Black violence Black boys face during play by minimizing racialized narratives concerning Black people's experiences and the play experiences of Black boys.

Pinckney et al. (2018) noted that Black boys (and girls) suffer three types of losses during play and recreation. They included: (1) loss of innocence; (2) loss of freedom; and (3) loss of life. The loss of innocence, freedom, and life connotes that Black boys (and girls) are more prone to adultification, hypersurveillance, and physical murder than their White counterparts during play and recreation.

Because BlackBoyCrit Pedagogy requires educators to acknowledge the ways in which Black boys are victimized during play, it is important to bring attention to the fact that Black boys' play styles have often constructed Black boys as those who victimize others instead of being victims themselves (Mayeza, 2017). For example, Bhana and Mayeza (2016) conducted an ethnography on 35–40 Black/African seventh graders in a South African township. These boys engaged in what Bhana and Mayeza suggested was homophobic violence against Black boys who defied hegemonic masculine expectations of play. Mayeza (2017) studied the play behaviors of 64 Black boys (and girls) on a playground in a South African township, and found that these children worked to create gender boundaries, meaning that the children were adamant about ensuring they played according to gender norms and expectations, and chastised children who transgressed those boundaries.

While studies like this one are important to the literature on Black boys' play, they reify deficit tropes about Black boys as victimizers, which are already solidified in dominant narratives. Such deficit tropes play themselves out in classrooms and school playgrounds, thereby explaining why Black boys are disproportionately suspended and expelled from schools as early as early childhood education and play time and recess are often restricted (Bryan, in progress; Gilliam et al., 2016; Wright & Counsell, 2018; Wright & Ford, 2016).

Black boys have also been socially constructed as those who internalize anti-Black misandry or uphold the dominant deficit beliefs about Black boys during play. Consider Kenneth and Mamie Clark's (1947) doll study, which is widely known for its contributions to Civil Rights arguments, and was a key component in judicial arguments for desegregating schools (Tuck, 2009). The study purported to demonstrate the negative impact of white supremacy on the psychology of Black children (Clark & Clark, 1947; Tuck, 2009). During the study, Black boys (and girls) were presented with options of Black and White dolls. They were asked to consider the doll that best described and represented who they were. The children consistently selected the White doll. Most of the children even characterized the Black doll as the "bad" doll. In other words, they internalized anti-Blackness and misandry, the disdain for Black people and boys in particular (Curry, 2017; Dumas & ross, 2016). Replications of Clark and Clark's work (Sturdivant & Alanis, 2021) continue to produce similar results, which means that the play experiences of Black children and especially boys are informed by internalized anti-Black misandry. BlackBoyCrit Pedagogy requires early childhood educators to collaborate with Black boys to work against anti-Black misandry and dominant deficit beliefs about their play styles, behaviors, and experiences.

Moreover, play therapy in the lives of Black boys and, by extension, Black boyhood play styles and experiences has recently become an important topic. In his book titled *Playing with Anger: Teaching Coping Skills to African-American Boys Through Athletics and Culture*, Stevenson (2003) proposed that play can be used to assist Black boys in confronting anger, which often stems from race, racism, and anti-Black misandry in their lives and the ways they are socially constructed in schools and society writ large. As such, he provides culturally relevant strategies through play-based interventions. However, I believe these interventions uphold what Stevenson himself has termed "the essentialistic becoming of Black male identity" (p. 4), or the tendency to construct Black boys based on male group identity and/or in homogeneous and one-dimensional ways. In other words, not all boys play sports and/or are athletic; however, they do engage in play experiences that may defy rigid hegemonic masculine norms and expectations (Bryan, 2020). Stated more pointedly, Stevenson (2003) narrowly defined play (e.g., sports and athletics), but did not provide much allowance for the varying ways Black boys engage in play beyond hypermasculine constructions. Unfortunately, to ignore the diversity of Black boyhoods and play experiences is an act of anti-Black misandric violence.

Because BlackBoyCrit Pedagogy centralizes the diverse expressions of boyhoods and play, early childhood educators must begin to acknowledge the diversity of Black boys' play. Most people generally have a one-dimensional, biased, and stereotypical view of Black boys' play, which I have described as anti-Black misandric in nature (McCready, 2004). In my own work (Bryan, 2020), I have argued in favor of Black boys who defy rigid Black masculine constructions of play by performing multiple masculine expressions of it. Indeed, Black boys are narrowly constructed as being interested in playing basketball and football, and those who do not engage in these activities are often perceived as less masculine. Important work on the play experiences of Black boys who self-identify as non-gender conforming and/or queer has started to emerge and become an important topic (McCready, 2004). Curry's (2017) critique of multiple masculinities has suggested that

> while male descendants of colonizers (i.e., White men and boys) are recognized for the naturally occurring varieties of masculinities within their group, this insistence on multiple masculinities has often been denied to Black men [and boys] who are the descendants of [enslaved Africans]. (p. 3)

In other words, White men and boys are freely able to express varying masculinities in ways that Black men and boys are not, and this can even occur during play (Curry, 2017). Consequently, we need a theory that attends to the myriad ways Black boys are raced and gendered during play.

We are also starting to learn more about the play experiences and styles of children with disabilities (Trawick-Smith, 2020). The play styles and experiences of Black boys with disabilities is a crucial topic to consider in discussions of play. If Black boys without disabilities are disenfranchised during play both in and beyond early childhood education, imagine the experiences of those with disabilities. The deafening silence on the play experiences of Black boys with disabilities is not only an act of racial violence but also of anti-Black misandry. We owe it to this population to honor the diversity of Black boyhood play by focusing on Black boys with disabilities like Ameer, who I introduced in Chapter 4. Ameer has autism. Toward that end, early childhood educators must work to support Black boys with disabilities in classrooms.

Conclusion

In conclusion, play is an important element in the lives of all children; it leads to a host of academic and social benefits for those children who actively play. However, for Black boys, play is a complex racialized and gendered phenomenon that leads to severe consequence including death. We must change this reality for Black boys by helping those who actively engage with them to confront their anti-Black misandry of Black boys play. Considering the need to further understand play, types of play, and the focus on the mischaracterization and concomitant consequences of Black boys' play, in Chapter 8, I extend BlackBoyCrit Pedagogy by introducing what I term *BlackBoy (Play)Crit Literacies* to address the anti-Black misandry Black boys face, and to celebrate the rich histories of the diverse ways in which they play.

References

Adair, J. K., & Doucet, F. (2014). The impact of race and culture on play in early childhood classrooms. In L.Brooker, M.Blaise, & S. Edwards (Eds.), *The SAGE handbook of play and learning in early childhood* (pp. 354–365). SAGE.

Alim, H. S., & Smitherman, G. (2012). *Articulate while black: Barack Obama, language, and race in the U.S.* Oxford University Press.

Bergen, D. (2013). Does pretend play matter? *Psychological Bulletin*, 139(1), 45–48.

Bergen, D. (2002). The role of pretend play in children's cognitive development. *Early Childhood Research & Practice*, 4(1), 1–8.

Bergen, D., & Fromberg, D. (2009). Play and social interaction in middle childhood. *Phi Delta Kappan*, 90(6), 426–430.

Bhana, D., & Mayeza, E. (2016). We do not play with gays, they're not real boys … they can't fight: Hegemonic masculinity and (homophobic) violence in the primary years of schooling. *International Journal of Educational Development*, 51(1), 34–42.

Boykin, A. W. (1994). Afrocultural expresseion and its implications for schooling. In E. Hollins, J. King, & W. Hayman (Eds.), *Teaching diverse populations: Formulating a knowledge base* (pp. 243–273). State University of New York Press.

Bronfenbrenner, U., & Morris, P. A. (1998). The ecology of developmental processes. In W. Damon (Series Ed.) & R. M. Lerner (Vol.), *Handbook of child psychology: Theoretical models of human development* (5th ed., Vol. 1, pp. 993–1028). Wiley.

Broughton, A. (2017). Being hip to their hop: Tapping into young minds through hip-hop play. *International Journal of Early Years Education*, 25(3), 323–335.

Bruce,T., Hakkarainen, P., & Brediktye, M. (2017). *The Routledge international handbook of early childhood play*. Routledge.

Bryan, N. (in progress). Investigating teachers' exclusionary practices in black boyhood play.

Bryan, N. (2020). Shaking the bad boys: Troubling the criminalization of black boys' childhood play, white hegemonic masculinity and femininity, and 'the school playground-to-prison pipeline.' *Race, Ethnicity, and Education*, 23(5), 673–692. doi:10.1080/13613324.2018.1512483

Bryan, N., & Jett, C. (2018). "Playing School": Creating possibilities to inspire future black male teachers through culturally relevant play. *Journal of Multicultural Education*, 12(2), 99–110.

Bulotsky-Shearer, R. J., Manz, P. H., Mendez, J. L., McWayne, C. M., Sekino, Y., & Fantuzzo, J. W. (2011). Peer play interactions and readiness to learn: A protective influence for African-American preschool children from low-income households. *Child Development Perspectives*, 6(3), 225–231.

Cannella, G. S. (1997). *Deconstructing early childhood education: Social justice and revolution*. Peter Lang.

Clark, K., & Clark, M. (1947). *Racial identification and preference in negro children*. In T. M. Newcomb, & E. L. Harley (Eds.), *Reading in social psychology* (pp. 169–178). Holt Rinehart and Winston.

Cohen, L., & Uhry, J. (2007). Young children's discourse strategies during block play: A Bakhtinian approach. *Journal of Research in Childhood Education*, 21(3), 302–315.

Connell, R. W. (2005). *Masculinities*. University of California Press.

Curry, T. (2017). *Man-not: Race, class, genre and the dilemmas of black manhood*. Temple University Press.

Dumas, M., & Nelson, J. (2016). Reimagining black boyhood: Toward a critical framework for educational research. *Harvard Educational Review*, 86(1), 27–47.

Dumas, M., & ross. K. (2016). "Be real black for me": Imagining BlackCrit in education. *Urban, Education*, 51(4), 415–442.

Earick, M. (2010). The power of play and language on early childhood racial identity in three US schools. *Diaspora, Indigenous, and Minority Education*, 4(2), 131–145.

Fiedstadt, E. (2018, October 16). Columbus PD says video of officer stopping two black boys with BB guns serves a 'lesson.' *NBC News*. https://www.nbcnews.com/news/us-news/columbus-pd-says-video-officer-stopping-two-black-boys-bb-n920671

Gaunt, K. (2006). *The games black girls play: Learning the ropes from double-dutch to hip-hop*. New York University Press.

Gilliam, W. S., Maupin, A., Reyes, G. R., Accavitti, M. and Frederick, S. (2016). *Do early educators' implicit biases regarding sex and race relate to behavior expectations and recommendations of preschool expulsions and suspensions?* Yale Childhood Study Center.

Gregory, E., Volk, D., & Long, S. (2013). Guest editor's introduction: Syncretism and syncretic literacies. *Journal of Early Childhood Literacy*, 13(3), 309–321.

Hale, J. E., & Bocknek, E. (2016). Applying a cultural prism to the study of play behavior of black children. *The Negro Educational Review*, 67(1), 77–105.

Hartman, S. V. (2007). *Lose your mother*. Farrar.

Hauser, C. (2018, October 17). 'I could have killed you,' Ohio officer warns two boys with BB gun. *The New York Times*. https://www.nytimes.com/2018/10/17/us/bb-gun-boy- police.htmlwww.nytimes.com/2018/10/17/us/bb-gun-boy- police.html.

Howard, J. (2019). Just playin': Black mixed-race boys and the injustices of boyhood. *Race, Ethnicity, and Education*. https://doi.org/10.1080/13613324.2019.1679760

Howard, T. (2014). *Black maled: Perils and promises in the education of African American males*. Teacher College Press

Lewis-Ellison, T., Solomon, M., & Rowsell, J. (2018). Digital play as purposeful production literacies in African American boys. *The Reading Teacher*, 71(4), 495–500.

Lillard, A. S., Lerner, M. D., Hopkins, E. J., Dore, R. A., Smith, E. D., & Palmquist, C. M. (2013). The impact of pretend play on children's development: A review of the evidence. *Psychological Bulletin*, 139(1), 1–34.

Lorde, A. (1984). *Sister outsider: Essays and speeches by Audre Lorde*. Crossing Press.

Mayeza, E. (2017). "Girls don't play soccer": Children policing gender on the playground in a township primary school in South Africa. *Gender and Education*, 29(4), 476–494.

McCready, L. (2004). Understanding the marginalization of gay and gender non-conforming black male students. *Theory Into Practice*, 43(2), 136–143.

Milner, H. R. (2020). Disrupting punitive practices and policies: Rac(e)ing back to teaching, teacher preparation, and Brown . *Educational Researcher*, 49(3), 147–160.

Paley, V. (1992). *You can't say, you can't play*. Harvard University Press.

Pinckney IV, H. P., Outley, C., Brown, A., & Theriault, D. (2018). Playing while black. *Leisure Sciences*, 40(7), 675–685.

Rogoff, B. (2003). *The cultural nature of human development*. Oxford University Press.

Rosen, R. (2017). Between play and the quotidian: Inscriptions of monstrous characters on the racialised bodies of children. *Race, Ethnicity and Education*, 20(2), 178–191.

Smitherman, G. (1999). *Talkin that talk: Language, culture, and education in African America*. Routledge.

Souto-Manning, M. (2017). Is play a privilege or right? And what's our responsibility? On the role of play for equity in early childhood education. *Early Childhood Development and Care*, 187(5–6),785–787.

Souto-Manning, M., & Martell, J. (2016). *Reading, writing, and talk inclusive teaching strategies for diverse learners, K-2*. Teachers College Press.

Stevenson, H. (2003). *Playing with Anger: Teaching coping skills to African-American boys through athletics and culture*. Praeger.

Sturdivant, T., & Alanis, I. (2021). "I'm gonna cook my baby in a pot": Young Black girls' racial preferences and play behavior. *Early Childhood Education Journal*, 49(3), 473–482.

Sumison, J. (1999). Critical reflections on the experiences of male early childhood workers. *Gender and Education*, 11(4), 455–468.

Tobin, J. (1997). *Making a place for pleasure in early childhood education*. Yale University Press.

Trawick-Smith, J. (2020). *Young children's play: Development, disabilities, and diversity*. Routledge.

Tuck, E. (2009). Suspending damage: A letter to communities. *Harvard Educational Review*, 79(3), 409–427.

Ulen, E. N. (2016, July 25). When play is criminalized: Racial disparities in childhood. *Truthout*. www.truth-out.org/articles/item/36947-when-play-is-criminalized-racial-disparities-in-childhood

Van Ausdale, D., & Feagin, J. (2001). *The first r: How children learn race and racism*. Rowman & Littlefield.

Worthington, M. and van Oers, B. (2016). Pretend play and the cultural foundations of mathematics. *European Early Childhood Education Research Journal*, 24(3), 51–66.

Wright, B., & Counsell, S. (2018). *The brilliance of black boys: Cultivating success in the early grades*. Teacher College Press.

Wright, B., & Ford, D. (2016). "This little light of mine": Creating early childhood classroom experiences for African-American boys PreK-3. *Journal of African American Males in Education*, 7(1), 5–19.

Yancy, G. (2017). *Black bodies, white gazes: The continuing significance of race* (2nd ed.). Rowman & Littlefield.

8

FACILITATING *BLACKBOY (PLAY)CRIT LITERACIES* IN EARLY CHILDHOOD CLASSROOMS

Roland's Portrait of Mr. Henry

Centralizing BlackBoyCrit Pedagogy to understand the landscape of Black boyhood play was laid out in the previous chapter and included the physical murder of a child, Tamir Rice; racist warnings given to Black boys at play by police officer Peter Casuccio; my own spiritual murder at age 10 by a White women who, in clicking her car locks, communicated her disdain for and fear of me; the misrepresentation of Black boys at play in early childhood classrooms; and the attempts by so-called cross cultural research to extrapolate findings about children from a range of cultural and national groups to Black children. So, how does a Black male teacher create a counter play space for a Black boy in an early childhood classroom, and, in so doing, academically engage him? Similarly, how does a Black male teacher use the notion of play as a social justice tool to deepen the anti-Black misandric consciousness of Black boys in early childhood education? To answer these questions, I highlight the perceptions of Roland on Mr. Henry's use of play. Mr. Henry provided Roland a counter play space and demonstrated the use of play as a social justice tool to deepen Roland's anti-Black misandric consciousness. As such, Mr. Henry drew on elements of BlackBoyCrit Pedagogy to engage in what I term *BlackBoy (Play)Crit Literacies* in his early childhood classroom. Table 8.1 provides an overview of the characteristics of BlackBoy (Play)Crit Literacies as a praxis of BlackBoyCrit Pedagogy. Furthermore, similar to Chapters 4 and 6, the "Zoom out" section of this chapter highlights italicized sub-headings that acknowledge the characteristics of BlackBoy (Play)Crit Literacies as a praxis of BlackBoyCrit Pedagogy.

Because few scholars have investigated how Black male teachers use play in the early childhood classroom, Roland's perceptions of Mr. Henry's critical use of play in the classroom is an important phenomenon. While some studies (Black et al., 1999; Leavell et al., 2012) have highlighted the ways in which Black fathers have used play to build relationships with their sons, even fewer studies (Broughton, 2017) have

DOI: 10.4324/9780429287619-9

TABLE 8.1 BlackBoy (Play)Crit Literacies as a Praxis of BlackBoyCrit Pedagogy

- Helping Black boys understand anti-Black misandry
- Deepening the anti-Black misandric consciousness among White children
- Integrating play examples into a children's book to simply complex topics
- Holding space for Black boys' emotions
- Encouraging a stand against anti-Black misandry
- Acknowledging Black mothers' concerns for the play lives of Black boys

recorded the ways Black male teachers in early childhood education have taken up play to engage Black boys in the academic enterprise and build relationships with them. Given that play is an essential component of children's lives and the early childhood curriculum, and that Black male teachers remain underrepresented in early childhood classrooms (Bristol & Goings, 2019; Trawick-Smith, 2020; Lynn, 2006), Black male teachers' facilitations of play continue to be a ripe area for exploration in academic literature. As such, Roland's perceptions of Mr. Henry's use of play help us better understand how Black male teachers use play as a pedagogical tool in the classroom. To that end, I begin this chapter by sharing Roland's perceptions of Mr. Henry's critical use of play as a foundation for the description of *BlackBoy (Play)Crit Literacies* that follows.

Portraits of Black Male Teachers

Zoom In

"I couldn't play with Kate."

—*Roland*

During a literacy discussion circle in his kindergarten classroom at Ponce De Leon Elementary, Mr. Henry led 6-year-old Roland (who was introduced in Chapter 4), and two of his classmates—Kate and John (a White girl and a White boy)—in a critical discussion about segregation. Mr. Henry's literacy discussion circles typically consisted of three to four students, which enabled Mr. Henry to build intimate relationships with them and informally assess his students' progress in reading. These literacy circles took place at a round table in the back of his classroom. The round table was situated in front of cabinets and shelves, where Mr. Henry stored books and other teaching resources for easy access. During the literacy circle, Mr. Henry's teacher assistant, Mrs. Wheeler (pseudonym)—a middle-aged White female—assisted the other students with independent assignments. (In addition to literacy discussion circles, Mr. Henry also used Morning Meetings [Kriete & Davis, 1999/2014] as a teaching tool to build classroom community and to center issues of social justice. Morning Meetings are most frequently used by early childhood teachers to facilitate similar critical discussions with the entire class.)

Mr. Henry used the children's book by Meltzer (2016) titled *I am brave: A little book about Martin Luther King, Jr.* to engage his students in the important conversation on segregation. The book highlights the life and legacy of Dr. Martin Luther King, Jr., and, by extension, Black people's collective struggle for civil rights. Mr. Henry frequently used such literature to engage young learners in critical conversations and to draw on their personal lived experiences in his early childhood classroom.

When Mr. Henry read a page from *I am brave: A little book about Martin Luther King, Jr.*, he paused briefly to give his students opportunities to react to what was being read and to make connections to their own lives and experiences. On that day, he used illustrations from the book to introduce the small group to the word *segregation*. *Segregation* is a complex one for most kindergarteners, and many of the young learners, including Roland, grappled with Mr. Henry's explanation of it for several minutes. Mr. Henry soon intervened with a child-friendly elucidation of the word, and used several relatable examples to help them understand. As Mr. Henry explained, during segregation, he would not have been allowed to teach Kate and John because he is a Black man.

Responding to Mr. Henry's example, Roland asked, "So you mean you couldn't be their teacher?"

Mr. Henry explained that laws prevented the integration of White and Black people in public spaces, including schools, and even though those laws have since been changed, segregation is still present in our society. Nevertheless, he added, the children's ability to attend school with students from diverse backgrounds was evidence of the nation's progress. Using the friendship bonds Roland and Kate had forged and the social play in which they engaged during recess, Mr. Henry explained to Roland that, during segregation, he would not have been allowed to play with Kate.

Roland was shocked. "I couldn't play with Kate?"

Mr. Henry acknowledged Roland's emotions and affirmed his statement, adding that segregation prevented Black and White children from attending the same schools and playing on the same playgrounds. The young learners continued to ask questions about segregation and its implications, and Mr. Henry explained that, although, as American citizens, we have made progress, we still have more work to do to ensure social equity for all American citizens. As such, Mr. Henry encouraged his students to be a part of the change we still need, and he helped them understand their roles in producing that change.

This was not the first time I saw Mr. Henry use play in the teaching and learning process. In fact, play was an integral part of his classroom, and he often incorporated it into the curriculum in several content areas, including math (as was described in Chapter 6). I believe Mr. Henry centered play in his instructional process because of his own history playing sports in high school and college and his current position as high school football coach, which helped him understand the power and importance of play in the lives of Black boys. In a way, Mr. Henry's classroom gave way to the school playground, and for his students, the two spaces had a symbiotic relationship.

Roland's experiences living and playing in an anti-Black misandric world is also one of the concerns of his mother, Mrs. Boins (introduced in Chapter 4). For this reason, she appreciated Mr. Henry's sharing his lived realities with Roland, which she explained during one of our conversations. As she related,

> Well, I am very concerned about my son because of recent events and race relations and [Black boys/men] being killed and shot in the streets and when they play. I'm raising a black man and a black youth. That concerns me tremendously … his safety in life and during play. Being stigmatized and generalized because he is a Black male—that worries me all the time. I try to raise my son accordingly, acknowledging those fears, but that scares the death out of me. I also worry because my son is Black and very smart; at some point, someone will try to dim his light because he is very intelligent. It's very scary for a lot of people, whether we want to admit it or not.

She further added that most White teachers and police misunderstand, generalize, and stigmatize Black boys (and men), and that Black boys (and men) are left to suffer dire consequences, including physical and spiritual murder. She constantly shared these kinds of conversations with Mr. Henry.

Zoom Out

BlackBoyCrit Pedagogy positions Black male teachers as effective pedagogues who are able to meet the academic and social needs of Black boys in early childhood classrooms. Because of the one-dimensional view (i.e, disciplinarians) of Black male teachers overshadows their pedagogical acumen as described in Chapter 3, Black male teachers are rarely constructed as those who know how to effectively teach. Similarly, considering that they were once young Black boys and most of them were stereotypically presumed nonreaders, Black male teachers are perceived to be unable to teach early literacy. However, Mr. Henry's literacy discussion circle that led to a focus on children's play, raises several key pedagogical considerations in the teaching of early literacy that are worth exploring. I would suggest that it is not by happenstance that, by positioning himself in the lesson, Mr. Henry gave his students a glimpse of his experiences as a Black man, and illuminated how, both historically and presently, there are consequences for living and teaching while Black. In other words, by drawing on his current reality (e.g., being the only Black male teacher on faculty) as well as what would have been his historical reality (e.g., not being able to teach Kate and John during segregated schooling), he helped his students understand how anti-Black misandry historically and presently operate in American society and in schools. In that regard, he was intimately connecting the past and present by helping his students understand both realities. BlackBoyCrit Pedagogy requires Black male teachers to be aware of themselves in such a way, and to use their lived anti-Black misandric experiences to not only inform the teaching and learning process, but to support the anti-Black consciousness development of their students. Roland is not the only student who benefits from the ways in which Mr. Henry draws on his experiences; Kate and John who are also part of the literacy practice. This demonstrates the flexible nature of BlackBoyCrit Pedagogy; any student can benefit from its use and application.

Helping Black Boys Understand Anti-Black Misandry

While the glimpse into Mr. Henry's professional life was important to share for all the students in the literacy discussion circle, it was especially important for Roland, a Black boy. As he transitions from boyhood to manhood (Ladson-Billings, 2011), Roland will need to understand the consequences of living in an anti-Black misandric world. And, BlackBoyCrit Pedagogues like Mr. Henry draw on their personal lived anti-Black misandric experiences to interpret the world *with* rather than *for* boys like Roland. When Black boys are younger, most White people consider them to be cute instead of intelligent (Ladson-Billings, 2011). However, when they are older, they are perceived as men, and receive adult consequences in and beyond schools. Like Mr. Henry, Roland have faced and will face consequences for his Black boy and Black male subjectivities. This is the knowledge Mr. Henry wanted to impart to Roland during the literacy discussion circle as well as during other moments where he engaged with him and other Black boys in the classroom.

Deepening the Anti-Black Misandric Consciousness among White Children

BlackBoyCrit Pedagogy is a pedagogical tool that can be used to support the anti-Black misandric consciousness of all children. While the glimpse into Mr. Henry's professional life was an important teachable moment for Roland, it was also a crucial teachable moment for Kate and John so that they too could understand the pervasiveness and historical and contemporary workings of anti-Black misandry. In other words, Roland is not the only student who benefited from the ways in which Mr. Henry drew on his lived professional experiences to help the children understand anti-Black misandry. This example was useful in deepening the anti-Black misandric consciousness of both Kate and John who are not only constantly bombarded with anti-Black misandric messages, stereotypes, and biases about Black men and boys, but rarely have opportunities to discuss issues of anti-Black misandry during literacy circles in early childhood classrooms. It is important to reiterate that most early childhood teachers uphold color evasive practices in classrooms, which means they avoid teaching about issues such as race, racism, and anti-Black misandry (Boutte et al., 2011). They also believe children are too young to engage in such conversations. As such, most early childhood educators opt for developmentally appropriate frameworks and practices rather than a specific focus on countering anti-Black misandry. As adopted by the National Association of the Education of Young Children

(NAEYC), developmentally appropriate practice is a framework that uses developmental theories as a foundation for young children's teaching and learning processes (Gestwicki, 2017). Oftentimes, in early childhood education, educators sacrifice teaching that counters anti-Black misandry for developmental practices, and presume that such teaching is antithetical to developmentally appropriate practice. Mr. Henry's pedagogy proves that this is far from the truth and that early childhood teacher can and do challenge conventional early childhood beliefs, ideologies, and curricula to deepen children's consciousness.

Furthermore, given the color evasive nature of early childhood education, most children's literature books tend to romanticize sociopolitical issues like segregation, and often whitewash the work of activists like Dr. Martin Luther King, Jr. Much like they believe children are too young to discuss issues of social injustices, most early childhood educators falsely assume that young children do not understand issues of social justice (Boutte et al., 2011). Black male teachers who use BlackBoyCrit Pedagogy challenge such myths as they center issues of anti-Black misandry, lessons that young children need to deepen anti-Black misandric consciousness in and beyond early childhood education.

Similarly, because BlackBoyCrit Pedagogues like Mr. Henry understand the importance of engaging *all children* in discourses about anti-Black misandry, the glimpse into Mr. Henry's professional life was also useful in demonstrating the flexible nature of BlackBoyCrit Pedagogy; it is clear that despite its focus on Black boys, BlackBoyCrit Pedagogy is far from exclusionary but can benefit *all children* in early childhood classrooms. As such, Mr. Henry's use and application of BlackBoyCrit Pedagogy can have a long-term positive impact beyond early childhood education, and especially for White children who will grow up to become adults and will most likely continue to perceive Black men and boys to be threats and threatening (Curry, 2017). Consequently, if early childhood teachers do not deepen their anti-Black misandric consciousness, White children will become adults who will weaponize their White privilege and entitlement by enacting anti-Black macroaggressions such as calling police officers on Black boys (and men) who they perceive to be threatening. Recently, Amy Cooper, a White woman, was walking her dog in a park, and Mr. Christian Cooper (not related to Amy) warned her about the illegality of her failure to leash her dog. Amy proceeded to call police to falsely claim she had been threatened by a Black man (Vera, 2020). These anti-Black misandric macroaggressions need to be disrupted and early childhood teachers, like Mr. Henry, can do so through the use and application of BlackBoyCrit Pedagogy to deepen the anti-Black misandric consciousness of *all children* in early childhood classrooms.

Integrating Play Examples into a Children's Book to Simplify Complex Topics

Although the book *I Am Martin Luther King, Jr.* was not specific to play, Mr. Henry was able to connect the themes presented in the book to the notion of play to help the children understand the term "segregation," In other words, by sharing the glimpse into Roland's and Kate's play relationship, Mr. Henry was able to draw on students' prior knowledge and experiences to facilitate the teaching and learning process and the children's understanding of the term "segregation." When Mr. Henry indicated that Roland could not play with Kate during segregation, he was intentionally pointing out the historical and contemporary nature of anti-Black misandry in the play lives of Black boys. As such, Roland later admitted that, after the play example, Mr. Henry "helped him understand he couldn't play with Kate." Roland's confession is an extremely powerful one. It demonstrated that Mr. Henry was not simply teaching an academic lesson on segregation, but a life lesson to deepen Roland's anti-Black misandric consciousness about the operation of anti-Black misandry in his own life.

Given that Black boys have been victims of anti-Black misandry during play with White girls (and boys) on and off the school playground, Mr. Henry's ability to deepen Roland's anti-Black misandric conscious through the use of a play example is a notable teachable moment. For example, in my own work (Bryan, 2020), I detailed a playground incident where a White girl was playing with Black boy twins. During an imaginative play experience, she pretended to choke the boys, and while swinging her head back and forth, she inadvertently headbutted one of the twins. She immediately began to cry, and blamed the boys for the mishap. Because White girls are often socialized into anti-Black misandry and deficit understandings of the ways in which Black boys play, such anti-Black misandry continuously occurs on and off the playground (Bryan, 2020). Black male teachers who employ Black-BoyCrit Pedagogy are intentional about drawing on children's books and other texts to help Black boys (and other children) to understand the consequences of anti-Black misandry in every aspect including play of the lives of Black boys.

Holding Space for Black Boys' Emotions

When Mr. Henry initially suggested that Roland could not play with Kate during segregated schooling, Roland was originally shocked, which is a typically reaction to such a discussion for young children who struggle to understand complex issues like segregation. However, Mr. Henry acknowledged Roland's emotion, and held space in a humanizing way for Roland as he worked through his emotions during the literacy discussion circle. BlackBoyCrit Pedagogy validates Black boys' emotions, and provides teachers who employ it opportunities to heal and humanize Black boys from anti-Black misandry in and beyond early childhood classrooms.

Encouraging a Stand against Anti-Black Misandry

Employing BlackBoyCrit Pedagogy, Mr. Henry also encouraged all of the children to take a stand against anti-Black misandry. He helped them understand their responsibilities to work toward countering anti-Black misandry, thus encouraging them to engage in the on-the-groundwork of dismantling social injustices—in ways similar to the praxis of enslaved African and young Black children on plantations (and during various civil rights movements). Enslaved African children played with White children to learn to read and write to help their enslaved parents to escape plantations (Perry et al., 2003).

Acknowledging Black Mothers' Concerns for the Play Lives of Black Boys

BlackBoyCrit Pedagogy positions Black families and communities as partners in the academic enterprise of Black boys. Mrs. Boins, Roland's mother, wrestled with the ongoing and intentional state-sanctioned murders of Black men and boys. The anti-Black misandric deaths of 14-year-old Trayvon Martin who was killed for walking while Black and 12-year-old Tamir Rice who was killed for playing while Black caused her to be concerned for Roland's life and safety during play. Much like he had done for Roland, Mr. Henry listened to, heard, understood, and empathized with Mrs. Boins who was concerned for her Black son. Unfortunately, Mrs. Boins' concerns are still valid because, at the time of this writing, Ahmad Arbery, a 25-year-old Black male, was shot while jogging in his own community in Brunswick, Georgia, by two White men who allegedly thought he was responsible for a recent rash of community burglaries (Fausset, 2020). As discussed in Chapters 2 and 4, when Black mothers (and fathers) are seen as informants and partners in the academic enterprise, their wisdom, worries, and pains can assist Black male teachers in supporting their sons in and beyond early childhood education.

Imagining *BlackBoy (Play)Crit Literacies* in Early Childhood Education

In Chapter 2, I proposed the expansiveness of BlackBoyCrit Pedagogy. By this I mean that when any curricula are topics of focus in curriculum planning or further theory development, it is then possible to place the subject matter in parentheses to demonstrate the expansiveness and the particular focus as the framework is considered across all elements of teaching and learning in early childhood education. Because Mr. Henry engaged in a range of literacy practices that provide exemplars for teachers employing BlackBoyCrit Pedagogy, I believe a few of those practices inspire the expansiveness of BlackBoyCrit Pedagogy and a new literacy practice that centers play. Based on Mr. Henry's use and application of children's books and other texts to acknowledge, celebrate, and bring attention to anti-Black misandry in Black boyhood play, his ability to deepen his students' anti-Black misandric consciousness through play examples, his willingness to acknowledge and hold space for Black boys' emotions during play and the critical examination of play, and to construct play as a social justice tool to confront anti-Black misandry in boyhood play in his early childhood classroom, I call for us to consider the potential of *BlackBoy (Play)* [1] *Crit Literacies*.

In his conception of Critical Race English Education (CREE), Johnson (2018) expressed the importance of integrating into the English Language Arts (ELA) curriculum Black literacies—language and literacy practices through books and other texts (i.e., videos, film, posters, and protests) that make explicit Black cultural ways of knowing and being. Johnson further defined Black literacies as an embodied and social practice, meaning that language and literacy is "who we are and what we do." It may also be inclusive of "tattoos, poems, novellas, graphic novels, technology/social media sites, oral histories/storytelling, body movements/dance, music, and prose" (p. 109). Borrowing from Johnson's notion of Black literacies, as well as Mr. Henry's literacy practices, I define BlackBoy (Play)Crit Literacies as literacy practices which center a multiplicity of Black historical and contemporary texts that specifically address anti-Black misandry and highlights and celebrates the beauty, diversity, and positive contributions of Black boys' play. In this way, BlackBoy (Play)Crit Literacies is a critical literacy tool (Boutte, 2016) to deepen the anti-Black misandric consciousness of Black boys (and other children) by confronting anti-Black misandry and deficit perceptions of Black boys' play as reflected in texts. Because expressing emotions is a language and literacy practice, BlackBoy (Play)Crit also encompasses all the emotions Black boys may experience during play and the critical examination of play. This includes the ability to be shocked (much like Roland) and to "giggle, play, cry, pout, and be just as silly and frivolous as other children" (Dumas & Nelson, 2016, p. 39).

Practical Recommendations for Early Childhood Educators

Similar to what I have done in previous chapters that highlighted the pedagogies, literacies, and schooling practices of Black male teachers through the eyes of Black boys, I provide practical recommendations/examples for teachers in order to encourage them to apply BlackBoy (Play)Crit Literacies as a praxis of Black-BoyCrit Pedagogy in their classrooms. While Mr. Henry has provided clear examples including helping Black boys understand anti-Black misandry, developing anti-Black misandric consciousness among White children, integrating play examples into a children's book to simplify complex topics, holding space for Black boys' emotions, encouraging a stand against anti-Black misandry, acknowledging Black mothers' concern for the play lives of Black boys, and implementing BlackBoy (Play)Crit Literacies in his early childhood classroom, early childhood educators are encouraged to consider the recommendations I

TABLE 8.2 Practical Recommendations for Early Childhood Educators

- Acknowledge the importance of play
- See play as a tool to name and dismantle anti-Black misandry
- Integrate Black literacies into play
- Allow Black boys to express all types of emotions
- Integrate the teaching of BlackBoy (Play)Crit literacies into teacher education programs

provide in Table 8.2, and develop their own practices supporting BlackBoy (Play) Crit Literacies as a praxis of BlackBoyCrit Pedagogy.

Acknowledge the Importance of Play

Most early childhood educators are removing play from the early childhood education curriculum (Broughton, 2017). However, Mr. Henry is intentional about centering play in and across the curriculum. He consistently integrated play into literacy, math, and other subject areas. Early childhood educators who employ BlackBoy (Play)Crit Literacies as a praxis of BlackBoyCrit Pedagogy must acknowledge the importance of play in the lives of children, and especially in the lives of Black boys. Because there are a host of academic and social benefits to play as discussed in Chapter 7, teachers should maximize instead of minimize play time among Black boys in early childhood education.

See Play as a Tool to Name and Dismantle Anti-Black Misandry

Through his literacy discussion circle, Mr. Henry not only demonstrated how play can be influenced by anti-Black misandry, but also how it can be used to dismantle it. He helped his students (Roland, Kate, and John) deepen their anti-Black misandric consciousness and to understand the need to counter anti-Black misandry and all other forms of oppression in their lives and the lives of others. Teachers and other educators who employ BlackBoy (Play)Crit Literacies as a praxis of BlackBoyCrit Pedagogy must help all children see play as a tool to name, identify, and dismantle anti-Black misandry.

Integrate Black Literacies into Play

Mr. Henry used a children's book about Dr. Martin Luther King Jr. to address a critical topic—segregation—through the use of play examples. Teachers can employ BlackBoy (Play)Crit Literacies by integrating historical and contemporary texts to support their own learning and student learning to "love on Blackness" (Johnson et al., 2017, p. 60), and to challenge anti-Black misandry, and deficit perceptions of Black boys' childhood play. A few examples of BlackBoy (Play)Crit Literacies include children's and youth literature that highlight anti-Black misandric experiences and the positive contributions of Black boys during play, such as Smith's (2007) *12 Rounds of Glory to Glory: The Story of Muhammad Ali*, and Abdul-Jabbar's (2017) *Becoming Kareem: Growing Up On and Off The Courts*. Similarly, early childhood educators may find compelling Clint Smith's—an American writer— TED Talk titled "How to Raise a Black Son in America," which elucidates his play experiences as a young Black boy whose father assisted in his anti-Black misandric consciousness—an awareness of his social, racial, and gendered positioning in the world—during play with his White friends. Teachers can also put Smith's story in conversation with the story of James Thompson and David Simpson, two Black boys who were accused of raping and kissing a White girl in 1958, while playing in a White community in Munroe, North Carolina. As a result, the boys were arrested. This case is widely known as the "The Kissing Case" (Sherouse, 2016).

Because Mr. Henry used a children's book to facilitate his literacy discussion circle, I want to help teachers consider other texts that can be useful in employing BlackBoy (Play)Crit Literacies. Since teachers who employ BlackBoyCrit Pedagogy and subsequently BlackBoy (Play)Crit Literacies must see texts broadly, they can also use historical and contemporary texts including posters, songs, and toys. For example, early childhood educators can use posters of Black men who used play and sports to stand up for social justice. They can place the poster of Colin Kaepernick, a Black male football player, in conversation with posters of the Black male Olympians including Tommie Smith and John Carlos who, in 1968, took a stand for justice by raising the Black power fist during the medal ceremony to acknowledge the mattering ogf Black lives (Brown, 2017). Given songs are also a type of literacy, teachers can teach Black boys the history of and critique of racist play songs, including "Eeney Meeney, Miney Moe," which originally referred to Black people as "niggers" (Raphael, 2015). Teachers can encourage Black boys to identify racist toys such as Pradamalia, a line of figurines and other accessories released in 2018 that featured racist keychains and toys that evoked racist imagery, such as monkeys (Albanese & Williams, 2018).

Allow Black Boys to Express All Types of Emotions

When Mr. Henry explained to Roland that he could not play with Kate during segregation, Roland was shocked. And, Mr. Henry held space for him to deal with such emotion. As such, BlackBoy (Play)Crit Literacies should include all the emotions that Black boys may freely experience during critical lesson on play. This includes the ability to be shocked and to "giggle, play, cry, pout, and be just as silly and frivolous as other children" (Dumas & Nelson, 2016, p. 39). To that end, when Black boys express such emotions, they should not be perceived as less masculine and/or stereotypically feminine. Rather, Black boys' expressions of emotions should be seen as valued male traits.

Integrate the Teaching of BlackBoy (Play)Crit Literacies into Preservice Teacher Education

Although much of what Mr. Henry learned about integrating play critically into the early childhood education curricula he learned by drawing on his own experiences and those of his Black boy students, teachers who desire to employ BlackBoy (Play)Crit Literacies as an extension of BlackBoyCrit Pedagogy must be prepared to do so in preservice teacher education programs. That means that preservice teacher educators should infuse such pedagogical and literacy frameworks into their courses. Each semester, I introduce and infuse Black-BoyCrit Pedagogy and BlackBoy (Play)Crit Literacies and others critical literacy frameworks into my language and literacy courses. Early childhood educators should also be inspired by my preservice teachers at Miami University in Oxford, Ohio, who, after learning about BlackBoy (Play)Crit Literacies in a course titled *Teaching Language and Literacy across the Early Childhood Curriculum*, were themselves inspired by the literacy practice, and decided to develop lesson plans to academically and socially support young Black boys with whom they worked during their field and practicum experiences.

Ms. Janae Sneed, a Black junior early childhood major who was enrolled in my literacy course, developed a lesson plan centering on BlackBoy (Play)Crit Literacies to deepen the critical consciousness of a Black third grade student in an urban elementary school in Cincinnati, Ohio. Understanding the young boy's interest in videogaming, Janae engaged Caden (pseudonym) in a lesson on the video game *Fortnite*, a lesson grounded in Ohio State's Reading Standards. According to Janae, she noticed that, during their lessons, Caden often spoke about the notion of *skins*, an important component of *Fortnite*. Caden's explanation of the notion of skins to Janae led her to believe that the game perpetuated anti-Black misandric ideologies. As such, Janae wanted to further explore *Fortnite* and the notion of skins with Caden, so she constructed a lesson designed to support not only Caden's ability to read, but also his ability to read the world of videogaming.

Similarly, Brittany Wade, a Black female early childhood major in her junior year, who was also enrolled in my course, developed a lesson plan grounded in BlackBoy (Play)Crit Literacies. Understanding that many young boys in early childhood education are interested in wrestling, and drawing on her own interest in wrestling as a young child, Brittany was aware of the ways anti-Black misandry was perpetuated through the sport. For example, she noticed that many Black male wrestlers were referred to as having "nappy hair" by White wrestlers. As such, she wanted to confront such injustices, and deepen the anti-Black misandric consciousness of as well as build Black pride among the Black boys she taught during her practicum experience at an urban elementary school in Cincinnati, Ohio. Tables 8.3 and 8.4 are examples of the lesson plans developed by both Janae and Brittany. It is important to note that both used Ohio State Literacy Standards to facilitate these BlackBoy (Play)Crit Literacies lessons. Teachers oftentimes fail to address critical issues in early childhood education because they believe such issues are not aligned with state standards (Baines et al., 2018). However, Janae's and Brittany's lessons make clear that teachers can tie state standards to critical lessons in and beyond early childhood education.

Conclusion

Black boys deserve to play, and those rights must be extended to them in both schools and communities. Grounded in critical race theories including BlackCrit, and

TABLE 8.3 Janae Sneed's Lesson Plan: Challenging Anti-Black Misandry in Videogaming through BlackBoy (Play)Crit Literacies

Name of the Curricular Structure:	*BlackBoy (Play)Crit (Fortnite)* *Read-aloud: Skin Again by bell hooks.*
Specific Concepts to be Taught:	*I want the child to understand that …* The online game *Fortnite* can perpetuate anti-Black misandric and racist and prejudice ideologies.

Standards:	R.2.2 Analyze literacy text development.
	
	  a. Determine the lesson or moral.
	  b. Retell stories, including fables and folktales from diverse cultures.

Rationale:	Caden enjoys playing the online game *Fortnite*. In casual conversation with him, he frequently mentions the game and how good he is at playing. In one conversation we had about *Fortnite*, he explained to me that he was at Level 57 in the game, which meant he was at a high level and he is able to get new skins. He further explained that he only has default skins right now, and the other skins let people know how good he is at playing the game. He stated, "Default skins means you're trash! And even if you high level, you're still trash!" After he explained the skin concept, it led me to think about how the game implicitly perpetuates anti-Black misandric and racist ideologies. In *Fortnite*, skins are certain characters and costumes, which are organized into tiers based on the level a player is on. There are certain skins available to all players, regardless of their level. These are the default skins, and other players are not able to distinguish the level the player is on. To be considered "good" at the game, you must be on a higher level and have certain skins. This concept is similar to anti-Black misandry and racism, as it reinforces the idea that people of Color—more specifically, Black people—can be highly skilled, yet still be viewed as less than because of the color of their skin. One can change their skin to advantage themselves in the game; however, in real-life, people of Color cannot change their skin to advantage themselves in the world.
Materials and Other Resources:	• *Skin Again* by bell hooks https://youtu.be/Gbp yxxds95E • Discussion question for read-aloud • *Why do you think the author keeps saying "The* • *skin I'm in is just a covering"?* • *Has a person ever said things about you that were not true? How did that make you feel?* • *Sometimes, people say mean things about people because of their skin color. Has anyone ever said anything mean to you about your skin color? How did that make you feel?*

(*Continued*)

TABLE 8.3 (Cont.)

Name of the Curricular Structure:	*BlackBoy (Play)Crit (Fortnite)* *Read-aloud: Skin Again by bell hooks.*

Step-by-Step Procedures:	• Read the book *Skin Again* and read discussion questions on the Post-It notes on certain pages.
	• After the reading the story, ask Caden for other ways people may judge someone because of their skin. (Recall Fortnite conversation if he does not.)
	• "The last time I saw you, you were telling me about being a high-level player in Fortnite, but you only have default skins so people do not know that high level. But, if you had the different skins you can buy, then other players would know how good you are, right?"
	• Continue the conversation, being sure to mention how:
	
	  • This reinforces someone judging another person based on their skin.
	  • Often Black people and other people of Color are not treated fairly and are not always recognized for the things they are good at because of the color of their skin. In the game, he is able to buy a new skin so that players can identify how good he is; however, in real life he is not able to change his skin for his benefit.
	  • Recall his statement, "Default skins means you're trash! And even if you high level, you're still trash! And I'm still high level and I'm still trash. But if you have a skin, you're not that trash." Connect to how people may internalize being judged based upon the color of their skin. Connect to the book's repeated phrase: "The skin I'm in is just a covering."

Cultural Relevance, Social Justice, and/or Linguistic Pluralism:	It is a myth that it is difficult to teach social justice topics to students in grades K-2, as the students are already talking about these concepts by simply discussing their life experiences. It is important that teachers are committed to teaching towards social justice by critically listening to the conversations students have, and engaging them in critical literacy education. This lesson is a demonstration of how curriculum is more than standards, textbooks, or courses of study. The curriculum is built from the multiliteracies that students bring to the classroom.
Assessment:	To take action on this issue, the student can be encouraged to write a persuasive letter to Epic, the creators of *Fortnite*, persuading them to change their term "skins" to something more inclusive. He can also be assessed through observing how he responds to the lesson, and by recording anecdotal notes from the conversation.

TABLE 8.4 Brittany Wade's Lesson Plan: Challenging Anti-Black Misandry in Wrestling Through BlackBoy (Play)Crit Literacies

Name of the Curricular Structure:	*BlackBoy (Play)Crit Literacies (Wrestling)* *Read-aloud*
Specific Concepts to be Taught:	*I want the child to understand that …* Wrestling can perpetuate racist, anti-Black misandric, and prejudice ideologies.

Standards:	English Language Arts (ELA) R.L.K. 1 with prompting and support, ask and answer questions about key details in text.
	    Social Studies
	    1. Heritage is reflected through diverse cultures and is shown through the arts, customs, traditions, family celebrations, and language.

Rationale:	Wrestling is a popular play literacy amongst students in the early childhood education age range. Wrestling is also a show that I grew up watching. While viewing *Understanding BlackBoy (Play)Crit Literacies In Early Childhood* lecture notes, I began to think of the types of play geared toward boys. It occurred to me that wrestling is very popular and that there are even toys and video games to expand the franchise. While wrestling is fictional, the storylines created for the characters have many anti-Black misandric stereotypes. There has even been written scripts where African-American male wrestlers are talked about because of their "nappy" hair. In fact, there have only been 2 Black WWE champions ever in 62 years, the latest to win was in 2019.
Materials and Other Resources:	• *Chocolate Me* by Taye Diggs • 1:40–3:30 – https://www.youtube.com/watch?v=1a84tpu_RpA • Pencil • Crayons • Paper

Step-by-Step Procedures:	1. First I will read *Chocolate Me* by Taye Diggs
	2. Discussion questions for read-aloud
	    a. Why do you think he wanted a different name?
	    b. Has there ever been a situation where you were not comfortable in the skin you're in?
	    c. How did the boy's perception of himself change from the beginning to the end of the book?
	3. Have students split up into small groups of three to discuss the questions asked in the book (visiting each group)
	4. The students will then regroup and watch the YouTube video attached above
	5. Next, the students will collaborate with a partner and recreate a T-shirt design and discuss/present how they made it more inclusive compared to the original design.

(Continued)

TABLE 8.4 (Cont.)

Name of the Curricular Structure:	BlackBoy (Play)Crit Literacies (Wrestling) Read-aloud
Cultural Relevance, Social Justice, and/or Linguistic Pluralism:	This topic is relevant because students will be enlightened on intentional and unintentional possible anti-Black misandric biases or racism specifically in WWE as well as in general. Students will be able to collaborate with peers and learn how to interrupt such stereotypes.
Assessment:	I will assess my students during the time they are in small groups. I will listen to how well they interpreted what they've seen and heard. I will also assess students by their presentation of the T-shirt designs and how they decided to recreate them. The T-shirts are representative of countering narratives about Black male wrestlers.

Black Male Studies, BlackBoyCrit Pedagogy serves as a tool to address anti-Black misandry in the teaching and learning process. An extension and praxis of BlackBoyCrit Pedagogy, BlackBoy (Play)Crit Literacies is a pedagogical framework, which acknowledges, celebrates, and confronts anti-Black misandry in Black boyhood play. Teachers should be inspired by the portrait of Mr. Henry as he applied BlackBoy (Play)Crit Literacies in his early childhood classroom. All and all, although BlackBoyCrit Pedagogy—and, by extension, BlackBoy (Play)Crit Literacies—are new pedagogical frameworks in early childhood education, teachers can use them to develop the anti-Black misandric consciousness of young learners. Black boys' historical and contemporary play is full of rich experiences, and it can be connected to books and other texts so that all children can see play as a phenomenon they can enjoy, and through which they can address issues of anti-Black misandry.

Note

1 Readers should be reminded that the term "play" is enclosed in parentheses because it demonstrates the expansiveness of BlackBoyCrit Pedagogy.

References

Albanese, C., & Williams, R. (2018, 14 December). Prada will stop selling $550 monkey figure decried as racist. *Bloomberg.* https://www.bloomberg.com/news/articles/2018-12-14/prada-will-stop-selling-550-monkey-figure-decried-as-racist

Baines, J., Tisdale, C., & Long, S. (2018). *"We've been doing it your way long enough": Choosing the culturally relevant classroom.* Teachers College Press.

Black, M. M., Dubowitz, H., Starr, R. H. (1999). African American fathers in low income, urban families: Development, behavior, and home environment of their three-year-old children. *Child Development, 70*(4), 967–978.

Boutte, G. (2016). *Educating African American children: And how are the children?* Routledge Press.

Boutte, G., López-Robertson, J., & Powers-Costello, E. (2011). Moving beyond colorblindness in early childhood classrooms. *Early Childhood Education Journal*, 39(5), 335–342.

Bristol, T., & Goings, R. (2019). Exploring the boundary-heightening experiences of black male teachers: Lessons for teacher education programs. *Journal of Teacher Education*, 70(1), 51–64.

Broughton, A. (2017). Being hip to their hop: Tapping into young minds through hip-hop play. *International Journal of Early Years Education*, 25(3), 323–335.

Brown, D. (24 September 2017). They didn't #TakeTheKnee: The Black Power protest salute that shook the world in 1968. *The Washington Post*. https://www.washingtonpost.com/news/retropolis/wp/2017/09/24/they-didnt-takeaknee-the-black-power-protest-salute-that-shook-the-world-in-1968/

Bryan, N. (2020). Shaking the bad boys: Troubling the criminalization of black boys' childhood play, white hegemonic masculinity and femininity, and 'the school playground-to-prison pipeline.' *Race, Ethnicity, and Education*, 23(5), 673–692. doi:10.1080/13613324.2018.1512483 (Original work published 2018).

Curry, T. (2017). *Man-not: Race, class, genre and the dilemmas of black manhood*. Temple University Press.

Dumas, M., & Nelson, J. (2016). (Re)-imagining black boyhood. Toward a critical framework for educational research. *Harvard Educational Review*, 86(1), 27–47.

Fausset, R. (2020, June 23). Suspects in Ahmaud Arbery's killing are indicted on murder charges. *The New York Times*. https://www.nytimes.com/2020/06/24/us/ahmaud-arbery- shooting-murder-indictment.html

Gestwicki, C. (2017). *Developmentally appropriate practices: Curriculum and development in early childhood education*. Cengage Learning.

Johnson, L. (2018). Where do we go from here? Toward a critical race English education. *Research in the Teaching of English*, 53(2), 102–124.

Johnson, L., Jackson, J., Stovall, D., & Baszile, D. (2017). "Loving blackness to death": (Re)imagining ELA classrooms in a time of racial chaos. *English Journal*, 106(4), 60–66.

Kriete, R., & Davis. (2014). *The morning meeting book: K-8* (3rd ed.). Center for Responsive Teaching. (Original work published 1999).

Ladson-Billings, G. (2011). Boyz to men? Teaching to restore black boys' childhood. *Race, Ethnicity and Education*, 14(1), 7–15.

Leavell, A. S., Tamis-LeMonda, C. S., Ruble, D. N., Zosuls, K. M., & Cabrera, N. J. (2012). African American, white and Latino fathers' activities with their sons and daughters in early childhood. *Sex Roles: A Journal of Research*, 66(1–2),53–65.

Lynn, M. (2006). Education for the community: Exploring the culturally relevant practice of black male teachers. *Teachers College Record*, 108(12), 2497–2522.

Meltzer, B. (2016). *I am brave: A little book about Martin Luther King, Jr.* Dial Books.

Perry. T., Steele, C., & Hilliard, A. III. (2003). *Young, gifted, and black: Promoting high achievement outcome among African-American students*. Beacon Press.

Raphael, A. (2015, April 16). Losing count: "Eeny meeny, miny mo" and the ambiguous history of counting-out rhymes. *The Paris Review*. https://www.theparisreview.org/blog/2015/04/16/losing-count/

Sherouse, A. P. (2016, March 24). It started with a kiss. *Huffpost*. https://www.huffpost.com/entry/it-started-with-a-kiss_b_9541646

Trawick-Smith, J. (2020). *Young children's play: Development, disabilities, and diversity.* Routledge.

Vera, A. (2020). White woman who called police on black man bird watching in Central Park has been fired. *CNN.* https://www.cnn.com/2020/05/26/us/central-park-video-dog-video- african-american-trnd/index.html

9

BLACKBOYCRIT PEDAGOGY

A New Way Forward for Black Boys

Although we have come to the end of this book, we have only just begun our journey toward making early childhood education a more affirming space for all Black boys. The Black male kindergarten teachers we have had the opportunities to learn with, about, and from have modeled the essence of BlackBoyCrit Pedagogy and the empathy needed to support Black boys in early childhood classrooms. Based on such models, and in addition to the practical strategies provided throughout this book, I take this opportunity to further flesh out BlackBoyCrit Pedagogy for readers. I remind early childhood educators that BlackBoyCrit Pedagogy is not prescriptive; rather, it provides opportunities for early childhood educators to pause and ponder— or, better yet, reflect on themselves—about their own practices in order to undo the harm caused through anti-Black misandric pedagogies, literacies, and schooling practices. I hope this will help us move toward a new way forward in early childhood education. I agree with Boutte (2016), who has suggested that the harmful actions of most early childhood teachers are not intentional and often not even recognized. Instead, they are enacted due to a lack of robust preparation for critical pedagogies such as BlackBoyCrit Pedagogy in teacher preparation programs, the majority of which have built, maintained, and sustained mechanisms of racism, white supremacy, and anti-Black misandry through both curricula and instruction (Ladson-Billings, 2009). Even when they are provided opportunities to learn critical pedagogies, teachers often lack confidence in their own execution of them, and end up failing Black children and boys in this case (Howard, 2014; Siwatu, 2011; Wright & Counsell, 2018). However, we can change this outcome by listening to Black boys who have long told us how best to educate and empower them, and by learning from teachers like the Black male teachers presented throughout this book, who are unapologetic about confronting white supremacy, racism, and anti-Black misandry in and beyond early childhood classrooms.

DOI: 10.4324/9780429287619-10

Because BlackBoyCrit Pedagogy may challenge existing pedagogical, literacy, and schooling practices with which teachers are comfortable and often see as tried and true in early childhood classrooms, many teachers may be hesitant to consider it. However, I encourage teachers to use what Stovall (2018) has called a *radical imaginary* to reframe what we currently know about early childhood education to see a different kind of schooling not yet in existence. In the words of Baines et al. (2018) "We've been doing it your way [e.g., the White way] long enough" (p. xiv), and in the words of Dillard (2016), it is time to "turn the ships around" (p. 406). In this way, early childhood teachers can undo the anti-Black misandric violence that confronts Black boys in classrooms across the nation. Otherwise, early childhood educators invite into their early childhood classrooms the same racism, white supremacy, and anti-Black misandric violence to which Black boys are often subjected.

BlackBoyCrit Pedagogy through the Pedagogies, Literacy, and Schooling Practices of Black Male Teachers

In Chapter 2, I introduced the developing ideas of BlackBoyCrit Pedagogy, the guiding pedagogical framework for this book. Here, I reintroduce them through the pedagogies, literacy, and schooling practices of the Black male teachers as told by the Black boys presented in this book. BlackBoyCrit Peadgogy:

1. Acknowledges the inter-curricular nature of anti-Black misandry in ECE and underscores the necessity to work collaboratively with Black boys to confront and dismantle these social constructions and to develop anti-Black misandric consciousness in teaching, learning, and literacy practices.
2. Centers teaching, learning, and literacy practices that are simultaneously influenced by Blackness, maleness, diverse expressions of Black masculinity, and the experiences of boys and male teachers that move beyond the language of hypermasculinity, thereby creating a symbiotic relationship between Black boys and male teachers in and beyond early childhood classrooms.
3. Humanizes and heals the wounded spirits of Black boys (as committed by anti-Black misandry) as a way to contest the consequences of anti-Black misandric violence in early childhood schooling, curricular, and literacy practices.
4. Positions Black families and communities as informants and integral partners in the academic and social enterprise of Black boys in early childhood education.

Guided by these developing ideas, I address collectively the practices of all three Black male teachers through the eyes of the Black boys presented in the book. While there are so many examples upon which I can draw, I select a few of them to elucidate how BlackBoyCrit Pedagogy was infused through the teaching and learning processes of the Black male teachers as perceived by their boy students. Table 9.1 provides an overview of a few of the examples of BlackBoyCrit Pedagogy I have selected from all three Black male teachers.

TABLE 9.1 Examples of BlackBoyCrit Pedagogy

Developing Ideas of BlackBoyCrit Pedagogy	Examples of BlackBoyCrit Pedagogy
1.) Acknowledges the inter-curricular nature of anti-Black misandry in ECE and underscores the necessity to work collaboratively with Black boys to confront and dismantle these social constructions and to develop anti-Black misandric consciousness in teaching, learning, and literacy practices.	• Building Black boys' anti-Black misandric consciousness • Connecting Black boys' interest across the curriculum • Using Black boys' engagement with motivating texts to assess them as readers
2.) Centers teaching, learning, and literacy practices that are simultaneously influenced by Blackness, maleness, diverse expressions of Black masculinity, and the experiences of boys and male teachers that move beyond the language of hypermasculinity, thereby creating a symbiotic relationship between Black boys and male teachers in and beyond the early childhood classrooms.	• Developing a broad understanding of Black boy interests and male masculinity when selecting books • Providing a model of Black men as readers • Using Black Masculine Literacies to support math and reading growth
3.) Humanizes and heals the wounded spirits of Black boys (as committed by anti-Black misandry) as a way to contest the consequences of anti-Black misandric violence in early childhood schooling, curricular, and literacy practices.	• Demonstrating love and caring for Black boys • Building relationships with Black boys as foundations • Seeing the importance of decriminalizing practices
4.) Positions Black families and communities as informants and integral partners in the academic and social enterprise of Black boys in early childhood education.	• Being appreciated, valued, and respected by Black families • Positioning Black families as partners • Acknowledging Black mothers' concerns for the play lives of Black boys

The Inter-Curricular Nature of Anti-Black Misandry

It goes without saying that anti-Black misandry is overtly and tacitly embedded within early childhood curricula. It raises its ugly head in literacy, math, science, social studies, and play. Consequently, Black boys are socialized into a White-esteemed curriculum, which privileges the experiences of White children (Asante, 1992). Due to the consequences of anti-Black misandry, Black boys allegedly underperform in every academic area in and beyond early childhood. So, how can Black boys have male privilege in a schooling system that is anti-Black misandric in nature, and when every aspect of said system disenfranchises them? Much like the Black male teachers introduced in this book, we must all work to dismantle these social constructions. Like the scholar-activist Angela Davis, I believe that anything that has been socially constructed can be socially deconstructed and destroyed (Davis, 2016). It just takes courage, willingness, and a deep commitment to do so (Baines et al. 2018).

Examples from the classrooms of Mr. Tal and Mr. Henry elucidate such courage through the teachers' infusion of the interests of Black boys to counteract the consequences of anti-Black misandry in early childhood curricula. For this reason, Braden suggested that the race cars books that Mr. Tal gave him were important. He was able to see how Mr. Tal infused race car books and race cars into the math and science lessons that he taught as a way to give him autonomy, engage him, and draw on his interests in the teaching and learning process while simultaneously challenging the White-centric math and reading curricula that often disregards the interests and experiences of Black boys. Mr. Tal, himself, noted the unmet academic and social needs of Black boys, which he suggested was akin to his own experiences as a young Black boy growing up in a schooling system that was designed to disenfranchise Black children. Similarly, Roland asserted that he was better able to understand why he could not play with Kate, his White female classmate, during segregation, after Mr. Henry infused play into an already White-centric, and anti-Black misandric literacy curriculum. By centering anti-Black misandry in his literacy circle, Mr. Henry was able to help unveil to his students the insidious and inter-curricular nature of anti-Black misandry in boyhood play and literacy curricula.

Centering Teaching, Learning, and Literacy Practices That Are Simultaneously Influenced by Diverse Expressions of Black Masculinity

Much like the Black male teachers in this book, early childhood educators need to understand how the teaching and learning process marginalize and disenfranchise Black boys. Every aspect of early childhood curriculum has made this clear and evident. Therefore, teachers can let Black male teachers be their guides and work to intentionally center diverse expressions of Black masculinity and Black boyhood experiences in the teaching and learning process. Take, for example, the words of Ameer, who related that Mr. Javien not only gave him good books, but also good advice, both of which were based on his own lived realities and experiences as a Black man living in America. Mr. Javien asserted that he needed to center this kind of wise advice, drawn out of his own experiences, in the teaching and learning process as a way to protect Black boys from the anti-Black misandric violence they face presently and will perhaps face later in life. He also mentioned that, although he considered himself to be an upstanding Black man, he understood that not everyone saw him that way. He described an experience in which the White parents whose children he taught often stereotyped him, and would not speak to him during school dismissal. As such, Ameer was able to see Mr. Javien as a caring Black man who had his best interest at heart. This moves beyond dominant narratives and images of hypermasculine Black men, who are stereotypically constructed as uncaring disciplinarians whose roles and expectations in schools are to keep Black boys in line (Brown, 2012).

Similar to Roland, Maurice suggested that he desired to pursue teaching as a professional option in the future because Mr. Tal was extremely patient with him in the classroom and "gave him many chances" there. Additionally, Mr. Tal was not afraid to hug and hold Maurice's hands during times when he most needed such affection. White male teachers in early childhood education have not been allowed to express such affection toward young children without being subjected to negative suspicions about their sexuality (Baum et al., 2014). Mr. Tal mentioned that he took this approach with Maurice and other Black boys because, in his own schooling experiences, teachers were not patient with him. Although he admitted that he had caring teachers, he also recalled having some teachers who were extremely dismissive of him as a young boy. He added that he has also witnessed such practices in his current professional capacity, where most White teachers perceive Black boys to be problems. As previously mentioned, the anti-Black misandric notion of Black boys as problems is consistent in the experiences of other Black male teachers, and often drives Black male teacher recruitment and retention initiatives (Woodson & Pabon, 2016). Therefore, like Roland, Maurice was able to see a caring Black male teacher who was intentional about protecting him from anti-Black misandric schooling. Maurice, too, was able to see Mr. Tal beyond the notion of hypermasculinity.

Returning to the pedagogies, literacy, and schooling practices of Mr. Henry, it is important to note that when Mr. Henry made connections between historical and present-day anti-Black misandry in the experiences of Black male teachers, Roland's anti-Black misandric consciousness became deeper. In other words, by centering his lived realities in the teaching and learning process, Mr. Henry helped Roland understand the everyday lived realities of Black men in America, which is information he can use in his present and future life.

Humanizing and Healing Black Boys

Humanizing and healing the wounded spirits of Black boys is far from the purpose of early childhood classrooms, despite DAP that suggests it purports to meet the academic and social needs of all children. In this case, the notion of *all children* becomes a way to ignore the needs of Black boys in early childhood classrooms; thereby, it is an anti-Black misandric phenomenon. Nevertheless, at the heart of the practices of the Black male teachers introduced in this book was their abilities to humanize and heal Black boys from those anti-Black misandric wounds that early childhood education naturally imposed on their innocent Black boy bodies. Roland admitted that he was motivated to come to school because he had a Brown teacher, Mr. Henry, who looked like him. The mere presence of Mr. Henry in his classroom was a humanizing and healing balm Roland needed to become motivated. Mrs. Boins, Roland's mother, admitted his previous challenges and lack of desire to attend school when his teachers were White. Roland's lacking desire suggests so much about the violence of Whiteness and anti-Black misandry and the ways in which they can negatively impact Black boys' motivation to attend early childhood education. Given that most teachers are White and female (Sleeter & Milner, 2011), this is concerning. Therefore, we need Black male teachers who are able to humanize and heal Black boys in and beyond these early learning spaces, much like all of the Black male teachers presented in this book.

According to Ameer, the good books that Mr. Tal gave him were humanizing and healing as they reflected his interest in hip-hop and Black culture. The same is true for Braden, who also enjoyed the Black boy-centric race car books, and the images of Black athletes that made him feel humanized and healed in Mr. Tal's classroom. Much like my own experiences, literacy experiences for Black boys, in early childhood classrooms are far from humanizing and healing, but are rather dehumanizing and sickening.

Black Families and Communities as Informants and Integral Partners in the Academic and Social Enterprise

It is also clear that Black mothers and fathers are not often provided space in and beyond early childhood classrooms to be listened to, heard, and understood (Braden et al., 2020; Bryan, 2020; Reynolds, 2010). However, these Black male teachers were intentional about seeing Black mothers and fathers as informants and integral partners in the academic and social enterprise of Black boys. In other words, they ensured that they made their classrooms welcoming spaces for both Black boys and their family members. For example, in terms of Mr. Javien, Mrs. Martha often served as a substitute teacher during his absences, and had built a strong relationship with him prior to her grandson's enrollment in his classroom. Given this symbiotic relationship, she knew she wanted her grandson, Ameer, to be Mr. Javien's student. She also gave Mr. Javien many recommendations on how to support Ameer, and he applied those recommendations in his classroom. One of them was to help Ameer develop Black pride and pride in general in himself, of which she admitted Mr. Javien did an excellent job. Mr. Raton, Braden's father, also gave Mr. Tal recommendations on how to support his son in the classroom (e.g., do whatever to reel him in), a recommendations that Mr. Tal used to instill a love for reading in Braden. Consequently, Braden was able to build his reading skills. Mrs. Aretha suggested that she felt far more comfortable having Mr. Tal as Maurice's teacher because he seemed open to listening to her and had an open line of communication with her about Maurice's progress in his early childhood classroom. She felt that she could talk about ways she and Mr. Tal could partner to better support Maurice both academically and socially. Collectively, Black male teachers held space for Black mothers, fathers, and community members who are often socially constructed as uninvolved in the educational lives of their children, to challenge anti-Black misandric narratives about their involvement in their children's lives.

Conclusion

We must not forget the vital importance of Black male teachers like my own kindergarten teacher, Mr. C., and the three Black male teachers whose pedagogies, literacy, and schooling practices reminded me of him. Much like Mr. C. made a difference in my life, these teachers made a difference in the lives of the Black boys presented throughout this book. The boys' perspectives of their teachers illuminate this fact, and remind us all of the importance of recruiting and retaining Black male teachers who teach against White norms and expectations, and particularly against anti-Black misandry. We cannot afford to fail at this; Black boys across the nation long to (re)-member, and to experience the kind of teaching and learning that center their realities. BlackBoyCrit Pedagogy draws on those realities to challenge the norm in early childhood classrooms. We need more of all of these things, as well as more Black male teachers, and even more of Black boys' perceptions on those teachers' pedagogies, literacies, and schooling practices in early childhood education. Black boys are counting on us to ensure that they are well in and beyond early childhood education. Will you ensure and commit to it by moving toward a BlackBoyCrit Pedagogy in early childhood education? I hope you will!

References

Asante, M. K. (1992). Afrocentric curriculum. *Educational Leadership*, 49(4), 28–31.

Baines, J., Tisdale, C., & Long, S. (2018). "We've been doing it your way long enough": Choosing the culturally relevant classroom. Teachers College Press.

Baum, A., Welsh, K., & Freeman, N. (2014). Men in the field of early care and education: Perceptions of male and female early childhood professionals. In L. Watson (Ed.), *It takes a team effort* (pp. 17–28). Information Age Press.

Boutte, G. (2016). *Educating African-American students: And how are the children?* Routledge.

Braden, E., Gibson, V., Gillete, R. (2020). Everything black is not bad! Families and teachers engaging in critical discussions about race. *Talking Points*, 31(2), 2–11.

Brown, A. L. (2012). On human kinds and role models: A critical discussion about the African American male teacher. *Educational Studies*, 48(3), 296–315.

Bryan, N. (2020). Remembering Tamir Rice and other black boy victims: Imagining Black PlayCrit literacies inside and outside urban education. *Urban Education*. https://doi.org/10.1177/0042085920902250

Davis, A. (2016). *Freedom is a constant struggle: Ferguson, Palestine, and the foundation of a movement.* Haymarket Books.

Dillard, C. (2016). Turning the ships around: A case study of (re)membering as transnational endarkened feminist inquiry and praxis for black teachers. *Educational Studies*, 52(5), 406–423.

Howard, T. (2014). *Black maled: Perils and promises in the education of African American males.* Teacher College Press.

Ladson-Billings, G. (2009). *The dreamkeeper: Successful teachers of African American children* (2nd ed.). Jossey-Bass.

Reynolds, R. (2010). "They think you're lazy," and other messages black parents send their black sons: An exploration of critical race theory in the examination of educational outcomes for black males. *Journal of African American Males in Education*, 1(2), 145–163.

Siwatu, K. (2011). Preservice teachers' sense of preparedness and self-efficacy to teach in America's urban and suburban schools: Does context matter. *Teaching and Teacher Education*, 27(2), 357–365.

Sleeter, C., & Milner, H. R. (2011). Researching successful efforts in teacher education to diversify teachers. In A. F. Ball & C. Tyson (Eds.), *Studying diversity in teacher education* (pp. 81–103). Rowman & Littlefield.

Stovall, D. (2018). Are we ready for 'school abolition'? Thoughts and practices of radical imaginary in education. *Taboo: The Journal of Cultural and Education*, 17(1), 51–61. https:// doi.org/10.31390/taboo.17.1.06

Woodson, A., & Pabon, A. (2016). "I'm none of the above": Exploring themes of heteropatriarchy in the life histories of black male educators. *Equity and Excellence in Education*, 49(1), 57–71

Wright, B., & Counsell, S. (2018). *The brilliance of black boys: Cultivating success in the early grades*. Teacher College Press.

AFTERWORD

There are times in history when certain books must be written! *Toward a Black-BoyCrit Pedagogy: Black Boys, Male Teachers and Early Childhood Classroom Practices* is one of these books! The famous words of W.E.B. DuBois (1903) are still relevant today where he noted, "how does it feel to be a problem?" Given the current state of our nation's political and educational climate, Black students (Black boys in particular) in our nation's educational system have been relegated to a substandard system where they have garnered media attention and a national spotlight not for the positive attributes they bring to the educational setting but for negative stories and headlines that are oftentimes manufactured to get likes and clicks.

I want to be crystal clear. Many Black boys are facing an academic death in our nation's K-12 public, charter and private schools. Unfortunately, in many schools, Black boys never see Black male educators as classroom teachers in early childhood and elementary settings (Lewis & Toldson, 2013). As a result, educators continue to make excuses why it is not their fault that Black boys are not achieving academically. However, they never discuss what is in their power to change when Black boys enter schools and school districts across this great nation to provide the essential literacy practices needed for success. As a result, this book is a welcome addition to the education knowledge base as it provides a new and fresh perspective on how to effectively serve Black boys, the essential need for Black male teachers and the literacy practices that must be in place in early childhood classrooms.

It is my hope that this book reaches the educators and other stakeholders that it needs to reach to make a positive difference for Black boys to achieve academically in the most affluent country in the world. We can no longer, in this age of educational accountability, continue to stand by and watch the achievement levels of this student population be at or near the bottom of every major academic barometer and be comfortable with our work as education professionals. Once the education

DOI: 10.4324/9780429287619-11

profession chooses to fully embrace the educational potential of Black boys, we will see transformation happen for Black boys that want to achieve at a high level but are in schooling environments that do not develop their full potential.

This book, *Toward a BlackBoyCrit Pedagogy: Black Boys, Male Teachers and Early Childhood Classroom Practices* is also for parents who send their children to school expecting something great to happen only to be met with disappointment at the door of the school building. The greatness they expect for their Black boys is why many work one, two or even three jobs to make sure their children have food on the table and a roof over their head just so they can make it to school! Unfortunately, when their Black boys matriculate through our nation's schools, they are met with "educational rhetoric." This educational rhetoric tells the parents all that is perceived to be wrong with their child(ren) rather than how the schooling experience will put them in the best position to have a positive impact on their lives.

Finally, this book embraces the voices, hopes and dreams of so many who have died for Black students to have a right to a quality education in this country. We thank you for making the ultimate sacrifice so that one day the education profession can reach its full potential by serving the educational needs of Black students. I have come to learn that we have to continue to push until this change happens. This is why I commend Dr. Nathaniel Bryan for this valuable contribution to the education profession. An intentional focus on BlackBoyCrit Pedagogy is exactly what we need at this moment. It is my hope that this book will spark a new movement of Black academic success!

Chance W. Lewis, Ph.D.
Carol Grotnes Belk Distinguished Professor of Urban Education
Director, The Urban Education Collaborative
Provost Faculty Fellow for Diversity, Inclusion and Access
University of North Carolina at Charlotte http://www.chancewlewis.com

References

DuBois, W. E. B. (1903). *The souls of black folk*. Random House.

Lewis, C., & Toldson, I. (Eds.). (2013). *Black male teachers: Diversifying the United States' teacher workforce*. Emerald Group.

APPENDIX

On Portraiture Methodology and the Construction of Black Boys' Portraits of Teachers

In this Appendix, I further explain portraiture methodology, my role as a portraitist, and how I co-constructed Black boys' portraits of their teachers. In so doing, I hope to be instructive to readers, including early childhood practitioners, scholars, doctoral students, and researchers who may be interested in applying this method to their own research and practice.

What is Portraiture?

As mentioned in this book's introduction, I used Lawrence-Lightfoot and Hoffman-Davis' (1997) notion of portraiture methodology to co-construct Black boys' portraits of male teachers. According to Lawrence-Lightfoot and Hoffman-Davis (1997), portraiture is a postpositivist method that conjoins art, science, and social critique to examine the lives and lived experiences of people of Color. Furthering this definition, Dixson, Chapman, and Hill (2005) describe portraiture methodology as the blending of several qualitative methodologies, including lift history, naturalist inquiry, and ethnographic methods. All in all, this methodology is consistent with Black education research traditions, and aims to acknowledge that Black people's "ways of knowing provided by the arts and humanities are often more useful in informing the understanding of our lives" (King, 2017, p. 6). In particular, portraiture methodology has been useful in exploring the experiences of Black boys and the pedagogies, literacies, and schooling practices of their Black male teachers in early childhood classrooms.

My Role as a Portraitist

Lawrence-Lightfoot and Hoffman-Davis (1997) also identified those who construct and/or co-construct portraits as portraitists. My role as a portraitist required me to position myself in this research; to build relationships with research participants and co-construct stories of hope, joy, possibilities, and pain; to listen *for* a story rather than listen *to* a story; and to highlight the "good" in both the research and the research participant (Lynn, 2006). By positioning myself in the research, I challenged the notion of objectivity, which oftentimes requires researchers to ignore issues of race, gender, and social identities in the research process. Challenging objectivity allowed me to make clear that the self is an important part of the research process and research has a personal agenda (Milner, 2007). For this reason, I was intentional about sharing my early childhood memories of my kindergarten teacher, my boyhood experiences, and my experiences as both a teacher and teacher educator.

Building relationships with the research participants was an important aspect of developing each Black boy's portrait of his teacher. In building such relationships, I spent a period of nine months in each teacher's early childhood classroom getting to know him and his students. I also spent time in other areas of the school building relationships with the boys' caregivers, school personnel, and community members who were able to confirm the boys' and teachers' stories and experiences.

As a requirement of portraiture methodology, I was also intentional about highlighting the "good" in the research and the research participants in order to push back against biases and stereotypes that too often frame the lives and experiences of Black boys and male teachers. I wanted to tell previously untold asset-based stories about both groups in early childhood classrooms. This idea is not only the hallmark of portraiture methodology, but is consistent with Black Male Studies, which aims to contest pathological assumptions about and misrepresentations of Black boys and men through a Black Public Philosophy (as described in Chapter 2).

To illuminate the "good" in the research, I used data sources such as semi-structured and unstructured interviews, field notes, classroom observations, and focus groups to challenge pathological assumptions about Black boys and male teachers in early childhood classrooms. These data sources are consistent with portraiture methodology, Black Crit, and Black Male Studies.

Constructing the Portraits

To construct Black boys' portraits of their teachers, I followed Lawrence-Lightfoot and Hoffman's (1997) recommendation and read the transcript four times during a process they call *the four phases of data analysis* (Lynn, 2006). During the first phase, I read all of the transcribed semi-structured and unstructured interviews, field notes, classroom observations, and focus group notes. I then highlighted information regarding the pedagogical, literacy, and schooling experiences of the Black male teachers. From there, I noted places wherein pedagogical, literacy, and schooling experiences aligned with the literature and other transcribed data. I engaged in three rounds of coding including in vivo, emotion, and descriptive coding, which allowed me to use respondents' actual words and emotions, and to describe detailed classroom events relating to the boys and their teachers. I finally constructed what Lawrence-Lightfoot and Hoffman-Davis (1997) termed *initial impressionistic records*, which I used to organize and scrutinize the data.

In the second phase, I made analytic memos, which I used to develop emerging themes and develop questions for addressing issues that arose in the data. I then created preliminary analytical categories to test the data. From there, I reread transcripts of the semi-structured and unstructured interviews, field notes, classroom observations, and focus groups to include missing information from the initial impressionistic records. I searched for ideas that continued to emerge in the data, and I organized those ideas based on areas the boys and their teachers addressed relating to pedagogical, literacy, and schooling experiences. Finally, I constructed preliminary portraits of the Black boys' teachers.

In the third stage, I made a list of themes relating the pedagogies, literacy, and schooling practices addressed by the boys and their teachers. I also reread and coded field notes and classroom observations, which I then compared to the semi-structured and unstructured interviews' codes, addressing pedagogical, literacy, and schooling practices. From there, I developed overall themes that addressed the pedagogical, literacy, and schooling practices shared by the boys and their teachers. I finally constructed the Black boys' preliminary portraits.

Finally, in the fourth phase, I reread interview transcripts, classroom observations, field notes, impressionistic records, and initial and preliminary portraits. I then coded for themes that aligned to Black Crit and Black Male Studies. I was intentional about locating evidence of pedagogical, literacy, and schooling practices that supported the boys in early childhood classrooms. I then created the boys' final portraits of their teachers, which I shared with the boys, the teachers, and the caregivers. This enabled me to revise the portraits based on the comments of all three groups.

References

Dixson, A. D., Chapman, T. K., & Hill, D. A. (2005). Research as an aesthetic process: Extending the portraiture methodology. *Qualitative Inquiry*, 11, 16–26.

King, J. (2017). Education research in the black liberation tradition: Return what you learn to the people. *Journal of Negro Education*, 86 (2), 95–114.

Lawrence-Lightfoot, S., & Hoffman-Davis, J. (1997). *The art and science of portraiture*. Jossey-Bass.

Lynn, M. (2006). Education for the community: Exploring the culturally relevant practice of black male teachers. *Teachers College Record*, 108(12), 2497–2522.

Milner, H. R. (2007). Race, culture, and researcher's positionality: Working through dangers seen, unseen, and unforeseen. *Educational Researcher*, 36(7), 388–400.

INDEX

Page numbers in **bold** refer to tables, those in *italics* indicate figures.

Made in the USA
Middletown, DE
11 October 2023

40526975R00113